'A supremely beautiful book that spins its particular story to tell a universal one about a more innocent and natural time, the swift passing of that time, and about the people who make us and whom we never thank' *Sunday Times*

'Rare, visceral writing that inspires one to try to match his capacity for observation' *Herald*

'Beautiful, richly satisfying writing' *Sunday Telegraph*

'The book glitters with memory, like some marvellous parade that marches around the small boy' *Irish Sunday Independent*

'[A] glowing and beautiful memoir of a childhood in a Scottish fishing village ... Poetry leaks from Rush's pen at every turn ... if the purpose of memoir is to make real a forgotten world, then Christopher Rush has done everything that could be asked of him' *Mail on Sunday*

'A vivid, powerful account' *Belfast Telegraph*

'Delicate and inquisitive' *Big Issue in Scotland*

'Vivid and lyrical ... A masterly work that enlivens the past with beauty and emotion, yet never sags into soft focus sentimentality. Instead its realism, and the author's heartfelt candour, make it one of those rare books that successfully evoke the human spirit' *Economist*

CHRISTOPHER RUSH was born in St Monans and for thirty years taught literature in Edinburgh. His books include *A Twelvemonth and a Day* (recently listed as one of the one hundred greatest Scottish books ever), the highly acclaimed *To Travel Hopefully* and the newly published *Will*. He now lives near his childhood home in Fife.

By the same author

Peace Comes Dropping Slow
A Resurrection of a Kind
A Twelvemonth and a Day
Two Christmas Stories
Into the Ebb
Venus Peter
With Sharp Compassion (with John Shaw)
Where the Clock Stands Still (with Cliff Wilson)
Venus Peter Saves the Whale
Last Lesson of the Afternoon
To Travel Hopefully
Will

Hellfire and Herring

A Childhood Remembered

CHRISTOPHER RUSH

Christopher Rush

For Alan and Jennifer
Shelley ~
with the gratitude of the
author ~
and great-great aunt Elspeth!
5th August 2008
Fife Ness.

P

PROFILE BOOKS

This paperback edition published in 2008

First published in Great Britain in 2007 by
PROFILE BOOKS LTD
3A Exmouth House
Pine Street
Exmouth Market
London EC1R 0JH
www.profilebooks.com

1 3 5 7 9 10 8 6 4 2

Designed by Geoff Green Book Design
Typeset in Bell by MacGuru Ltd
info@macguru.org.uk
Printed and bound in Great Britain by
CPI Bookmarque, Croydon, CR0 4TD

A CIP catalogue record for this book is available from the British Library.

ISBN 978 1 86197 974 2

For my mother's family

And for little Jenny, who never knew them

CONTENTS

Another Time, Another Place

You could smell God on the air in St Monans as surely as you could smell herring. That was in the forties, though, when I was born there, on 23 November 1944, to be precise. Not that precision was required of you in those days, unless you were in school or in church, counting your tables or your blessings, or in either case your sins. A rule-of-thumb philosophy prevailed in most practices, from cheese-cutting in the grocer's to sex in the fields – you got it right by instinct. And if you got it wrong on occasion then somebody ended up with a bundle of dubious joy or an extra ounce of cheddar from that monolithic yellow slab on the counter.

It surprised me how, in spite of post-war poverty, things often worked out on the side of superfluity, illegitimacy included. Even the undertaker bustled in and scanned the deceased with the deadly blue measuring-tape of his eyes (inch-tapes were for tailors and the snipping out of Sunday suits, also voluminous): alive or dead a body always gained the benefit of the doubt. Especially dead. Nobody went cramped into eternity in a James Miller coffin. Boat-builder and coffin-maker, the ships were tight but the boxes were comfortable. 'An extra inch or two won't harm him – he'll grow into it.' That was the usual joke, meeting death with a quip and an open-handedness that boasted a generous supply of wood.

There was a good foundation for it. The historian Sibbald,

ignoring Gaelic and old Icelandic and other etymologies, derived the name of Fife from an old Danish word meaning 'the wooded country'. James IV had shorn it of its former glory when he built *The Great Michael*, the Goliath of Scottish waters, in 1511. But the wasted woods of Fife recovered – fortunately for me, as I carried out in their close and leafy coverts some of my earliest experiments in poetry and in sex (sometimes simultaneously), each of which required the utmost secrecy from the envious eyes and harsh judgements of critics, the self-appointed gods of metre and morality. And of God himself, the severest critic of all.

We've come back to God. That's no accident. You couldn't get away from Him in the forties. Time's whirligig always brought in God and his revenges. The air was impregnated with him and with his mint-sweet and moth-ball evange-lists. Just as it was with herring, as you might expect in a fishing village on Scotland's repressed east coast where fishing was an act of faith and not yet a computer-science industry designed to suck the last drops of life out of the sea. The only echo-soundings to be heard then were the desperate plummets of prayer (*Out of the depths, O Lord, I cry to Thee!*) from those in peril on the sea. Or on the slate. Fishermen with light nets and heavy bills were known to string themselves up from the rafters like stranded fish, staring at the sky, in those dark lofts where they stored their gear, and which also smelled of the sea.

The oldest fishermen swore they could smell a shoal of herring in the breeze as accurately as a gannet, diving from two hundred feet into the waves, could detect the glimmer of a fish another two hundred feet beneath the surface. That was nothing to these old men of the sea, who had birds' beaks for noses. Faith and science were tucked neatly up their snouts, a faculty per nostril, the aspect of some secret symbiosis. They'd snuff the air when at sea and give the order to shoot the nets, or not. Even the old-timers sitting on stanchions at the pier-ends would remove their pipes from their mouths, lift their grizzled muzzles, sea-dogs questing the air, and tell you they could detect a shoal of herring ten miles off shore. 'There's herring out there – I'm fucking sure of it! As sure as God's my judge!' Their language was not exclusively scriptural.

But there was more to it than just smell. The old salts of St Monans sometimes struck me as steering that narrow course between lunacy and genius. Later, in my teens, I learned from Dryden that this was entirely likely. *Great wits are sure to madness near allied / And thin partitions do their bounds divide.* In spite of this my old men were scholars without degrees, madmen without a dangerous bone in their bodies, unless they choked on a fishbone. As a matter of fact we were all mad to a degree, on the scale of eccentricity to insanity, and yet nobody ever came to any harm in this place of open doors and wild, free fields, roamed by children who'd never heard of paedophiles and who had no cause to worry about them. Our world was a protective cocoon, like intoxication. You fell and got up again, amazed and unhurt. God was around anyway, looking after you while spying you out. He was in charge of the asylum that was our village and he ran a Captain Bligh-style ship, a thousand souls under his commandments. Obedience was the operative word, discipline – and 'fishency, Kipps, 'fishency, in this fishermen's world that lived by fish and smelled of fish and dreamed of fish as Ahab dreamed of whale, blowing his drowned brain.

Ahab was another sea-captain, but an ungodly one, like the Old Testament king he was named after. I knew all about both Ahabs, just as I knew I hadn't come from God, or from the Bass Rock, or from the back of beyond, as some of the early explanations had it. The truth was simpler and more shocking, in fact. And more mundane.

A stinking drop. That's what I came from, or so I was advised by a hellfire-and-herring-breathing preacher in the braehead kirk, where the Congregationalists sweated in the dark for their share in eternity. 'A stinking drop!'

he thundered, smashing the prow of the pulpit like a dog-collared Viking, giving no quarter to any horny rams or ewes in his flock who planned on being on the giving or receiving end that Sunday night. Six days shalt thou labour and do all thy work, but on the Sabbath day thou shalt not shag – this seemed to be the sub-text of his sermon. Maybe he was just trying to be as discouraging as possible, adding his tuppenceworth of sulphur to anything that lassitude and weariness of the spirit might achieve in the way of Sunday self-restraint. The fear of conception was the beginning of wisdom at the end of the week. And to make it sound as absolutely pointless as possible, he added (shocking the matrons of the congregation), 'Copulation is friction of the members and an ejaculatory discharge, that's all.'

You could hear their knicker elastic go twang with holy horror, in the echoes of which there sang a terrible glee. And this proved to be his undoing, as nothing, not even communion cloth, was as sacred as knicker elastic in the East Neuk of Fife, where nobody admitted that sex even existed, though the bible was awash with it and the bulls were hard at work in fields that were green to our very back doors.

As for the effect on the innocents of the flock, if disincentive was his game, it failed to achieve the desired result. Not in me, at least. Too young, I was also too ignorant and sexually untutored to understand exactly what he meant by friction of the members. Even so, something in the language excited me and I came out of church longing to meet a member and rub it up the wrong way. Not the right way. There was never any doubt when you emerged from the holy place with a half-hour-long sermon still burning your ears that everything in the world was wrong – and nothing was more wrong than your loathsome self.

That self-loathing quickly burned off in the sunny days of adolescence, or at least was tempered by sudden surges of self-love. But it occupied a large portion of early childhood, and fairly kept me sweating in the dark too. Not entirely inappropriate, though, when you come to think of it, that concept of original sin – entirely and especially congruent, indeed, to a world which, as I entered it, appeared to have got itself into something of a mess.

1

Glimmer of Cold Brine

There was one week left in November when I was born, and eight hundred miles away or more, as the Spitfire flies, a Soviet-betrayed Warsaw was trying on for size yet another form of military subjugation, Stalin preparing to take over where Hitler had left off. Poles percolated west, a clutch of them fetching up in our little seafaring townships, together with the occasional German or Italian prisoner-of-war who'd opted to stay on and give Scotland a try. Germans, Poles, whatever, they seemed the same to me, Fritz and Stanislaw sharing the same pale thin grins and pensive eyes. One of them, gathering potatoes in a field once, held out to me an enormous smoked sausage, the like of which I'd never seen, and begged me to share it with him. *Vill you bite, please?* A peace offering, perhaps. They never took to the sea, though, these solid Continentals, preferring the life of farm labourers, sensible Scots earth under their feet, to the unstable element on which my mother's people took their chances. An understandable choice in the case of men whose whole world had slid from under them, leaving them staring into hell. Not that I fathomed any of this with five weeks still left to run in '44, when the war was also in the winter of its course. One way or another there was a nip in the air.

At my baptism there was ice in the font. Of all the churches the length and breadth of this sceptred isle, the old kirk stands closest to the sea, a rock built on a rock, its latticed windows lashed by spray, its leprous gravestones leaning like masts, encrusted with centuries of salt, lichens and old rhymes about death and hell that were quite literally the first literature I ever read; while inside the church the constant sound of the wash of waves appeared to be saying something in its muted melancholy way to the spartan pews and pillars. What was it saying exactly? It had something to do with death.

The interior was only marginally more inviting: one of those echoing Presbyterian barns, the whitewashed stone silence unheated sixty years ago by anything so pagan, so mundane, so modern as a radiator. Alec Fergusson, the old lobsterman who doubled as beadle and sexton, had placed the water there the night before, so that when the Reverend Kinnear removed the lid and made to perform the sacrament, he found himself staring at a frozen white shield.

But his arm was strong to smite, as all the Sunday schoolers knew (he was an ex-miner who'd suddenly seen the light, deep in the bowels of hell, and left off smoking and drinking, if not swearing), and his fist was as great as his faith. He brought it down into the stone font with force enough, my mother said, to kill a whale. The circle of ice splintered but yielded no water – it had frozen solid. There wasn't a drop to be had in the vestry either, the vestry being one step up from a latrine, the pipes iced up too in merry December, when milk comes frozen home in pail, and Mr Kinnear stood breaking the third commandment between his teeth and threatening to break others that God hadn't even thought of. So old Alec legged it down the outer steps of the church, to where a bursting sea was spraying the tombstones of my ancestors. He brought back a glimmer of cold brine in a brass collection plate. That was how it happened that the waters of the firth, which had been wetting the bones of my forebears for uncountable tides, were used that morning to baptize me – in the name of the Eternal Father (strong to save), and of the Son, and of the Holy Ghost. Amen.

My own father could not attend the ceremony and sent his regrets on a postcard. At that point he himself was in peril on the sea, somewhere on the other side of the globe, unavoidably detained by the Emperor Hirohito; and sparing a thought for the absent father, the Reverend Kinnear asked God to listen as they prayed to him to still the restless wave (*but jigger the fucking Japs!* hissed a youngling of the flock) and bring the father safely back to his infant son. A noble and heartfelt thought – but he should have saved his breath. (So should my uncle Billy, aged all of seven, who'd added the entreaty on behalf of the Japanese and who was soundly thrashed afterwards.) When the father did come home in one piece and greeted the son he'd never seen, the son lashed out with his little fist and hit the invading stranger across the face. Was it that, I wonder, that started us off on the wrong foot? Five years of war, to return to an ungrateful little wretch, a mummy's boy who'd slept with his mummy for the best part of a year and burrowed blindly into her breasts? Well, now the maternal reign was over. To the victor the spoils, as they say, and to the occupying enemy the young girl's bed. My mother was twenty-three. I can still summon up some of the cold smouldering rage I felt then, when I was torn from the sleeping place and dropped behind bars, betrayed. Real or imagined, I can't be sure. But I remember looking through the bars all right, and seeing the expression on that alien face that had swum so suddenly into my ken.

Faces, then. These are the first things that you see, floating and bobbing about you as you lie in pram or cot, or cradled in somebody's arms, faces with phases and aspects of their own, all of which you grow to know. They were neither young nor old in my brave new world of consciousness without cognition. Nor were they ugly or pretty, wise or stupid, they were simply there, constellating the microcosm that was the family. They were kindly, though, that much I could tell, apart from that one face that I came to fear,

the one with the strange grating accent, the face staring
unlaughingly at me through the scabby green bars of my
cot, the face that made me cry.

That's all I was to start with – a wafer-thin cry, a winter
wailing that went up through the thick green panes of our
skylight windows in that house on the hill, up from Shore
Street, where it mingled with the smoke from all the other
village chimneys, drifted out over the clusters of red pantiled
roofs, the reek from the kippering sheds, and was lost among
seagulls and steeples and the huge fluffed-up towers and
castles of clouds that the fishermen called Babylonians.

It was the time of the winter herring. The sea was busy with
boats and from early on I could hear them, the steam drifters
hooting in the harbour and the crews calling to one another.
I could hear the clamouring and hammering coming from
the boat-building sheds too, the muted sylvan sound of axes
on wood. There were horses snorting and stamping in the
streets, horses bringing the morning milk, horses carrying
carts laden with farm produce, horses hauling fishloads in
boxes up to the station, where the steam trains puffed and
whistled through, horses being shoed in the smiddy right
beneath our house, horses clothed in fire, stamping among
the sparks. And scarcely any distance away the sea-spray
wetted the fields where jingling horses gave way to tractors,
two eras in tandem for the briefest possible time, a childhood
glimpse of social history on the move.

But the sound that ran through my brain most of all,
the sound that I could easily disentangle from the whole
natural and social symphony, was that of water: the sound
of the living firth. This was my first language and my first
university, my alma mater, my alpha and omega, my eternal
mother, the sea, the sea.

And my actual mother, she who bore me – that was Christina: Christina Scott, telephonist, eldest daughter of Margaret Marr Gay and Alexander Scott, born 21 December 1921, a child of the winter solstice, now married to Christopher Rush, able-bodied seaman, born 9 May 1919, now engaged in war service. So I'm told sixty years later by certificates of birth and marriage, on whose ageing parchment their love in black ink still shines bright. As I stare now into the laughing teenage eyes of my mother, looking out at me from a 1930s photograph (clad in the garb of her straitened time and place, a coarse heavy coat, and shoes without stockings), I can feel again that warm wave of love she gave out all her life, and with which she must have enveloped even my father. Five years after that photograph was taken, outside my granny's house, the iron gate she leant against was gone, as were they all, gone to foundries every one, turned to guns, and turning young Huns to corpses – and young Christina was wheeling a pram.

Our house, as I've said, was on a hill, a steep winding street with the harbour glinting at the foot. Down we came in winter, in the dark, my mother pushing the pram and me in it, looking up at the bright freezing lights in the sky, among which her young face shone like a lamp. *Twinkle, twinkle little star*. The words of the song drifted from her lips in hot frosty clouds and hung between us. I reached out for them as the skidding pram ran past the sharp harled wall of the house. That was first blood – a red glove with which I could have touched the stars, but no sensation of pain, just a song in the air, still hanging there, and my mother's changing face, the sweet love in her mouth turned to an O, and those stars tingling at my fingertips.

Then came the snowdrops. It must have been February 1945 at the latest, and I'd have been all of three months. I was wheeled the mile inland to Balcaskie woods, a gloomy cathedral of evergreens, vaulted over by the interlocking boughs of ash and elm and oak, and wheeled another mile along the nave of this gothic affair, a moss-soft path, deep-piled with needles and the sea-drift of leaves, generations of birch and beech casting their carpets over the marvellous avenue along which the endless altered people came to buy snowdrops from the estate.

First a girl in a green-caped hood, bending over me and crushing the flowers into my face. Why? Who was she? Many years later I saw a white-haired lady at a local gathering and knew in myself that it was she, raped by age. The flood went over me, the memory of how they'd then loaded the pram with snowdrops, a froth of sea under which I was wheeled home, sucking in the green white scent. How valid this is as a piece of recollection I have no idea, but stuck in a pram in the winter of '45, a wordless little world, I know only that I was aglow with the knowledge of snowdrops, into which no cancerous worm had yet bitten the bitter recognition that I should surely die.

It was Epp who passed on that knowledge to me, both by instruction and by example. Epp was a great-aunt of my mother's and our landlady at Shore Road, for the house was not our own. She was Queen Victoria at No. 16, well into her eighties when I knew her and dead before I was three, but it wasn't necessary to possess a memory like mine to remember Epp. A hibernating spider, stuck in a corner, would have remembered her. She was unforgettable.

It was Epp who began my literary, religious and sex education, all rolled into one. And in all three respects as in every other, she was an anachronism. Throned on her massive moss-green velvet armchair, all curves and buttons, she presided over me in a black waterfall of lace and silk, her skirts spilling across the floor and rustling over my feet. Her fists were knotted over the head of an African cane, up which a brace of wicked-looking snakes wriggled and writhed, standing out like the veins on the backs of her hands. From this position she thundered at me every morning about how well Horatius kept the bridge in the brave days of old, and other heroic stand-offs:

> *Half a league, half a league, half a league onward . . .*
> *At Flores in the Azores Sir Richard Grenville lay . . .*
> *On Linden when the sun was low*
> *All bloodless lay the untrodden snow . . .*

Years later, coming across many of these lines at school, I realized with a shock that I was not learning them but remembering them. And suddenly I was back in front of the armchair, standing to attention, no higher than old Epp's knee, stormed at by the shot and steady shell of her wrathful cannonades, and watching once again the trembling of her dreadful dewlaps as her frail white fists descended on the arms of the chair, beating out the rhythms of the verse. She held the windowed sky in her spectacles and her head was lost in clouds of snowy white hair. She was God's mother, for sure.

'Be a brave wee man,' she lectured me when I cut my thumb and cried, 'or you'll never be a sailor like your father, or a soldier like my bonny brothers!'

'I don't want to be a soldier! I want to be a fisherman!' I howled back at her.

'A fisherman!' she scoffed. 'You might as well be a tinker!'

She never failed to pour scorn on my role models, my grandfather and his sons, who went out like matadors to face the bucking white bull of the sea.

'And you'll never get a wife either if you bubble like that! None but the brave deserves the fair!'

> *None but the brave,*
> *None but the brave,*
> *None but the brave deserves the fair.*

I wept all the louder.

When I was bad and uncontrollable and all the men in the house were at sea, I was taken to Epp.

'Oh, you scoundrel!' she scolded me. 'You bad wild boy!'

Then she would tell me that the horned and hoofed devil had flown over the rooftops on scaly black pinions of soot, that he was sitting on our roof right this minute, listening to me, and would be down the chimney at my next word. His mouth was full of sinners and that was why I couldn't hear him mumbling, but at the next swallow there would be room in his jaws for one more gobbet of begrimed humanity, and that would be me. Didn't I hear the soot falling? Open-mouthed, I turned my head to the lurid red glow of her grate. Sinister scrabblings seemed to be coming out of the awful tall blackness of the chimney, which led up to the universe, the unknown corners of God's coal-cellar. Quaking, I turned my eyes back to my torturer, her pale old face laved by flames.

'You will go to hell!' she leered. 'You will be crying for a single drop of water to cool your parched mouth as you lie in the lake of fire. Your throat will be like the Sahara. But Satan will just laugh at you before he crunches you up. And not one drop of water will you get! Not one! Oh yes, my bonny man, you'll get something to cry for in hell!'

When I ran to her, screaming, she never softened. My hands clutched at her knees, my face buried in her black lap, wetting the velvet. She smelled of moth-balls.

'Go away, you bad lad,' she said softly, sternly, stroking my hair. 'You're like every other boy that was born, picked up from the Bass Rock you were, that's where you came from, that's where your father got you, didn't you know? Why didn't he go to the May Island, the stupid wee beggar that he was, and bring us all back a nice wee lass, instead of you, you nasty brat!'

Avoiding the biology of stinking drops, Epp assured me that boys came from the Bass and girls from the May. My father's ship had gone off course. Someone had blundered, some hand at the helm. I had not been intended, that was all. Ah well, it had been wartime and many errors had been made, many wrongs committed. I was one of them.

'Ours not to reason why,' she proclaimed.

And then she was off again at her poetry and her preaching. When she came out of it she told me that since I was a boy I had better make the best of it and behave as well as I could. But like all boys I was born to be bad. There's your bairn, God had said – make a kirk or a mill of him for all I care. And like Pontius Pilate he went and washed his hands.

Poor Epp. Her two brothers had run away from home, following their father, and had died in scarlet in the Zulu wars, leaving their mother naked in her age. They'd left Epp to grow into an unmarried battleaxe, grinding out her grudge against the entire male race in those tireless tirades of hers. But if she blamed them with one breath, she glorified them with the next, and every breath in her body was dedicated to their reproach and their renown, the latter articulated unconsciously perhaps in the wild volleys of heroic poetry. These were her only concession to their selfish and stupid bravado in throwing their lives away. She was a stern Eve. She had known a sharper sting than the serpent's tooth, and the apple of life had turned to ashes in her mouth. So she bit back with venom.

But she unbent for the ceremony of the pan-drop.

I was summoned to the hearth. Taking one of the large white mints from a glass jar, the holy grail of her sideboard, she would place it on the whorled bronze corner of the fender and pulverize it with the head of the poker. And always I feared for the precious pieces, scattered amongst cinders and ash. Epp waited there to the end, watching me haughtily as I picked them out and sucked away the last white shards.

'Away you go now, you young rascal, that's all there is!'

She lifted the poker and waved me away, shaking her free fist at me. I ran from the room. I was terrified of her in those moods.

But Epp was my first queen and I her adoring subject. Her sceptre was the gleaming poker, her court the flickering hearth with its high-backed buttoned throne. The pan-drops were the favours she dispensed. And how could she or I have known then that I would one day pay tribute to her in the only coins I have ever had to spare – memory's mintage of hard-won words? Why is it, Epp, that the old lady and the little boy have to meet again after all these years? And will go on meeting until the last day's tribute has been settled.

Is it because of what happened one winter's night, that still grips me like some dreadful disease? I remember that night when the grown-ups faced one another across a bare table, all of them as dumb as stones for sheer poverty. The fishing had failed that season and there was nothing to eat. I was up whining for food and there were no toys either, nothing to distract me between ceiling and floor. I roamed the distempered walls, following my gaunt shadow beneath the gas mantles, glancing narrowly at the grown ones as they sat there in that grim-faced gathering that angered me to the bone. Why didn't they do something? I sensed it instinctively -- that this was what adults were *for*. Not my father, of course, who wasn't around that night, out drinking himself drunk again, as somebody said, pissing what little money we had up against the wall, not part of their real world of sea-stress and struggle to survive. But that was their function and burden, to shoulder the heavens that were falling on us, and instead they were sitting there like statues, while I scoured those bare unpapered walls, passing the mouse-hole over and over, out of which no mouse ever came. It had slung its tiny hook and buggered off, my uncle Billy said. And so I was the one who heard the little silver chiming at the door – so small a sound that the others did not even lift their faces out of their fists. Blotting myself against the wall, I glided to the door and stared down at two shining circles on the floor, two bright winter moons that lit up the linoleum. Two half crowns.

Down on her knees, where the grey draughts struck like daggers between the ribs, my great queen had knelt in her empty hall, on the other side of the door. She had laid her old bones down there in the dark, unseen, and had pushed back our rent money that we could not afford to pay. Through the door it had come again, from the probing tips of her white ringless fingers, from Epp, who never said a word, though everybody blessed her for that tender mercy which became her in the end better than her reign of terror.

But she breathed her last, old Epp, before she could receive the thanks of her meanest vassal. Such is the breath of old queens – brief in the bitter mornings of little boys.

One morning I was not summoned for the usual audience. When there was still no summons on the second morning I balanced pandemonium against pan-drop and decided the sweet was worth the death of the six hundred, or even my own in the sulphurous pit. Where's Epp? I pestered my mother repeatedly and she tried to calm me with a quatrain.

> *God saw that she was weary,*
> *And the hill was hard to climb,*
> *So He closed her weary eyelids*
> *And whispered, 'Rest be thine.'*

A sentimental snippet from a church magazine? An epitaph picked off a gravestone? It chiselled itself into my brain, all right, revealing itself decades later when pen on paper acted like the key in a lock. But at the time the words merely drew mysterious veils over something which I knew to be ultimate and awful, and I pursued my quest relentlessly for the vanished Epp, keeper of the pan-drops, drawing whispered riddles out of the mouths of everybody in the house. Old George, my great-grandfather, said she was now a pilgrim before God, my grandmother told me she had gone to a better land, and grandfather said she was being made ready for the kirkyard. No. 16 Shore Road was a sprawl of family, and artless infants don't need a who's who. It was years before it even occurred to me to unravel the relationships, the aunts and uncles who put the sacred seals and stoppers on Epp's passing, rather than show me a mystery. Asleep in Jesus, gone to glory, singing hymns at heaven's gate – Epp haunted me from a thousand hiding places.

At last my father, tired of my questions, told me.

'She's dead.'

Dead. What's *dead*? What does it mean, being dead? I'd asked the big one, the one that most human beings spend their lives ignoring, preferring not to think about it. What could they answer, after all? Extinction? Putrefaction? Translation? Resurrection? Judgement? Eternal bliss? Eternal torment? The lake of fire? A state when totally irreversible chemical changes have taken place in the body? That last's for sure. But none of that was on offer and I expect my upturned face and persistent questioning must have preyed on their nerves.

Yes, but what is it? What is *dead*?

So they took me to meet death.

My father snatched me up roughly under his arm and my protesting mother followed us, through the hallway, past the parlour, and into Epp's presence. It has never left me – the total blackness of the room in which she was laid out.

The silence was electric – though there was no electricity in that house of gas mantles where at that moment there was no shilling to feed the meter. A match was struck – and failed. The tight little whispers of my parents still deafen me today. Another match, breaking open the blackness and the silence. Criss-cross patterning of the trestle on which lay a big dark shape. Blackness again and another match. And then there she was, in the flaming dark, old Epp, my queen, clothed in whiteness to the wrists, the first time I had ever seen her out of black, her chosen mourning, or her stern eyes so softly closed. Now she was the bride she had never allowed herself to be. And finally, in the plunging confusion of more darkness and exploding matches, a heavy lid thudding shut, the inscrutable workmanship of shining oak, the brass mirror of the polished name-plate, Elspeth Marr, her name, her years. Where's Epp? That's where she is now, in there, in the box. And that's where she stays. Till the last trumpet. The rest was silence.

With Epp gone I ran wild for a few days before I forgot her, if I ever did forget that old queen of the night. My crimes were legion, apparently, though I remember only a few. I dry-shaved myself with my grandfather's old-fashioned open razor and wore the red results for weeks afterwards. I gulped down a bottle of Indian ink and thought it not too bad, stuck buttons up my nose beyond the reach of the local practitioner, put back a large quantity of my uncle Alec's home-brewed beer and was as sick as a pig. I also found the rum that my father had brought back from the navy and which had been put into a little brown bottle, left in the medicine-chest in the bathroom and forgotten – till I emerged reeling downstairs, clutching the bottle and the banisters. Jenny and Georgina shrieked at the tops of their voices, the house silvery with aunties' laughter. My grandmother raised her eyes to the skies, proclaiming the Apocalypse. Uncle Billy began singing a song about fifteen men on a dead man's chest. I saw fifteen rum-raddled sailors, each with a booted foot set in triumph on a dead pirate, his chest cracking like a crab's carapace as they caroused on his corpse. And I felt as drunk as all fifteen put together, and ready to take on the whole family, all nine of them.

Not the tenth, though. My father was never part of the family. He was the intruder from the open ocean whose ship had gone wrong, or so Epp had said. He should never have come here, someone had blundered. I wasn't the error, he was, though he never admitted it and always shifted the blame on to me. 'You're the nigger in the woodpile,' he'd say to me privately when something went wrong, 'you're the fucking fly in the ointment!' One adult day came the realization that he'd been swearing at me, verbally abusing me. But he'd always added, 'And you repeat that *if you dare!*' So I was forbidden to tell the secrets of my prison-house, on pain of the usual punishment, s*onny boy!* And that's what he called me as he gave me the instruction I heard a thousand times after that, heard it with fear and loathing. *Bend over that chair!* And I bent over the chair. I can see it, feel it, describe its green design, smell it, follow its damp thread-bare awfulness, its every loose thread. Off came the belt. And that's the first thrashing I remember. I wasn't even three, my bottom not even the size of his able-bodied hand.

The day of the thrashing, my first experience of inflicted pain, I escaped from the house and made my way down Shore Road, heading straight for the water, wiping away the tears, ignoring the cat-calls from the other kids. *Cry baby cry, put your finger in your eye, tell your mother it wasn't I.* I arrived on the wave-swept rocky shore, the sunken sea-dreams of my folk locked hard in my head.

The harbour crooked its arm around me. It was a safe haven but I left it, left the harbour and drifted east. Nobody stopped me as I made my way past the swaying forest of masts, the fish-curing sheds, the high sylvan din of the boat-builder's yard, where the scents and sounds of sea and forest met in a strange mingling and the men laboured minutely inside the giant curving rib-hulls of the boats, like Jonahs in the bellies of great wooden whales.

Leaving behind me the last black-painted house, I walked the last of the piers, the east pier, climbed the iron steps in the wall, came down on the seaward side and made my way out on to the zigzagging breakwater that took the batterings from the south-east seas and stood between the town and Poseidon. At the end of this Roman mole I found myself staring into the infinite depths of the sea, a calm cold world of wonder and weeds. It was a magic glass, so green and clear – if I just leaned over a little bit more and looked into it, I might see to the other side of the world . . .

Did I fall or did I simply let myself go? Better to be with Epp, perhaps, whose rage was all in her head, not in her hand, whose anger was all words. I could hear all the oceans of the world roaring in my ears. The dark tangles parted to let me go by, waved to me in passing, stroking my face, and Epp sure enough came floating up from the bottom of the world to meet me, her eyes still blind and jaw still bandaged but her arms extended. They wrapped themselves round me for the first time – she had never touched me once in all my short life – and I was surprised by her youthful strength and suppleness as she kicked us both up to heaven. My head broke back into the blue world of sunlight and air and suddenly there was water everywhere, changing its texture, a stinging blizzard of brightness and salt. Epp had changed too. I could see now that she had metamorphosed into a man – a fully dressed man, who became a boat and sailed us both back to land, where I vomited torrents of water. I was hurried to the nearest house and wrapped up by strangers, smothered in a grey army blanket whose crude red stitching I can still see out of the corner of my eye. A circle of faces, many voices, a large spoon with something in warm water – *Give him some more . . . put more brandy in . . . No, that'll do, I hear he's had enough already* – and then my mother arrived, trundling my old pram, in which I was wheeled home and put to bed.

From there I could hear the voices.

'I'll give him a bloody good thrashing when he wakes up!'

'You'll do no such thing! You've hit the boy too hard already and look what happened.'

'But Miller's lost his gold watch – do you know how much a thing like that costs?'

'It didn't cost a life, anyway, it was the other way about. Your son's alive, man. A thrashing's not going to bring the watch back. And Miller can stand it.'

My grandfather was home from the sea. I was safe. And I slipped into a warm sleep, unaware of the enormous debt owed to James Miller, boat-builder of St Monans, who'd been dressed for a funeral that day, fob watch and all. A debt my father sullenly reminded me of long afterwards. The calculation was easy, even for him. A son's life, a gold watch. And I had escaped a thrashing, though the next time he administered one and I thought it was over, he breathed for a moment before starting again, standing over me gloating and snarling, *And that's for the bleeding watch!* No justice in the world, then, but God's blind hammer and an implacable little bully. But James Miller lost a time-piece – and gave me a lifetime in return.

With my mother often putting in night shifts at the local telephone exchange in Anstruther and my father working by day and drinking by night, or vice versa, I was put in the care of old Leebie who, like the sibyl, had time on her hands. Nobody had ever worked out who exactly Leebie was – which was far from strange in a village of a thousand souls where inbreeding must have amounted to unconscious incest every now and then. Even Leebie herself didn't know, or pretended not to. 'Oh, I'm there or thereabouts on the

family tree,' was the most she came up with when questioned. Ironically it was Leebie who followed the branches
better than anyone. She could quote you the dates and places
and even times of the hatches, matches and dispatches, as she
called them, the names of the forebears, the progeny who'd
come and gone, the lines of descent, the cross-fertilization
and cross-relationships.

The task Leebie set herself was to bring me up proper,
so she said, by putting me in perspective. 'It's high time you
knew who you are,' she told me, convinced that if I knew
who I was, it would somehow confer on me the consciousness of how I should behave, and so save me from future
thrashings. This genealogical tutelage she carried out either
at the sewing-machine, her polished black shoes flying on
the treadles, or more usually while knitting one of her
long black Sunday scarves, the family line and the woollen
comforter growing longer together, knit one purl one, as
she sat there, patient and persistent as Penelope, hour by
hour, waiting for no man, but determined to make a man
out of a little boy.

On my mother's mother's side she took me back six
generations to seventeen ninety something, to a multitude
of Marrs and Gays who had never moved more than a
mile from St Monans and who had spawned shoals of local
offspring, all bearing the same bewildering names as their
forebears: William, Philip, David, Andrew, John; Helen,
Christina, Elspeth, Margaret, Georgina, Jenny, Jean. And
on my mother's father's side she reached back again into
the black bag of the past, into a time unthinkable, and came
out with a clutch of Alexander Scotts, one in every generation, who'd given my grandfather his name. The frightening
thing was that she'd known them all, all the way back to
that seventeen ninety something, before which was Adam,
and all the way down to the last Alexander, my uncle Alec,
born in 1928 and not yet out of his teens. William was the
youngest, my uncle at seven, and the one who'd sworn at

my baptism. My mother, Christina, was the eldest of the children of Margaret Marr Gay and Alexander Scott, and her sisters were Jenny and Georgina. Jenny had black hair, Georgina was fair and my mother was red. Alec was black and hairy and Billy was blond. Grandfather himself was still very dark. His spouse, as Leebie called my granny, was very grey. And then there was me, with my stupid English name that God didn't recognize because it wasn't in the bible. I was the son of Christina Scott and Christopher Rush – and of his line Leebie knew nothing at all and didn't want to. 'He doesn't belong here,' was all she said. 'But all these other lines now, they come out of the sea, and that's where you belong, my lad, just you remember that.'

Then she would tell me the story of Mary Buek on the side of my grandfather – whose mother, Bridget Burk, had hailed from Dundee. Mary Buek was a nurse in Dundee, back again in the 1790s, and Leebie had never known her because she had died in 1854, but she'd known her daughter, Margaret Watson, who'd lived till 1892 – and that, for Leebie, was only yesterday.

Always she started the story by asking for one of the pair of black-leaded cannonballs that sat on either side of the fireplace, so symmetrically placed that they looked like part of the decorative fittings of the grate, though I often initiated the narrative myself by bringing one over to her, carried with pride and difficulty to the chair where she sat smoking. Her long silky white hair was usually in a bun, but for some reason she let it down, combing it out for the story, and it came out yellow with nicotine, a weird contrast with the unblinking china-blue eyes and the chipped black teeth. She looked down at the ball, cast off the scarf she was knitting and took out the old bone comb.

'A fair-sized small shot,' she said, refilling her tiny white pipe. 'A present from the Spaniards, though not the biggest shot that hit the *Victory* that day. But it was just a wee musket ball that did the worst damage.'

Leebie struck another match and puffed. A coil of blue tobacco smoke hung round her head. Some of it drifted up to the blackened beams. The other wisps were sucked up the chimney by the draught from the fire. But her words stayed in the air like a fragrance, and the folk she told me about seemed to enter the room as she introduced them, one by one. Up the lum went the smoke, to fade into the stars – and down came Mary Buek, like a wraith risen from her grave.

Buek at least was the name on the gravestone in Kilrenny kirkyard, not much more than three miles away, but that was just the ignorance of one old local chiseller, according to Leebie. It should have read Burk and he'd put in an 'e' for an 'r', robbing her of the true sound of her immortality in an age when people still hung over the tombs and studied their stone pages. Well, you can't always believe what you read, but Buek she became, reborn in stone, and stone is stronger than paper, so Buek she stays – at least until people stop remembering, and when will that be, eh?

So Leebie's talk drifted on.

Mary Buek came down from Dundee and married a Cellardyke fisherman called Watson, Thomas Watson. He was press-ganged in 1797 and the jolly jack tars took Mary along too, mainly on account of her being a nurse. What could be better aboard a man-o'-war? So the pair of them became guests of His Majesty aboard HMS *Triumphant*, which took them to Leith. After that it was the high seas and the French wars. The century turned like a tide and lifted Thomas Watson to the position of bosun gunner on HMS *Ardent*, a line-of-battle ship with sixty-four guns. And it was below the decks of that ship, to the thunder of the guns, that their baby daughter Margaret was born, right in the thick of the Battle of Copenhagen in 1801. Some birth that was, in the middle of that death-ridden bedlam, down in the cockpit, the bloody womb of the ship, delivered among the dead and dying. Margaret Watson's cradle was a rolling man-o'-war that shivered and shook in the North Sea. Her lullaby was the iron song of cannonballs, the rending of timbers, the shrieks of mutilated men. Stranger still for all those suffering and doomed sailors, whose cries were filling the ship, to hear the wail of a new-born baby rising thinly into the world of terrors that they were just on the point of leaving.

So then they were three. And the battle was a victory for Nelson. Their employers would have let them go after that but Thomas and Mary stayed in service for another five years until six months after Trafalgar, and the little girl stayed with them, knowing nothing much of the wide world except ships and sailors during all that time. Her lasting memory was of Trafalgar itself.

Strange today to think that I was taught my first history lesson by one old lady who'd known another who'd been at the Battle of Trafalgar. It's now the year 2005 and that battle was exactly two centuries ago. Impossible? No. I'm sixty as I write this. Leebie was born in the 1860s and the Trafalgar baby lived to the age of 91. Leebie was in her late twenties when Margaret Watson died – the dove-tailing of eras was far from tight – and she'd heard her talk about Trafalgar often enough.

Margaret remembered the roaring and the rolling, the flashes of fire and clouds of smoke and the song of the guns among the shrieking beams. She remembered her mother standing with arms red to the elbows, helping the man with the shining blades who did such terrible things to the sailors. And she recalled their shouts, which Leebie repeated with stabbing actions of her pipe, the smoke curling out of her blackened mouth as she replicated the scene and gave the orders. *Close up, there! Two points abaft the beam! Point-blank, now, point-blank! Fire, damn you, fire!* And she remembered the man with the stars on his coat being brought down to the cockpit and laid out on some spare sails, where Captain Hardy kissed him. He asked for lemonade and wine and water, but he never finished it. The tide had gone out of his body and no sun or moon could bring it in again. Soon afterwards the ship burst out into a round of sweet cheers for the victory that matched its name. But the cheers withered almost as soon as they began. Everybody was thinking about the great sailor, stretched out on his bed of sails.

What more fitting a bed to die on, for a seaman who'd stood beneath their billowing clouds through so many famous campaigns?

It was Mary Buek who dressed the corpse and embalmed it for burial back in England. Nelson had asked not to be given to the waves. And so to the famous barrel of rum and the tapping of the Admiral, the sailors sucking the life-force out of their leader, imbibing his seamanship all the way home. As for the Watsons, they'd had enough action and adventure for a lifetime. They returned to Cellardyke where, with their prize-money, they opened up an ale-and-pie shop at the harbour head. Margaret Watson married a cooper and became Mrs Camble. She had a large family but she outlived every single one of them and lived on to tell her story a thousand times.

'They're all lying up there now in Kilrenny kirkyard,' said Leebie. 'I'll take you one day and show you their headstones.'

She never did, but I found them out myself long after Leebie was dead, and there they still stand.

ERECTED
BY MARGARET WATSON
IN MEMORY OF HER HUSBAND
JOHN CAMBLE 1801–1859
ALSO
MARGARET CAMBLE 1801–1892
THREE OF THEIR CHILDREN LIE EAST OF THIS
STONE

That was the memorial I discovered first, and I knew that

beneath the simple stone lay the baby of the sea-battle, now a bundle of old bones. Later, as a student, I inspected Scotland's Census of 1856, and there, listed among all the familiar street names of Cellardyke houses – George Street, James Street, Dove Street – there she was: Margaret Watson, born HMS *Ardent*, 64-gun ship at sea, during Battle of Copenhagen, 2nd April 1801. And though I'd known it all already, it still came as a shock to see it so simply, so starkly, so officially recorded. And there I was, a child again, blowing away Leebie's pipe-smoke and feeling the weight of the small shot that had found its way from a Spanish battle-ship to No. 16 Shore Road.

The older stone always struck me with even more force by its matter-of-factness and understatement.

ERECTED
BY MARY BUEK
IN MEMORY OF HER HUSBAND
THOMAS WATSON MARINER
CELLARDYKE
DIED 17th DEC 1831 AGED 66
ALSO OF HIS WIFE
MARY BUEK WHO
DIED 28th FEB 1854 AGED 77

On the reverse side of the stone there was a simple epitaph:

> *What though we wade in wealth or soar in fame,*
> *Earth's highest station ends in 'Here he lies.'*

When I first saw that stone I was a secondary school pupil at Waid Academy, Anstruther, and I was about to sit a final history exam as part of my Higher Leaving Certificate, so I had with me a copy of Keith Feiling's *A History of England*. I lay down on the summer grass and leaned back

against the epitaph, thumbing through the tome. One of
Feiling's sentences leaped out at me. 'Few places are better
known in England than the cockpit of the *Victory*.'

How many in England knew about this simple Scottish
headstone? Few places could be more obscure. The stone
didn't even carry a record, however brief, of the things the
Watsons had done. Bosun gunner? Trafalgar? Nelson's
nurse? Not a mention, not the merest reference. Mariner,
Cellardyke – that was it, a simple seaman, nothing more.
That's when I first realized that history in the long run is
made up of people, and by people – not the Napoleons and
the Nelsons but little people like the Watsons who'd been too
busy living and dying to think about making history. That
was for their leaders to worry about. The French marvelled
at the superiority of the British naval gunnery when their
own ships and guns were technically better. Some would say
it took men like Nelson to work the witchcraft. Old Leebie
took a different line, that gunners like Thomas Watson and
women like Mary Buek were what made the difference.
What did it matter for them now? People would pass by
their stones and never know the greatness they had touched,
and their own touch of greatness too. But Leebie made sure
I knew it and that I'd not be blinded by the icon of English
naval history. 'Your father's an English sailor,' she grimaced
at me, sucking the last of the pipe, 'just another able-bodied
tarry-breeks. But that's not where you're sprung from. You
go back through your mother to a time when ships were
made of wood and men were made of iron.'

'What were the women made of?' I asked.

'The women were made of sterner stuff, and that's all you
need to know. And now you know just who you are.'

So then I knew who I was: the scion of a female fore-
runner who'd sunk the world's greatest sailor in a butt of
grog, to be reborn in every drop, in every mouth, all the
way to England.

How much effect Leebie's family slant on history had on my behaviour is hard to calculate. But there was no doubting the efficacy of her other method of bringing me into line. She threatened me with the *Mars*. The *Mars* was a floating borstal, a grey hulk to which bad boys were sent instead of going to jail. I never saw the *Mars* but Leebie let me know whenever it happened to be anchored just off the harbour, which was whenever I was threatening to misbehave, and the night was dark and the curtains drawn. It was then that I hovered anxiously between the devil on the chimney and the *Mars* on the deep blue sea.

On the *Mars* boys were made to scrub the decks all day long. That was all they ever did – scrubbed until their kneecaps wore whitely through the red rags of their skin, like the elbows of old women, and their hands were sodden lumps of carbolic soap, soggy and scarlet from the dawn-to-dusk immersions. They were made to use freezing water and if there was a single speck of dirt left on deck by any boy, that boy was tied to the mast and flogged. Buckets stood ready to catch the blood as it leaped from the cat-o'-nine-tails that they used for the flogging. The *Mars* boys lived on hard tack, with maggots for meat. They slept with rats in their bunks, but when they had been especially bad they were put in the bilge in chains, and the wobble-eyed crabs came and linked claws round their necks, fringed their raw wrists and tore off their toes one by one.

By this time Leebie had left juvenile correction methods so far behind as to convince me. I could picture those living necklaces and bracelets, and I knew exactly what it would be like to have no toes. An old man called Tom Tarvit used to hobble up the hill to see my great-grandfather. He was an ex-whaler and had lost all ten toes in the Antarctic. He

came in on two sticks bent in half, dripping from the nose
and drooling from the mouth.

'You'll be just like Tom Tarvit,' Leebie would say to me.
'Not a toe to your foot and not a tooth to your head.'

In which unfortunate circumstance – Leebie always
added – I'd be unable to go to the shops. Eager for the
shops, not so much because of anything that was actually on
offer on those late '40s shelves, as because of the adventure
they presented in getting there, I settled down to earn the
kingdom of heaven, the right to keep my toes, and also to
leave the house on my own.

Battling to the baker's then through heavy seas of wind
that pitched me from side to side of the street and did with
me what they wanted. Clutching the coppers tightly in my
pink freezing fist, I pushed open our front door, only to be
knocked flying as it came back at me like a cannon on the
recoil. My mother held it open for me and I edged my way
through the blue murder-hole and found myself in the grip
of my first screaming north-easter.

It ripped off my cap, diminishing it to a speck halfway
across the harbour, to be intercepted by a disappointed gull.
It tore at my hair, tugging at the roots, shredding it to spikes,
forcing the tears from screwed-up eyes. It punched me full
in the face, bullied the legs from me, knocked me flat on my
nose, spun me round like a top, lifted me up by the seat of my
pants and catapulted me to the corner of our street. I tried
to turn up the narrow wynd but the wind shot down like
a battering ram and thudded me against the harbour wall,
panting for breath. When I wanted to walk it made me run.
If I tried to run, it drove me back. If I stood still it rocketed
between my legs, sending me sprawling, splay-footed, into
the gutter. As I lay there reeling, some words from Epp ran

through my dazed brain. *The wind bloweth where it listeth and thou hearest the sound thereof, but canst not tell whence it cometh and whither it goeth.* And that much, so I reckoned, was for sure.

At last I came somehow to the foot of the big broad wynd and began the ascent. Up at the top of the hill I could see all the houses puffing like steam drifters, chugging a passage through the storm. The crews were snug inside, fathers, mothers, youngsters, munching their yesterday's bread. Only I was out and about this morning, riding the dawn, bobbing like a berserk cork in the invisible rivers of wind, and still not a roll for breakfast in our house. I had to reach the bakehouse or we would perish one and all. But the storm wind stood in the way. There was only one thing to be done. I spread my arms wide, turned myself into a gull and flew straight up the brae, landing in a perfect pouncing dive right at Guthrie's door. Why was it that I could never perform that feat again, except in dreams?

They never understood my heroic undertaking, the men in the bakehouse that day, safe in their quiet solid world of dough that rose no further than their oven doors. It was a dim windless little world, the bakehouse, dusted with snow-flour and icing-sugar. The bakers stood white-elbowed among the slow storms of yeast, their faces red as their fires. And the freshly baked bread stood in battalions behind them in beautiful order, piping hot and waiting to be bought and eaten. I passed through to the shop, under floury hands that tousled my hair.

'My mother's rolls, please.'

Mrs Guthrie picked a baker's dozen from the last piping tray, passing them to me with an expert swirl of the paper bag.

'Run all the way home now,' she said.

But then she took a cream cookie from a very small tray of cakes, put it in a separate bag and handed it over the counter with a wide pearl-strung smile.

'That's for you.'

I stood before her, open-mouthed with gratitude and worship – Mrs Guthrie, now my queen, the apple-cheeked baker's wife with the flashing teeth, apples in her face and apples in her pink brocaded bosom, as she rested her breasts on the high counter, displaying her cleavage, and placed her broad bare arms across the wood, bending to say goodbye. Flour on her wedding-ring touching my face, flour sprinkling her butterfly spectacles, snow-blinding her flashing eyes till I wondered how she could see, flour in her hair, lending it its only whiteness, raven-haired Mrs Guthrie, queen of the apple-tarts, now queen of my heart, Mrs Guthrie, now white bones in the green mound of the kirkyard hill, still smiling beneath the white unbroken bread of the January snow.

Or I was sent to Agnes Meldrum's shop and house in Virgin Square, off the east pier. Agnes served between endless cups of tea, sipped from the saucer, while her mother, who had seen out a century by the time I was born, sat unblinking in a basket chair, her hands knotted like Epp's round the head of her stick, never uttering a word. The customers always greeted her out of politeness but she came out of the corners of her hundred years for nothing and nobody, and I had never heard her speak. Some folk even said that she was dead – had died years ago and Agnes had had her stuffed, though nobody dared say so in the shop, even in a whisper. The opposing story was that, far from being dead, she had preternatural hearing and could hear your thoughts, even though you were at the other end of the village with your head under water. That at least was my uncle Billy's view. Alec belonged to the other camp – that she was stone dead. Although it was obvious, if you stared at her for a long time, that she was subject to certain minuscule movements, Alec attributed these to 'nerves', of the sort that kept a fish quivering long after you had killed it. But Alec was older. Billy by this time was all of ten – and gave out truths with the absolute majesty of his decade. To be ten seemed to me to be in the fullest glory of life.

Agnes herself was in her seventies. Her shop counter was really an enormous old dresser. In its dark mahogany drawers she kept her personals, as she called them, bits and pieces of linen and lingerie, together with whatever spinsterish secrets could not be sold over the counter to a mere boy.

'Don't you go near them drawers,' she was forever warning the boys who came into her shop, searching for sweets. 'Them's my unmentionables.'

All the goods that could be mentioned – and they were precious few – were laid out with neat precision on the dark wooden shelves that lined the house from wall to wall and ceiling to floor.

Agnes's father had been a master-mariner with an extraordinary taste for literature. He had brought back from his voyages books from all over the globe, amassing a library which might have graced a medieval monastery or a Renaissance university, along with other volumes of the nineteenth century. The ministers and schoolmasters of the time buzzed like bees about the Meldrum house, sipping the nectar of knowledge.

Nor for long, though. Captain Meldrum perished in the China seas in his early fifties and his library suffered an even worse fate. Agnes and her mother had no liking for books and no understanding of their value. The shelves were stripped bare and the books bundled off down to the cellar, where they lay for years in tea-chests for the dampness and the rats to do their worst. Periodically Agnes would rescue a few, pulling them from the chests, blowing off the loose tea, and placing them on the shelves of the house-turned-shop, next to the eggs. Not for any educational purpose. Egg boxes were an invention of the 1950s, and until they became available customers with a taste for eggs and the classics could consume interesting breakfasts. Agnes used the

contents of her father's books as packaging. Systematically
she tore out their pages, crumpling them into balls and using
them to separate the eggs, each egg individually wrapped in
a scholarly leaf, and the dozen or half dozen popped into
ordinary brown paper pokes that would not have been proof
against most message boys, including myself – not without
the additional protection of the academic wrapping.

An entire library was shredded in this way over a period
of decades, in the course of which a dozen eggs could have
improved a man's mind no end, and an egg a day for three
or four years produced a Master of Arts. But the eggs were
rationed, like everything else, the precious coupons limiting
your entitlement, and meanwhile the mice were nibbling
away at the roots of the tree of wisdom, and Agnes simply
ripped her way through the great works. Now, where leather-
bound, gilt-spined editions of Milton and Shakespeare had
once stood like palms in the wilderness of Virgin Square,
jars of humbugs and Chivers jellies offered themselves like
manna to us post-war indigents with nothing but holes in
our pockets.

Agnes went round the shelves with the list: a tin of
Lyle's golden syrup; a tin of Fowler's treacle; a half pound
of margarine; half a dozen eggs; a tea loaf; a packet of Rinso;
a bar of Sunlight; a packet of Wild Woodbine; and a quarter
of black-striped balls.

'That'll be nine shillings and elevenpence, and no doubt
you'll be getting the penny for going. Do you want to spend
it here?'

'The boat's not in yet, my mother said to say.'

'I'll put it on the slate. Your grandfather can pay me when
he goes to the lines.'

'My granny says he doesn't go to the lines until the
spring.'

'There will be no herring in the firth this winter,' said old
Mrs Meldrum suddenly, staring over the head of her stick
into seas of space a hundred years away. I looked into the

fathomless eyes and Agnes looked from her mother to me, and then down at the slate.

'You'd better tell your grandfather what she said. If she breaks her silence it's only to speak God's truth.'

As I reached the door the old woman repeated her prediction. The voice came out of an empty sea-shell, brittle and white and dry, as if the ghost of a crab had spoken. I opened the door and the bitter whisper followed me into the wind.

'There will be no herring in the firth this winter, you mark my words.'

The prophecy was fulfilled. The winter fishing started on the second day of January and lasted till the end of March. The days were gone that my grandfather talked about, when winter mizzen masts and sails were stepped and rigged. Now you could hear engines chugging in every boat, though still the change was made in the nets from black to white at the start of the year, white for winter. The fleet left the harbour every day and night, drifting up and down the firth in the hope of herring. From east to west, from north to south, from Fife Ness to Elie Ness, from close inshore to as far out as the May Island, and across to the Fidra, the Bass and Berwick Law, they shot their nets over and over, hauling them in heavy with living silver, or sometimes, as Leebie used to say, 'as empty as Kilrenny kirk'.

This particular January was a disaster, just as old Mrs Meldrum had foretold.

'Bloody old witch!' muttered grandfather. 'It's like hauling in the middle of the first week that ever was – before God even made the fishes!'

So he came into harbour that year and told me instead about his first night at sea, when he was a boy, and not much older than me.

Now in another millennium, when I shut my eyes in winter, I can hear the story and see its teller, sitting on a bench by the white bowling-green. Another old man was with us, an older man than my grandfather by far. Gloved and overcoated, capped and scarved, he was little more than a shrunken voice, trembling on the edge of the bitter wind that blew that day.

'It's a cold wind,' he said, 'a cold, cold wind.'

'It is that,' said grandfather, 'but it's turned westerly at long last.'

The old reedy voice became thinner still.

'Ah,' he said, 'it's farther west than that. It's farther west than westerly, let me tell you.'

Grandfather smiled, and I could hear the smile in his voice.

'How far west can the wind get?' he asked. 'How far west can a westerly wind actually go?'

The old head shook on its frail stalk, its eye sharing the secret with the invisible eye of the wind. *Thou canst not tell whence it cometh nor whither it goeth* – so Epp had said, quoting scripture. But this ancient seadog, long retired, seemed to know the secrets of the wind even better than God.

'Aye sir,' he said, 'it's a far west wind, farther west than westerly by far.'

Grandfather never answered. But I hear him speaking now.

It was on a boat called the *Regina* that I first went to sea – a sixty-foot boat made of Scottish larch, with a keel of American elm: 1071 KY, that was her number. Old Jock Dees was the skipper, Adam his son, Alan Keay his son-in-law, Ecks Ritchie, Rob Ritchie and my father. That was the crew for my first time at the winter herring.

It was the second day of the year. My father wrapped me in a huge jacket and I stood on the fo'c'sle trap. Cold? I've never felt cold like it, a westerly half-gale it was, and there was no appearance in the Mill Bay, off Kilrenny, or off the coves at Caiplie, or even at Crail, when we had all the lights in a line in the small hours of the morning. But just off Kilminning farm we saw five gannets that took a sudden dive, all together, like a white hand plunging into the water.

'That's the hand of God,' said my father.

'Let's follow that hand then,' Adam said.

So we went the way the hand pointed. We shot the anchored nets and left them there.

Head on then it was, coming home in the dark, with all the harbour lights lighted and the white spray flying in our faces. Lumps of it struck me between the eyes like ice, the white whips lashing my cheek till the flesh quivered and I wanted to cry. I wouldn't sit down though, and my father put his arm around me. Everybody was wondering what the morning would bring when we sailed back to the nets. Would we have anything to show for our tiredness and cold? Would we even be able to haul the nets at all for the weather?

Jock Dees, the skipper, was in no doubt.

'It'll be a fine morning the morn's morning,' he said, 'for the wind's far west now.'

We got three cran that morning, the first catch of the season and me ten years old. Each man got ten shillings and the boat got five. The skipper should have had two shares but he only took one. He gave me the extra shilling, the one that was left over, for my first time at sea. A mere pittance for a night and a morning of cold and exhaustion and wetness and sleeplessness and hunger. One shilling. But I've never spent it yet.

The first of an old man's stories, recalled in stark detail, even to the numbers he cited. And I still have that coin of his that he passed on to me, the one that he could never bring himself to break, with the head of Queen Victoria, and the date, 1875, I who pay more in taxes each month than my grandfather earned in his whole life.

At the turn of the year now, as I sit in rooms of amber before an embering fire, and I hear the wind veer from west-south-west to north-west, I take out the shilling and stare at it, and those old scenes and stories come creeping back into my mind. And the faintest feeling of guilt stirs as I remember one other saying. It was said to me by Leebie (who lived on into my teens) when I came home much too late one night, in the small hours, not from catching herring like my grandfather – the fish and the father-figure were both gone by then – but from a youthful party and smelling of drink.

'A far west wind, like all good young men, goes soon to its bed at even.'

That's what she said. Winds don't change their habits much, though young men do.

Later I lay back in my grey army blankets in the long night, listening wide-eyed to the loud hallooing of the owls as they tore their prey with rough strife up in the wild woods, beyond Balcaskie. And from farther west and up country I could hear the weird and wilder cries of the geese in their midnight arrivals at Kilconquhar loch, where they drowned the witches long ago. Once I nearly drowned too – and Miller's fat gold watch now lay at the bottom of the sea, beyond the breakwater blocks, its ticking long stopped. If Miller hadn't pulled me out in time, then I would have stopped too, just like a watch. Like Nelson and all his crew, like Thomas Watson and Mary Buek, in spite of the victory, in spite of the life-affirming rum.

I opened my eyes wider still, listening. Not far from where I was sleeping lay the dead of the village, frozen like fish in a black fathom of earth. Could they feel this terrible cold, tinkling on the jack-frosted panes? Could they hear these cries, these terrible thoughts of mine?

And old Epp was lying up there with them, a whiteness in a box, packed about by blackness, Epp who had said that the dead know not anything, denying her own stories of eternal torment. Agony or extinction, earth or fire, which was it? One day we would all be dead.

I closed my eyes tight in my terror, shutting out the stars.

2

Home from the Sea

We lived on in Epp's house while certain legal wrinkles appeared, and were ironed out again – on the deep brow of time, in Leebie's sonorous parlance. She may have mixed her metaphors but it wasn't hard for me to imagine a forehead under the steam iron – I simply thought of my father's. He had a way of raising his eyebrows any time I happened to squint at him out of the corner of my eye, as if to ask me what I was looking at, and the effect was ugly – a field of furrows in that arrogant pink flesh. I had already developed a tendency to play with images. They came at me in my dreams. But leaving Epp's house was no dream. It was a short journey up the hill, away from Shore Road and into one of the newly built council houses sitting in what had been the previous year a green sweep of field. The war itself now seemed like a bad dream, people said. Men had left the village and died, but even more had come in, men like my father, eager to pull off those bell-bottoms and be fruitful – and all those hopeful new families had to be housed.

The house itself was clean and light and without corners and cubby-holes and stairs, free from the dark retentions of the old house. All the new memories were waiting for us to make them, waiting to be impressed on the smart-smelling linoleum, the freshly papered walls. They came, in time, and were imprinted, indelible as the patterns themselves. And in time I came to hate it, that house, and left it without

regret, closing its door behind me one day with the toe of
my boot. It was a place where I merely marked time, not
lived. I stepped out instead into the brand-new decade of the
'50s – and into my grandfather's house.

Whatever the wrinkles were (and I never found out), they
split us up, forcing me out from under the strong gentle
wings of my mother's folk and into the clinical prison of No.
16 Inwearie Street, where my father now held sway – the
cock of the midden, as Leebie said. But whenever I had the
chance, I left the new house to its unformed identity and
made a beeline for the braehead.

Here my grandfather had bought a house further back
from the harbour than Shore Road but with a high windiness
which gave out on a gull's-eye view of the village and the
whole of the firth. A clutter of red rooftops jostled crazily
down to the shore, their chimneys sparkling in the sun or
puffing through the winter storms. The firth flashed its
fire at us. Or we watched its grey glimmerings all the way
from Earlsferry on the west side, up past Pittenweem and
Anstruther on the east. But always it was on the move, a
fluid kaleidoscope of sound and colour. Infiltrated in this
way, even the graveyards seemed not to stand still. All
along the coast the village steeples linked land and sea and
sky, fish and fishermen and fishers-of-men. Like forefingers
jutting from sturdy fists, they pointed at God, somewhere
up there. And to the south and east the big blue folds of
firth and firmament were pinned together by three blue
brooches – the May Island, the Bass Rock, from which I'd
been brought in error, and Berwick Law on the other side
of the world.

The house was actually two houses, which for some
reason they called the old house and the new house, though
both were ancient. The old was separated from the new by
the transe, a narrow funnel two feet wide which led to the
yard, and through which the north-east wind whistled like
an arrow, hitting you like Harold at Hastings, Leebie said,

giving you an instant cold in the eye and blurred vision for a week.

On the east side of the transe was the new house, lived in by the whole family. The other house was mainly used for old lumber, torn nets and broken creels, except for one room which was occupied solely by my great-grandfather. It contained a stove, a bed, a table and chair, and a small desk in the sea-facing window, on which his huge pulpit-bible was always laid out. An old sea-chest stood in front of this desk, serving as a seat. This he called his 'headquarters'.

The door of the new house opened on to what we called 'The Room', first off the hallway. This was my grandmother's holy-of-holies, cold and clean as a new gutting knife and joyless as an unbaited hook. Only at funerals was I allowed into this special room, which nobody but granny ever went into anyway, except sometimes Leebie, who sat there in the cold, revolving her memories, and Georgina, to play the old piano. The doctor was always taken in there first, whenever he came, and the minister and the undertaker; once a man in grey who my mother said was a lawyer – and they all carried death and depression in their terrible black bags, their soft white faces and hands. They sat there among the polished oak and cold brass, sipping tea and rehearsing for their coffins. Helping them along, staring at them from dresser and sideboard and mantelpiece, were my rusted brown ancestors in their heavy gilt frames, grimly assuring me that life was a deadly business. As I peered through the keyhole of the Room on these state occasions, the black-clothed visitors seemed to stiffen and grow tarnished and brown, merging with the gowned ghosts, the faded frock-coated phantoms in their frames, disappearing into the dimension of the dead, into Leebie's unthinkable history.

These were the Davids and Andrews and Alexanders, the Christinas and Elspeths and Jeans. Only one of them drew me like a moth to her pale flame – a young bride, sad and slender as a white willow, almost weeping, it seemed to me, on her wedding day. Her husband had such gigantic whiskers – how could they possibly kiss? He carried the commandments in his eye and a bible under his arm. His other hand grasped his young wife's with an inflexible caress, and with her free fingers she held a single brown rose to her bosom – tenderly, but so unlike Mrs Guthrie, with her floury fingers and flashing glasses and the apples in her dress, apples resting on the counter.

The young bride's breasts were buttoned up to the neck. An invisible sea was breaking on her beautiful brow. I touched her with my nose, wiping the breath from the flower, the rose that had been red on her wedding night. If only she could have known the ecstasy I might have given her, had I sailed backwards through the frames of generations on my grandfather's boat, saving her from life with that dreadful beard, that bible. But what would I do when I got there? What was the ecstasy that existed between man and woman, that made my mother sigh some sleepless nights? And what did the bible mean when it said that the sons of God *went in unto* the daughters of men?

'Come out of that room this minute, you young rascal!'

She was always there whenever I went back for her, always awaiting the rescue that could never be, for ever a bride and still to be plucked, her petals not yet fallen. And that stern sea beating on her brow. But I passed her by behind the closed door nearly every day, going straight through to the kitchen where everybody lived, eating and drinking, shouting and singing, telling stories and falling asleep and falling out, year by yesteryear.

Except that it wasn't a kitchen really, it was the heart of a ship, with its dark driftered beams brushing my grandfather's head, its sun-slanting, small-paned windows that let in the light but beat off the rains, and its winter-thick walls in which we were cribbed and cabined off from all the winds that the firth threw at us. Long long since, my grandfather said, in the long agos before the Flood, some bewintered

boat had been caught up by the biggest wave in the world
and flung right up on to the braehead. The sails had been
torn away, the masts toppled over, the hull splintered and
stove in. But the mariners, unwilling to abandon the ship
that had been their home, had built this house around its
knotted heart of oak, and we had inherited it.

The engine-room was the hearth, the heart of the ship
that never stopped beating. The first sounds would be
grandmother at the big black-leaded grate, worrying it
into life, raking out yesterday's white ash, blowing the cold
embers back into being. A few sticks thrown on and soon it
was crackling again without having to be relit. She would
never let it go out, superstitiously equating its pulses with
the family's, and she told me proudly that it was the same
fire as had burned in Epp's house, and in the house before
that, the house she and my grandfather were first married
in. Each time they moved home, grandfather had scooped up
the glowing embers of the very last fire and run with them
in a bucket to the new house. She made the doors of the grate
gleam with Zebrite and she polished its knobs and rails with
Brasso. She kept the blackened kettle on the boil. It was my
grandmother who first taught me to find faces in the fire,
golden long-haired heroes and ashen-faced old men, flickering sprites and soldiers on the march. And when everyone
was at home there was a circle of ten faces looking into those
other faces and listening to the heart's red beating against
the white and black beatings of winter. I have no memory of
my father sitting there – he was never part of that circle.

Everything in the kitchen had its appointed place.
Hanging from hooks in the low black beams, the various
mugs and pitchers constellated my childhood, the pots and
pans, the toasting-fork, the brass tankard, the potato-masher,
small handlines of brown twine rolled round bits of kindling
– and the odds and ends of clothing that were put on and off
at the last minute by the adults in their comings and goings,
my grandfather's cap on a nail nearest the door.

Between the kitchen and the Room a steep staircase wound
its way dimly up to the bedrooms, where the big ones of the
family, all beards and bosoms, slept out those few desperately short hours of their lives when they were not working
or worrying or putting food into those busy mouths that
murmured endlessly in front of the fire.

The back of the house faced the sea. It had a paved yard
with a coal-cellar, a barking boiler and a gear-loft built over
the wash-house. And it was the wash-house that was the
scene of the most furious activity in the life of the family.
My mother lit the fire beneath the washing boiler, and when
the water in the copper began to boil and bubble, the whites
were thrown in – the flannel shirts and vests, the long johns
for men on stilts, and nightgowns for spare sails; shifts and
sea-boot stockings, sheets and slips and pillowslips; and here
and there the scantier things worn by the young aunts, who
snatched them up with squeals and blushes, throwing them
in quickly to prevent their brothers running round the yard
with them on their heads. And there we all stood, knee-deep
in our own dirty washing, drowning under the warm waves
of bleach, winnowed by sunlight on the outside walls.

At the end of the long herring seasons the huge washings
of heavy woollens and beddings took place and every woman
in the house seemed to be washing every day for a fortnight.
Set upon set of working clothes piled up in an aromatic
jumble – thick brown kersey trousers and oiled-wool jerseys,
barked jumpers and reefer coats, all the boat's bedclothes in
which grandfather and his sons had slept hard in their bunks
in the nights broken by sea and herring. They came into the
yard and emptied their kit-bags upside down on the stones,
drawing the tie-ropes through the brass eyelets, shaking
the bags upside down until everything that had suffered the
direst cruelty of the sea, from woollen hats to pepper-and-

salt socks, came tumbling out in a sudden salt-stiffened bundle to be dumped straight into the dolly barrel.

Leebie directed operations and she and my mother and my aunts stood round the tub in a striving circle, armed with their wooden dolly sticks. They were like giant potato-mashers and Billy assured me that this is exactly what they were. Sometimes they sailed to South America, he said, and there the potatoes were bigger than your head. You needed a club this size to mash them up. Then you brought them back with you and they did for the washing. 'We cut them from Norwegian pines,' he added, 'deep in the fiords.' And as they thudded up and down in the barrel, beating the brine out of the blankets and three weeks' body-sweat from the clothes, the women were women no longer, but the white Lapland witches of Leebie's stories, singing and thumping in a circle of suds, scarlet-armed, their red faces like rising moons over a foaming sea.

'I'm forever blowing bubbles,' sang auntie Jenny, suds on her cheeks and in her hair, foam flying from her as she floated round the yard like a ballerina.

> *I'm forever blowing bubbles,*
> *Pretty bubbles in the air,*
> *They fly so high, nearly reach the sky,*
> *Then like a dream they fade and die.*

My grandmother stood watching out of the grey prison of her asthma as her three daughters heaved and sweated in the glory of their youth, their dresses drenched and clinging to their bosoms, hair flying in the bright wind, blowing bubbles like mermaids, just as Jenny sang. My mother wielded the scrubbing brush on the big aluminium board, larding the dirtier linen with monster yellow bars of Lifebuoy soap. And Leebie worked the mangle, rinsing and wringing with arms made of anchor-rope – she was tough and long and slippery as an old conger-eel, was old Leebie.

'All hands on deck!' she would shout on wash days, and the yard at once became warm and wet and wild with female life. Soon the pinned-up sheets would be walloping in the big-bellied wind, carrying us like sails over the roofs of all the other houses, into the far-flung foam of the clouds.

But it was the garret that was my favourite part of the ship. I stowed away up there, hidden among the piles of nets that belonged to grandfather's boat. There were over seventy of them. He used to say that if he shot his whole fleet of nets together he'd have fifty million meshes in the water, waiting for the fish to swim into them and drown.

'And if I had a herring come into every mesh,' he said, 'how rich a man do you think I'd be?'

'Rich enough to retire?' I asked.

'What would I have to live for without the herring to fish?' he said. 'It's what I was born for.'

All his best gear was kept in the garret: coils of net ropes and messenger ropes beneath the benches; canvas buoys and green glass floats hung from the rafters; herring baskets and barrels stacked in piles; lobster creels, partan creels, lanterns, dead-eyes and grappling irons. There were all kinds of lines too – small lines and great lines with their huge hooks that went down hundreds of fathoms, and sprools and jigs that sank into the sea unbaited but came up jerking with fish. Boxes of pirns, corks, mending needles; bottles of oil, tins of alum and cutch – and a great kist crammed with old sea-clothes. Oilskins hung from nails round the walls, the yellow forms of old fishermen, vanished heads haunting the empty sou'westers, thigh-length leather boots standing strangely upright, though the sea-legs had long gone that had steadied them on slippery decks. And across the rafters lay the giant cod, every drop of juice squeezed out of them by the June suns of the season past.

On summer days, when the high blue heat came in through the skylight, I lay back on piles of half-mended herring nets and closed my eyes. I could smell them, the spirits of the sea, and those strange wraiths of the deep that they talked about round the fire. They were everywhere, lingering in the lobster-creels, flitting in and out of the wickerwork through which the sunlight waved and winked like the sea itself, coiling into nostril and eye, salting my drowned brain that had so nearly stopped ticking. Even the shiny hooks that had hung deep down in the water, so many fathoms out of sight, had come up from the seabed flickering with stories, waiting to be taken off and fed on like fish. When it rained I put on the giant oilskins, opened the skylight, stuck out my sou'westered head from the wheelhouse roof and steered the ship straight into the blur that lay beyond the harbour – till down in the galley the cook called me to come below and take my tea. They made a makeshift bed for me up there, where I sometimes slept when my mother and father were working night shifts, and by night on my mattress, lying among nets, the rafters shivered in black waves, the dried cod came to supple life, swam in white shoals through my sleep, and the yellow oilskins were the drowned fisherfolk of the family past, floating in the night-sea of my dreams like golden ghosts.

We were a tight-knit crew. My grandfather was the skipper of the house, and the house followed the fortunes of his steam drifter, the *Venus*, as it breasted the seasons in search of herring, the mainstay of our lives. Nights of hard hauling streaked my grandfather's arms, the blue veins standing out like knotted string, and lay in the tiredness of his eyes. Days he tossed back like spray from his head. The years broke over him as though he would never be done but would keep on sailing into the skyline. No matter where you go, he used to say, there's always a horizon – in front of you, behind you, all around.

How can I describe him, lock him in a frame of words?

He looked like a Spaniard, my grandfather, the midnight blue of his hair streaked with foam. His skin was burnished by the burning suns of the high seas, the Bay of Biscay breaking in his eyes. They were eyes that held the lure and lore of the long horizons. The sea sounded in his mouth, in the tall lunge of his walk. Or it lay flat calm as he sat at peace, taking his sore sleep, upright in his chair. The big bones of his chest and shoulders showed up through the tightness of his navy-blue guernsey. Shrunk in the washes of all seasons that ever were, its sleeves came up over his knobbly wrists, and his elbows shone through. Two mother-of-pearl buttons fastened his jersey at the side of the neck, where he always wore his loose-knotted kerchief, dark blue with white spots. The trousers were two dark waterfalls plunging to his stockinged soles. In winter he stuck his huge feet on the fender and puffed dreamily at his rolled cigarettes, his stockings steaming away furiously, a raggedness of holes and darns. I touched them and they burned my fingers. But he never noticed. His eyes were lost in the red embers of that deep remembering that was always his.

Or he strode out like a Viking in his thigh-length leather boots that took him across the seven seas in one of his giant strides. He spread the black honeycomb of his nets wide on the waters, filled them with the salt sweetness of the sea, lifted them dripping with moonlight and fish. He came back smelling of tar and tangle, saltness and sun, sea winds and Woodbine and bottled beer. Then he lay down in his box bed, and the tides turned him in his sleep, the sea rolling his cigarettes for him as he dreamed and dozed.

It was grandfather who took me on my first teetering walks. He bestrode the burn in its foaming winter spate. Or I stared through the huge straddling arch of his legs in rainy July, his outstretched hands reaching to the other side for the ears of winter barley. He rubbed the grain between brown millstone palms, gently blew away the chaff, and urged me to eat. We walked on then, following the clamouring water, chewing in silence, the earth freshness in our mouths. I wondered if the farmer would be angry if he knew we were eating out of his field.

'The hell with the farmer,' grandfather said. 'The disciples ate corn on a Sunday, didn't they? Straight out of the field – and so did Jesus.'

There were times when he took me down on his shoulders, deep into the belly of his boat, where the dead fish lay in stilled shining legions, open-jawed with the horror of drowning in air, the silent protests emanating from a thousand accusing mouths and astonished eyes. The dead in the kirkyard swam at me again in a dense shoal. How awful to be a fish, or to be where old Epp was now – to be underneath the floor of the world, beneath the waterline, to be in the black wave of earth or sea, where the blind worm and the slippery eel never saw the sun. I shuddered, and grandfather took me into the little cabin.

It was full of men. Bulky as bears, they hunched round the tiny table in a red-faced circle, sipping scalding tea through their whiskers and laughter. Half a dozen half-pint mugs clattered on the wooden board, slammed down by scarred, knotted knuckles. Grandfather took me over to his bunk and showed me where he slept. A space too small for a man like him – a space between dark wooden boards, with blankets stitched together as though they were a shroud. So this was where he slept while his vessel drifted – in this narrow underwater coffin. But as I looked again at the bunk, I noticed the small strands of shag scattered about the pillow. My grandfather would lie smoking his cigarettes in death, rolling and puffing at his ease, while the old earth itself rolled like a ship and sped on into time through the dark blue seas of space. And when the good old earthship anchored at heaven's gate, journey's end, grandfather would sit up and nip out his cigarette, sticking it behind his ear. He would throw out a mooring line, stretch his legs, take two

mother-of-pearl buttons from the pearly gates to replace the
ones he'd lost from his guernsey last winter. Then he'd walk
in and ask God for a light.

When he was a boy he had a tame seagull, he told me,
which he'd taken from the nest when it was young, feeding
it on fish-scraps and crabs until it grew. After he let it go,
it kept coming back to perch on his chimney-pot every
morning and wake up everybody in the street, waiting
to see him on his way to school, landing on his shoulder
to be fed. It came to the schoolroom window, distracting
the class and turning the schoolmaster purple. He tried
to wring its neck and received a vicious pecking, almost
losing an eye. Grandfather received a terrible thrashing.
Then old George came up and thrashed the schoolmaster
and took grandfather off to sea, where the gull accompanied the boat, sitting on the mast day and night like the
albatross.

'I could shout out loud in the middle of the ocean,' he
said, 'and it would appear out of a clear blue sky and land on
my arm. It made me feel like a god.'

After that I longed for a baby seagull, but they could be
obtained only from the May Island, and I had to make do with
a sulky jackdaw with clipped wings. Apart from gobbling
crusts it did nothing, according to my great-grandfather,
but sit there in splendid black silence, brooding miserably
on the sins of the world. Uncle Billy came one day with
scissors to clip its tongue too and make it talk. Operation
completed, he lectured it relentlessly.

> *Nebuchadnezzar the king of the Jews*
> *Sold his wife for a pair of shoes.*

It paid not the slightest attention, glaring back at him
with an expression of bored contempt. It could stare out
anyone, even old George.

'You'd be likelier to get a word out of a bloody worm!'

snorted Billy, throwing back into the garden the wriggling morsels on which the bird refused to be fed.

Even when he liberated it from its rabbit-hutch on the clothes-pole, it refused to accept its freedom but stayed with us to become a source of nuisance, and eventually of outrage, raiding the paper bags of morning baps which Mr Guthrie, with unfailing expertise, hurled on to doorsteps and into open vestibules, standing up in the delivery cart while his horse ambled up the street without stopping. The neighbours began to swear murder. To save its life, old George came up to collect it. He walked more than a mile upstream to the burn woods, the jackdaw under his jacket, and left it there to work for its living at last.

'And if not, God will provide for it,' he said.

Within less than a week, to everybody's astonishment, the wingless wonder was back, sitting in the middle of the garden, one eye cocked expectantly at the house. I sacrificed my morning roll, dipping it in milk and taking it out in a saucer. My father had just come back from night shift and turned ugly with rage. He threw down his bag and stumped out of the back door, leaving it swinging. By the time I reached the door the bird was in his fist. It had no time even for a squawk. One vicious twist and I was looking at a bloodied pile of feathers, twitching on the grass, and a head pitched at a pathetic angle, one eye still cocked absurdly at the house. My father stormed back indoors.

'It's your neck that needs wringing!' he shouted at me. 'You brought the bloody thing here in the first place! It was you that wanted it!'

And he started cramming his breakfast into his mouth. He always wolfed his food. I went outside again and looked at the uneaten saucer of sops, sitting next to the mangled remains. My mother was dabbing her eyes.

'It didn't ask for much,' she said. 'What were a couple of crusts of bread a day, for pity's sake?'

I ran to her, hid my face in her dress, and filled up with black hatred.

'It was a sin.' Old George made this grim pronouncement when he heard of it. 'That bird came back like the dove to the ark. And not a sparrow falls without your heavenly father knowing it. He'll have something to say to *your* father, you can take my word for that!'

That was the only time I ever saw my great-grandfather up in Inwearie Street. Generally old George kept to his one room in the old part of grandfather's house, separated from the rest of the family by a streaming river of wind. There he lived on among broken creels and coils of rotten rope, deep into his eighties. He was a bible-boatman, old Geordie, who had given up the fishing in his youth to go to the whaling, and was now, as he put it, voyaging to eternity.

'The scriptures are my charts,' he said, 'the star of Bethlehem my guiding light, a broken Christ my figurehead.'

He never looked back a single day, rarely remembered things, as grandfather did, seldom referred to the past, unless it was the biblical past. His eyes were set on heaven, his haven.

And he never altered his gear. Every day he put on his old pilot-rig of navy blue – coarse trousers, waistcoat and reefer coat, polished black shoes and cheese-cutter cap set squarely on his head, though he scarcely needed to care for sun, wind or rain, for he sat on the old sea-chest most of the day, at the low table facing the sea, his back to the door. His arms were spread out stiffly on either side of the great open bible into which he stared for hours, the pearls of wisdom forming in the oyster-beds of that old deep-sea brain, the lips clammed shut behind the spiky silvery beard.

But though he was an iceberg of a man, nine-tenths of him sunk in the scriptures, the tip of his nose stayed alert to whatever was going on around him and he had a wild beast's sense of hearing.

'Is that you, laddie?'

I stood still as a stone among the heaps of old nets, baskets and creels that littered the room just under his. I was a magic fish, flitting among all those meshes, too subtle to be caught.

'Come on up now, I can hear you breathing.'

I went slowly up the bare wooden steps.

'What is it, Gramps?'

There was no need to ask. It was the same every time. I went and stood by his side, scenting his ninety years, near enough, and more than seventy of them spent at sea. He rose without stiffness and went over to the stove, where a black pot of broth was simmering. He dipped the ladle twice, filling the deep dish to the brim with rich steaming soup. Then he jabbed a large spoon into the bowl where it stood like a sword.

'Eat,' he commanded.

'I've had my dinner, Gramps.'

'Eat them up,' said the stern voice, 'they're good for you – they'll stick to your ribs.'

Soup was always plural in the mouths of the old folk. I ate as I was ordered, while he watched every mouthful with a kind of grim satisfaction. Then he pushed the plate to the side, lifted me on to his knee without tenderness, and began his sermon: Jonah and the Whale.

'Do you know what size a whale is?' he asked when he had finished reading the text.

'As big as this room?'

'Bigger.'

'As big as the whole house?'

'Bigger.'

I shut my eyes tight and tried to picture the leviathan.

'Go into Miller's boatyard,' the voice commanded, 'and stand beneath one of the big new boats they're building there now. Look up at it from where you're standing. That will give you some idea of the size of a whale and what its belly can swallow.'

I saw again the men in the boatshed, moving minutely, like worms in the great curving coffins that they built about themselves day by day – till the voice brought me back out of the mouth of the whale. Old George's eyes shifted to the window and seemed to touch the blue horizon.

'A whale can make the sea boil like that broth over there. A whale can lift a ship on its shoulder, crack it open like an egg with a toss of its head. It can deliver it to the deeps with a single whack of its tail, never to come up again. That's just one of the things a whale can do.'

There was something of Herman Melville in George's delivery. He claimed to have met the great author, whose grandfather was buried just a few miles from where we lived, in an upland graveyard at Carnbee, overlooking the blue sea. But George needed neither the bible nor Melville to tell him what a whale could do to a ship.

And what a whale could do to a man was even worse. To be swallowed like Jonah – imagine passing through those curtain jaws and them swishing shut behind you, ushering you into the awful underwater theatre of your own death, where your last act is played out in darkness. Imagine that darkness, deepening, ever deepening, as the great fish plunges downwards to the bottom of the sea, and you inside its belly, with the oceans of the world roaring round you, like being in a long thundering train in a never-ending tunnel. And as you roll and slither in your despair among the half-digested carcasses caught in those walls of flesh, some of them that are still alive even tear at you in your last agonies, though you are unable to make out, thank God, what monsters they are that rip into your flesh.

'It was disobedience to God's will that put Jonah in the

way of the whale,' the old man stormed at me. 'And that should teach you to obey and to fear the Lord with all thy might, and with all thy heart, and with all thy soul.'

But it hadn't always been that way with old George, my mother told me. He had turned to God in his age. As a young man he'd lived wild and wicked at the whaling. She told me the stories that grandfather had told her, pressing them to my lips like secret kisses at bedtime, warning me not to let on to George that I knew anything of his wild days without the Lord.

The best story was about one of his drinking episodes. In a public house in Stromness, just back from the Arctic whaling, he placed bets with an Icelander and a Dane that he could outdrink the two of them put together. Mug after frothing mug they lined up on the bar in two rows, one for George and the other for his opponents to share. They drank them down doggedly, desperate men glaring at one another dead in the eyes, searching for a glimpse of weakness, the bolting blue madness of despair. At last young George made his move.

'I'm tired of playing boys' games,' he said. 'To the cellars!' There he bought a barrel of ale for each man, and they lay down on the floor, the three of them, side by side, and turned on the taps. The flow was slow but steady. Their eyes bulged and their fists clenched, nostrils dilating. Their feet went rigid. Only their throats worked convulsively.

The Icelander was the first to go. He rolled over suddenly and started vomiting. The other two carried on, lying a little apart, yet locked in a terrible struggle, each determined to prove himself the drinker rather than the drunkard. The changing bets flew round the closing circle of men, the odds altering according to the slightest flicker of expression in the faces of the prostrate giants. Sovereigns, crowns and krona jingled in sweating fists, and the heads of kings and queens of the northern hemisphere were set at odds.

It was over without warning. The Dane's stomach

ruptured suddenly and he drowned and died where he lay, in
a torrent of blood and beer. The young George calmly stood
up, all eyes fixed on him. And with his head a red expanding
balloon, he walked back to his ship. He had drunk enough,
he said, to float it all the way to Baffin Bay.

'He was a knocker-out,' my mother said simply. 'Every
man was afraid of him. He just laid them all low.'

My bible-punching great-grandfather – a knocker-out of
men. I shut my eyes tight again, trying to fuse the sedate,
stern-jawed old scripturalist and the ale-swilling giant of
the Davis Straits.

Only once did the savage and the saint flash together in
one picture. That was the day the Jehovah's Witness came
to the door. It was a Sunday, after church, and everybody
was at home when the knock came.

'See who's there, would you, Kiffer?'

This was as far as I'd got in pronouncing my own name,
much to my father's irritation, but it had become my accepted
alias. On the doorstep stood a man grinning widely behind a
pair of glittering glasses.

'Do you want to buy a copy of *The Watchtower*?' he
asked.

'No thanks,' my grandfather said, coming up behind me
and shutting the door.

The man's boot got in first. I looked down at it, beautifully polished and black.

'If you wouldn't mind letting me in I'd be glad to explain
what it's all about – in the name of the Lord.'

Grandfather opened the door wide again, letting in the
last half dozen words.

'In the name of the Lord? I think you'd better see my
father,' he said.

He turned to me, his eyes twinkling.

'On you go, lad, take the man over to the old house, will
you?'

I led him up the old wooden steps while he patted my

head, humming a hymn happily to himself. He knocked with
his leather-gloved hand on the blistered door. Behind it sat
old George in his Sunday silence, steeped in the scriptures
up to his lips, the only part of him that moved, murmuring
the words to the sea-fronted windows, pondering the
prophets, nodding all to himself. There was no answer to
the first knock, so the glove knocked again. George didn't
like to be disturbed on a Sunday. I turned the handle and
went in.

The old one half turned in his chair and saw the man
standing behind me. His eyes were chips of ice.

'What do you want?' he asked quietly.

'I wondered if you'd like to buy a copy of *The Watchtower*,
sir?'

Old George moved faster than I'd ever seen him move
before. He sprang at the man like a lion, seizing him by the
lapels of his raincoat, drawing him up close to his bristly
jaws so that their eyebrows nearly touched.

'How much?' he spat.

'Sixpence.'

The man's voice shook with fear.

'Sixpence!' roared George. 'You want me to give you
sixpence, do you, for your own pathetic, perverted little
brand of the bible?'

The man's arms dropped limply to his sides and all his
pamphlets tumbled to his feet, littering the outside steps all
the way down in a holy river. My great-grandfather had him
by the throat.

'Have you ever read the bible?' he sneered.

'Yes, yes, of course, sir, many times. And if you'll just . . .'

'What are the first words of Isaiah, Chapter 55?'

'I don't know, sir, I mean, I can't think.'

'Think?' leered George. 'So you have to think, do you?
Well, think now!'

'I can't remember.'

'You can't remember!'

George's teeth were bared and his beard bristled with rage.

'Well I'll remember for you!'

He jabbed at the ceiling with his forefinger, his arm straight as a steeple.

'Ho! Everyone that thirsteth, come ye to the waters, and he that hath no money, come ye, buy, and eat!'

He let his victim go but remained with arm aloft, a magnificent ruin, dwarfing him, his finger still stabbing the sky like a spire.

'How can you have the brass neck to come to my door demanding money for preaching the scriptures, when scripture itself expressly forbids it?'

He was breathing quickly through his nostrils. The man in the raincoat twitched his mouth into a quick smile.

'Isaiah didn't have any overheads,' he said.

The desperate joke failed. George spun the man round, gripped him by his starched collar and the seat of his trousers, and trundled him down the steps, flinging him out into the street. Every member of the family was standing there awaiting the expected exit, doubled up and splitting their sides – all except my grandmother, who was hiding inside the house for the shame of it, she said. George looked at them all laughing, but the anger never left his face. He harried the fleeing figure with his rage.

'And if you dare darken my door again I'll break your bloody neck!'

The seller of pamphlets, bereft of his wares, hurried even faster on his way.

'Just count yourself lucky this was the Lord's day! If it hadn't been the Sabbath I'd have thrown you off the pier!'

And he stormed back up the steps to his room without a single word to any of us.

Cold porridge he was, old George, the fires of his youth burnt out of him long ago. When I wanted comfort and my mother was not at home, I went to my grandmother. Out of her grey frailty she doled kindness and warmth as if she had nothing else to live for.

Asthma was her curse. It shackled her to the house all day long. It was a chain you could hear rattling inside her, a chain forged from gaspings and wheezings and wild little cries. Some days it kept her in her chair for hours at a time, head bowed, hand over her eyes, her shoulders shaking, the drowning going on in her mouth as she battled for breath like a spent fish.

When she was a girl of twenty her father died at sea on the way home from Yarmouth. There was nothing to warn the welcoming family that the skipper lay dead in his boat. So when she heard that it was coming into harbour, she ran down to welcome him, waiting on the pier for the presents he always brought back at the end of the season. But it was a body draped in oilskins that was brought ashore and given to her. She fled home with her grief from the sea, shut herself in the cellar and threw herself face down on an old chaff mattress which had lain there for years. There she cried herself to sleep and lay till night, not answering the door, till they had to break it down and carry her into the house. Fever blazed through her for a week and when she came out of it her father was already buried. For a month or more she could scarcely walk and her health was ruined, the doctor said. She had been a prey to asthma ever since. When I was born she was barely fifty. Now I realize that she always looked eighty.

But a lifetime of illness did not make her indifferent to our aches and ailments. She was an expert on all the old homely cures that couldn't be bought from the chemist and which she prepared herself in patient stages, stripping the seasons of their offerings, for which Leebie was sent out. Leebie came back from obscure fields and humble hedgerows with scourings of ditches, baskets brimful with rose-hips and cowslips and hawthorns, dog roses and dandelions and poppies. Rarer scatterings were identified only by their efficacy or otherwise. 'I used that last year and it helped your uncle Alec's catarrh.' Whole seasons were laid to rest. Like the summery dust from butterflies' wings, they faded and fell into a fine powder in a blue-check cloth on the floor, encouraged by granny's pale sickle-bent presence – a waning moon by the mantelpiece, beneath which the mixtures matured. There was one which she called her all-purpose mixture. After it was boiled and distilled came the devil-may-care stage when almost anything could go in. 'The rest is just for taste,' she said, adding honey and vinegar and lemon, quince and crab-apple jelly, bruised sugar-candy and oil of sweet almonds, and pouring in port and old plum juice and rum and green ginger. This was the panacea, to be taken four times a day, no matter what you had or how bad you had it, or even if you only thought you were going to get it.

So she cared for her family by instinct and old world country faith, but she never took a drop of her concoctions herself, placing all her trust instead in the prescriptions which the doctor scribbled out for her on his frequent visits. She shook her head admiringly at the appalling scrawl left in Latin and black ink on the mantelpiece, saying how 'awful clever' he must be that nobody could make head nor tail of his spiderwork, and how this one was sure to work, to help her heart beat its murmurs and her lungs allow her a little more air.

They seldom did. But I ran down to Bett's the chemist twice a week for her medicine and her library books, much to old Bett's consternation. He passed the preparations in their dark brown bottles over the counter to me as if he were placing arsenic and antimony, mercury and lead, the complete Crippen's compendium all at once into my five-year-old hands. I reached up for the package, but still he held on to it, as if reluctant to let it go, looking fearfully into my face as he finally relinquished his hold.

'Don't drink it, now, whatever you do! For God's sake don't drink it!'

I handed him last week's library books and he let me have two or three others, all modern romances, first skimming the contents carefully for the passage where Gloria lay back in the bracken and Bob placed his burning kisses on her lips. Why did she lie there and get burned? It made no sense at all and I could see even upside down that p. 109 of *The Crimson Room* was a problem. Mr Bett was an elder of the Old Kirk and had an encyclopaedic knowledge of what each of his customers had already borrowed.

'Don't read them now, will you? For God's sake don't stop and read them. Are you reading yet?'

And he followed me anxiously to the door.

'Run all the way home now!'

I looked back and saw his worried hands stroking his red chin. The chemist had a highly inflamed face. Perhaps he had been the victim of burning kisses. Or had drunk one dose too many of his own medicines.

'Well, and what did Jockie Bett have to say?' asked my grandmother. Unable to go out, she was always eager for the slightest snippet of news.

'He said not to drink the medicine — and not to read p. 109.'

And everybody laughed.

Leebie was the only one who did not approve of grand-mother's potions, though she dutifully did the fieldwork. In the unwritten law of Leebie's medical lore, there was only one sure cure for anything: the kaolin poultice. If you'd lost a leg, Leebie would put a pot on to boil and offer her poultice as a cure for amputation. Doubtless if you applied it for long enough the leg would simply grow back. The trouble was that everything in her repertoire involved heat.

'It's got to be scalding hot,' she said grimly.

As the water came to the boil, the tin of kaolin bubbled like a volcano. An aunt or uncle guarded the door to stop me making a break for it, while Leebie spooned out the steaming grey lava, smearing it over large squares of lint with a kitchen knife, as though it were for eating. I blew on it frantically.

'Stop that, you rascal!' she roared. 'It's got no good in it if it isn't piping. Take off his shirt!'

Kicking and howling, I was held down by a ring of hands, while Leebie held the dressing across both palms, preparing to slam it on my chest, to be followed by another across my back and round my wheezing ribs, to beat off the coughs and colds, the boils and blisters and bouts of fever.

'Lay it on canny, for pity's sake,' pleaded grandfather. 'It'll take the boy's skin off like that.'

'Don't be soft in the head, man. Would you rather drown slowly or all at once?'

'I'd rather not drown at all at your hands.'

'Away you go back to your boat!'

And she slapped it on like a bricklayer throwing his mortar, a dead-eyed doctoring that had me drumming my heels on the table for thirty seconds while the flames engulfed me. But before a minute was up, there came the inexpressible relief of that barely bearable warmth which took half a day to dull down, by which time the squares of lint under shirt and jumper had lost their adhesiveness and the poultices had slid down to a rumpled clamminess encircling the waist. But for half a day you were a schoolboy hero, everybody wanting to sit beside you, even the girls, to breathe in the warm waves of kaolin, of which you were the fragrant Aquarius.

Leebie was the faded old signpost standing on the very edge of the family circle, outside which floated the faces of strangers. She appeared to have been approaching the grave for so long, her lifeline was now running parallel to it, if not inclining away. The polished nut of a skull, shining through the bunched white hair, the bare arms, tough as congers, the nippy spider-crab fingers, nimbly working the old Singer, the ancient shanks shuttling like pistons, little shiny black boots tip-tapping on the treadles – she seemed unkillable.

'We'll have to shoot her in the end,' grandfather would say.

She darned our stockings, patched our elbows, let down turn-ups, turned collars, let out gussets, took in waists, took up hems. Necks were knitted up or slashed away, sleeves lengthened, whole wardrobes remade, nothing was wasted. She was a hearth deity for sure. But as she sat in the corner, black-shawled and hooded, the thread in one hand, the snipping scissors in the other, she seemed more like the sisters of Fate all woven into one.

'They've been too long at sea, these men,' she would say when grandfather's boat was slow in returning, 'and I don't like the look of that sky.'

Then she'd go back to her sewing, muttering as she worked, and the others shifted their feet and told her not to be a silly old wife, and laughed. But their eyes would wander to the windows all the same, knowing her instinct for weather, and they'd go quiet all at once, and in the sudden silence the Singer sounded strangely sinister, and Leebie was the awful spinner of life and death.

Grandmother was the frail white witch of the family, but Leebie occupied the sharp end of its medical life, making up her hot bread poultices for boils or skelbs (splinters), afterwards extracting the shards with tweezers, or lancing the boils with red-hot needles. The uncles submitted to this for the salt-water sores ringing their hands and wrists where the oilskins rubbed constantly against their not yet hardened skins. And some of the village fishermen came to her with slow, gloomy feet, shuffling up the path, to be cured of their piles, caused by the endless wetness of life on deck. Treatments were carried out in the kippering shed,

out in the back garden. The best cure, Leebie said, was just
a bucket of scalding hot water.

'Take off your trousers, fill the bucket to the brim, boiling
hot, sit on it – then run like hell!'

But as few would face such an ordeal, Leebie had other
medications to offer. Her most famous was Stockholm tar,
normally used to seal the leaks in the bottoms of boats,
and in the human department applied in exactly the same
way: heated and rubbed well into the affected area – usually,
according to the uncles, with the toe of her old Wellington
boot. And may the Lord have mercy on your soul, they
always added. And pray to God you never have to go to the
kippering shed, except for kippers!

Leebie herself was matter-of-fact about it.

'A good dollop of hot Stockholm tar up your behind and
you won't be worrying about piles any more,' she would say.
'Go on, get your breeks down, boys!'

The fishermen came sheepishly but they left the kippering
shed with a lighter stride and with glad faces.

But it was grandmother who soothed me when I was ill,
held my head when I banged it hard against the sides of the
whirling world; she cleaned my cuts and wiped my nose; she
warmed my bed with a big stone hot-water bottle, always
wrapping it round twice with a towel so that it wouldn't
burn my toes. And when I came in dirty, she stripped me and
sat me in the kitchen sink amid a mountainous landscape
of bubbles, beating the blackness out of me with bars of
carbolic, rubbing me down in front of the fire till I was pink
and tingling and resurrected.

'There you are, your father's got nothing to pick on now,
has he? And I've mended the tear in your trousers – he'll
never see it.'

Still when I think of her, she is the provider, filling the
kitchen with her plain and wholesome fare. Broth and
potatoes were the staple diet, with the mutton removed from
the soup to serve as a second course along with the mash.

Or if there was no meat, she turned the tatties into a meal in themselves by beating them in with turnips and onions and lashings of pepper, whipping them into an explosive clapshot. A little dripping instead and they became stovies, all served up on the same faded azure narratives of willow pattern. I chose my morsels with care, slowly uncovering the pigtailed lords and love-lipped ladies, meeting by pools and gardens and on bowered bridges, allowing their blue stories to evolve, mouthful by mouthful.

Bannocks and baps and loaves of crusty bread came out of the side-ovens of the grate when we couldn't afford to buy from Guthrie. And she worked her way through endless quantities of fish. The king of fish, as she called it, the humble herring, became in her hands fish for a king. 'Never mind the king,' said grandfather, 'it's a fish fit for a Fifer.' She boiled them, fried them in oatmeal, roasted them on the brander, smoked them into kippers in the garden shed, shredded them into hairy potatoes, producing variety out of sameness. Herrings and haddock and cod landed on the chipped blue crockery day after day – and shoals of flatfish to be picked to the bone.

The fish were brought to the house in bunches of six or twelve, knotted together by their mouths, dangling like dumb silver bells from my grandfather's finger, their tails sweeping the path as he strode over the doorstep and into the kitchen, slapping them heavily into the sink. Grandmother wrenched off their heads, lobbing them through the open window to the prowling cats and the hysterical gulls. She cut off their tails and slit open their bellies with her flashing knife. She ripped off the scaly sheen of their skins as easily as my auntie Jenny peeled off her nylons after work. Then she filleted them and flung the bones after the heads, embracing the cats and birds as well as ourselves with the village motto, *Mare vivimus*: we live by the sea.

Long hours at a time she stood at her kitchen sink, working slowly, stood there while the tides came and went, her menfolk going out and coming home, the years passing as she grew older without ageing, because illness could age her no more. Often she paused, the knife in her hand, fighting away her asthma. I stood and looked at her – the bowed, beaten back, bent with suffering, the mouth opening and shutting in the same silent agony as the fish, now dead. She laid her hands on my shoulders for a few minutes at a time, for support of both kinds, and we stood together in silence, each of us incapable of finding words. Then she carried on patiently. She taught me how to gut and fillet. She showed me St Peter's thumb-mark on the side of the haddock. She gave me the top of my grandfather's egg.

But it is the crabs that remain, crawling horribly into the present. The big partan crabs were brought into the house like fallen knights, their armour-gauntleted claws folded quietly on their bellies, as though they were dead and laid to rest. But when they were picked up they sprang to attention, the claws wide open, waiting for the attack. Grandmother laughed at the panic that sent me to the other side of the kitchen. She dropped them into the pot, holding them by the back, where the blind waving pincers were unable to clutch and tear. I watched, horrified, as the water began to boil and the crabs crimsoned in death, the claws gripping grimly on to the rim of the pot as they tried to vault their way to freedom, to joust with me on the kitchen floor.

'Gran, they're getting out!'

So she put on the heavy iron lid with a flat stone placed on top. But still they come scrabbling out of the pot and into my dreams, those crabs that dined on sailors, all bubbling and bulging and red with rage and terror. Could some merciful stiletto not have been inserted between the armoured plates, to reach the vital parts and deliver a quick kill?

'Don't let it bother you, Kiffer, their nervous systems are not like yours. They're not so highly strung.'

She knew more about crabs and boys than I realized at

the time. All the same I was not convinced, and having failed
to secure a merciful end for them, I dreamed again of those
demon faces that would be visiting the sins of the grandmothers upon the children down the generations, starting
in sleep with myself, with infestations of eyes that wobbled
wickedly on stalks, and claws that tore me to gobbets where
I lay. For a time they made night hideous.

Between them my grandparents had produced five children
who had survived. After Christina, my mother, came Jenny
and Georgina, and then Alec and Billy. Jenny was the
wildest. With her whirlwind affection she had inherited
grandfather's dark colouring and nightfall shock of hair,
the big brown eyes, the brow of Egypt. They called her the
black tornado. She swept through the house leaving nothing
and no one uncleaned or unkissed. She lifted me like the
wind, clasped me kicking and howling to her bosom, killing
me with her red wounding lipsticky kisses.

'Let me be! Let me be!' I yelled, as she rocked me on her
blind undirected longings.

> *You do something to me –*
> *Something that simply mystifies me.*

Then she was out of the door and pedalling her four
furious miles to Cellardyke, where she worked in the oilskins
factory. And singing all the way she went, to the clouds
in their flying, the sun on the sea. Outside the house they
called her the Daft Diva.

Georgina was her opposite in every way: blonde, blue-
eyed, quiet as dew. She cupped her chin in her hands, rested
her elbows on her knees, fixed her eyes on a far strand, and
sighed quietly to herself. That was Georgina, a landscape

locked up, waiting for some spring to come and free her and fill her full of life. When she was at home she worked for Burgon the fish-merchant, but for part of the year she followed the southward passage of the herring as they shifted from Shetland down to East Anglia, Georgina walking in their wake like Ruth the gleaner, old George said, and often adding, 'But she'll never find a man like Boaz.' She came home with sand between her toes, her hair coarse with salt and her knuckles rubbed raw to the bone, ugly purple cuts from the gutting troughs disfiguring her pale fingers. I kissed them for her and she smiled.

Always she brought back with her sheets of music that were worlds apart from the old Scots songs which my granny loved to listen to. Then she went into the Room, where she sat by herself, practising her newfound treasures. I crept in quietly after her, creaking the uneven floorboards, and without looking round or interrupting the flow of a phrase, she lifted a hand and beckoned me to come. I stood behind her, watching the white bruised fingers running over the old brown keys. Her hands, playing these miraculous melodies, seemed to heal their own wounds. She accompanied herself in a slow tuneful voice, still not turning round, but smiling to me with the lilt of her head.

> *The poor soul sat sighing by a sycamore tree,*
> *Sing all a green willow;*
> *Her hand on her bosom, her head on her knee,*
> *Sing willow, willow, willow;*
> *The fresh streams ran by her and murmured her moans;*
> *Sing willow, willow, willow;*
> *Her salt tears fell from her and softened the stones.*

'Sing me another one, Georgina, please, another one.'
'Another one,' she said, closing her eyes and smiling. 'All right, another one, another one for Kiffer.'
She sifted through the new pile of sheet music, chose a

piece, and placed it above the keyboard, looking at it for a long time. Then she sang.

> *How should I your true love know*
> *From another one?*
> *By his cockle hat and staff,*
> *And his sandal shoon.*

> *He is dead and gone, lady,*
> *He is dead and gone,*
> *At his head a grass-green turf;*
> *At his heels a stone.*

The walls of the Room fell away and Georgina and I were the only ones left in the world. We sat together under the single sycamore tree that spread out in time's green field. I was her lost love for whom she mourned, so I kissed her on the cheek, telling her not to cry, and she bent her head, brushing my face with her hair. But now the new music came up out of the floor, filling the sky.

> *White his shroud as the mountain snow,*
> *Larded all with sweet flowers,*
> *Which bewept to the grave did go*
> *With true-love showers.*

The song went through my groin like a sword, thrilling with some sharp indefinable comprehension. It aroused in me something wafer-thing, tenuous as a ghost, the memory of a memory, something I had once known but forgotten. The tune, Walsingham. What was Walsingham? And Ophelia's song. Who was she? What was I remembering?

But they were broken up, these episodes, when the 'boys' came bursting into the house, bringing breezes from the sea.

'What are you playing that old rubbish for, Georgie?

Come and listen to the wireless – and make us a cup of tea.'

I watched Alec and Billy grow up, though I never knew it at the time. Alec was Jenny's counterpart, his beetle-black hair brilliant with Brylcreem, the hair on his chest running over his shoulders, on to the nape of his neck and all the way down his spine. He loped about the house looking for lost shirts and jumpers, naked to the waist, a genial grinning gorilla. He read books about explorers and talked of going to Australia. Billy was fair-faced like my mother, but he was the one who had my grandfather's deep abiding passion for the sea. He never Brylcreemed his hair, never hurried to climb out of his fisherman's gear, as Alec did, when he came home from the sea. He padded about in his thick white sea-stockings, exuding the fishing like a poem never recited but carried in his head, and which made his eyes shine. I always knew if he was at home the moment I came through the front door. The sea-scents clung to him, even after he'd bathed.

My mother too was out of the house for most of the day and sometimes at night. She worked the switchboard in the post office down at the harbour, taking the calls from the boats by radio, transmitting information. She was the mouth and ear of all the local fishing news and sometimes sent me round the houses with what she called The Word.

'The *Halcyon* had a good shot of cod behind the May this morning.'

'The *Shepherd Lad* has landed ninety cran at Peterhead.'

If the news was good there could be a penny a time in it for me. Otherwise it was a long nod of the head and a quietly shut door.

Later my mother moved to the little telephone exchange

in Anstruther, where she'd worked during the war. Night shifts were her speciality – she got by on very little sleep and improved her mind with reading. It was during the war, before I was born, that she'd fallen asleep over her book and dreamed that her cousin Andrew, who'd joined the airforce, had been hit in his Spitfire and had died. Sometime later the switchboard woke her and the message came through.

'I knew it was the hour he died,' she said, 'because of the chapter I was on.'

She accepted the immaterial as an unremarkable fact of life.

'Maybe it was just telepathy,' somebody suggested.

'Just telepathy? And what telephone wires does telepathy run on, I wonder?'

A clever woman, my mother. As soon as you say telepathy you've admitted to a form of communication that is not man-made.

Sometimes she took me to the sands, west of the village, where the gloomy ruins of Newark, a seventeenth-century castle, stood on the cliff edge, towering over the rocks below. One blue day I left her on the beach in her light summer dress and climbed up to the castle by the back route, the safe grassy bank, to play among the ruins. What had been the great hall was now a gaunt shell, grass-grown and open to the sky, and the walls were gone that kept you from one false step to a hundred-foot drop to rocks and sea and certain death. Flying around up there, my Spitfire wings outspread, dogfighting madly, blindly, I halted at the beetling edge just in time to see my mother, standing far below, one hand over her mouth and the other arm extended, as if to touch me. I waved to her and she waved back, beckoning me down to the beach.

She took my face seriously in her hands.

'You have to be more careful, Kiffer. If those children hadn't been dancing round you, you'd have gone right over the edge.'

'What children?' I asked, astonished.

She looked at me and smiled, her hands in my hair.

'I thought as much,' she said. 'I thought as much.'

Thirty years later I picked up a copy of Sibbald's *Bygone Fife* in a second-hand Edinburgh bookshop and dipped into the history of Newark Castle. There was talk of youngsters, six of them. At one time, the author said, the great hall must have rung to the sound of children's laughter. I had the sudden terrifying sensation of falling through space, and the bookseller ran to steady me and to offer me a glass of water.

'You look as if you've seen a ghost,' he said.

'Not me,' I said, denying experience, 'but my mother could see them – six at a time. And call them up too.'

The bookseller smiled. But I saw my mother again, the flimsy dress fluttering in the sea-breezes, a mere speck on the sands far below me, but one arm extended protectively, as if to save her son, by whatever means. Had she read the book, I wonder, Sibbald's local history, during one of her night-shift vigils? Read it and forgotten what she'd read, except in the unconscious mind, into which she plunged her arm at a mother's terrified moment, coming out with six children, dancing in a three centuries' old ring, a maternal thought-force around a small boy, fiercely jealous and full of love? And even if she had, would it explain the experience? It's easier sometimes to believe in ghosts. But it's not a ghost story – that's how close I was to my mother.

As for the sentimental little scene I concocted in my early prose, where I lie in bed with her, and she tells me all about my heroic able-bodied father, and how he'll be coming home one day – it had as little basis as the dream I never had, that my father telegraphed the village post office that he was on his way, and how his ship came swaying drunkenly over the morning horizon, sending the low sun spinning into space. It sliced the May Island in two and sank the Bass Rock, which went growling to the bottom of the sea. Then it crashed through our small harbour and kept on coming, right up the brae, battle-scarred and glorious, until the point of its prow splintered our window panes, and there was my father, under the white ensign, wearing white and gold braid, straddling the bowsprit with bell-bottomed trousers and waving madly to me from on high as I lay back in my bed in amazement . . .

No, I lay in bed with my mother, all right, and we spoke about my father, but it was usually after he'd beaten her up and was lying drunk asleep, and she'd moved into my bed, where we lay naked like lovers, stroking and kissing, unfolding each to the other in butterfly whispers while the blind winds wailed outside our window, and that beast in the next room snored and swore in his sleep. It wasn't his ship that came swaying drunkenly home with a bosun-gunner on board, battle-scarred and glorious, and powder's blue stains scattered on his skin, it was the drunken bastard himself, night after night, come home from the pub, to make my mother cry.

'Another night like this,' she wept, 'and maybe I'll go to Jesus.'

I lay there chilled to the bone by the thought that my mother could ever leave me and go to Jesus. And that's the first and last time in my life that I contemplated murder. The woodshed axe, the gutting-knife, the pickaxe through the eye. Then trip him that his heels may kick at heaven . . . And that is just how close I came to my mother. You can't get closer than that – to want to kill for a person, to love that someone to death.

3

Queer Fish

Somebody once said that heaven lies all about us in our infancy, but from what I can recall, it was more like growing up in a Bosch boneyard, with devils on the rooftops, hell beneath the floorboards, and the growing child well and truly trapped somewhere in between. Somewhere? There was nowhere else to go. Not that the priest and doctor came running over the fields exactly. One came on a bicycle and the other in an Austin Cambridge. But the medicine man and the God man were just figures in a many-peopled landscape, where the dance was a crowded one, and if Satan led the ball, as the preachers believed, he did so with a masterly and ceremonious humour. The place was crawling with weirdos.

Crawling is not completely metaphorical – one of them, called Bowfter Sandy, did actually get down on all fours and go around biting people's ankles. He even featured famously in a braehead church sermon, in which it was announced that Nebuchadnezzar was alive (if not well) in St Monans, an indication of the eternal cycle of truth to which the bible gave witness. There was nothing new under the sun. When the king lost his reason, his hair and his nails grew long, and he went down in the field like a wolf and ate grass.

As soon as church came out that day, I joined the gleeful pack of Sunday schoolers that went haring down to Bowfter's house, pulling up fistfuls of grass on the way, which we stuffed through his letter box, bidding him tuck in and clamouring for him to come out and bite our legs. He skipped the proffered meal but otherwise did his best to oblige us. The door burst open and suddenly he was among us as we whirled about his well-grassed front garden, avoiding the snapping mandibles. Surprisingly agile for a dimwit of sixty, he grazed one or two who'd come close enough to thrust their grass bouquets into his yellow-fanged jaws, as though they were feeding a mad cow. When summer came and lawns grew long, the poorest old men would come round the doors asking if they could sharpen your mower blades and earn a shilling or two for tobacco. 'Oh, never mind about the mower,' folk would say, 'we'll just get Bowfter to come along for an hour later on – he can cut the grass and have his dinner all in one!'

Unbelievable? I haven't even started. The really difficult thing to swallow, though I was assured of it from an early age, was that God not only made the world but made man in his own image and made every individual man and woman in it. In which case even God must have had his mad March moods. And why had he put so many oddballs all in the one place? There seemed enough of them in our little village to share out round the whole globe and still have some to spare. What I never realized at the time was that all our seafaring townships were swimming with shoals of queer fish and that the same was probably true of all the villages of the world. Were people 'normal' in cities, then? I have no idea. But if sanity is a mere statistic, then God couldn't count in the '40s, and still hadn't learned by the '50s. Not in St Monans.

St Monan. A martyred missionary maybe – who came out of the Celtic Dark Ages and found a spring to drink from, right on our doorstep. It washed a long salt voyage out of his mouth and also put iron in his blood and probably in his soul. Something must have given him staying power – other than crabs and black bread – on that windswept landfall, where the best living accommodation was a sandstone cave, now

concreted over by the cretinous North-East Fife District
Council in order to create a pointless little patio. King David
II, Robert the Bruce's son, liked the water too. Or it made
him well. Or the saint's spirit saved him from shipwreck. Or
a Neville's Cross arrow leaped miraculously from his wound
– as arrows do – simply at the mention of St Monan's name.
Take your pick. The fact remains the King built a chapel
over the shrine, hence our fourteenth-century church, the
Old Kirk. The spring remains too – and even as late as the
'40s you could still see an older fisherman soaking his nets
in its brownish water, believing that the iron would make
them more durable, and perhaps even secretly hoping for
the saint's blessing on his boat. Why not? He had nothing to
lose – except perhaps the sceptical pride of a self-respecting
Calvinist who didn't believe in Romish saints.

Anyway, the saint stayed, the name stuck (if it ever was his
name) and a village ticked over. St Monans, my birthplace.

Seagulls were what you heard in St Monans all the time,
bearing vocal witness to the quantities of fish landed in
those days, when the boatsheds rang with the sound of the
adze on freshly cut keels of American elm, the harbour with
the bartering of merchants and shouts of fishwives, and the
curing sheds were ecstatic with the reek of newly smoked
kippers. The little haven swayed like a forest, so many masts
you could step from east to west on the decks of stacked
and jostling vessels, and the fish gleamed from pier to pier
like heaps of bullion, breaking the sun a billion times. The
reflections were everywhere. It was the silver age of the
great herring boom, though nothing to what my golden-age
grandfather must have seen as a young man, when a single
boat gave work to a hundred hands. Still it seemed astonishing enough to me, the sea's bounty, a miracle of fishes

to go with the loaves in Guthrie's bakehouse. I soon came
to know a good catch, ninety cran, a hundred cran, and the
boats that were likely to make them. There were lucky boats
and unlucky boats, sober boats and drunken boats, and there
were religious vessels and irreligious ones, though most of
them had names that rang with the sound of scripture: the
True Vine, the *Magdalene*, the *Shepherd Lad*. They went out
without computers or echo-sounders to face wind and wave
and they shot their nets in the name of the Lord whether
they believed in him or not. Most of them did, but even if
they didn't they played it safe. *O, hear us when we cry to thee!*
Fishing was a dangerous business and an act of faith, and
the faith of the fisherman was recorded on his boat.

The faces remain: the douce Dutch faces of my ancestors,
the Nordic seas that glimmer in a pair of Viking eyes, the
suns of Spain that burnish this or that complexion. Faces
floating just beneath the surface of sleep, men drowned by
memory. Ancestral winds wrote wrinkles into their faces,
these yesterday's men. History got worked into the flesh,
like the lines of passage, entered on the log-books of their
parchment skins.

Faces. I remember sailors who are now turned to coral,
farmers that are kirkyard clay. I remember old wives who
kept the secrets of the town about their scrubbed doorsteps
– toothless sibyls who sat in the sun to stay alive an hour
longer and weave village gossip on the cracked old looms
of their tongues. And still in dreams I re-encounter them,
in the cobbled closes and on the bouldered beaches, where
their faces and forms first broke in upon my childhood.

Hodgie Dickson was the first to peep through the
blanket of the dark on those wild nights when the town
trolls strode through the corridors of my sleep like ghosts
in technicolour.

Hodgie lived with his brother Frankie, not far from us on
the braehead, in a house at the west end of the village, right
at the top of a steep hill. The house had a narrow paved

yard in front, where Hodgie used to work away with bits of
timber. Apparently he was building a boat, though nothing
remotely boat-like ever emerged — if it had, the tiny yard
would have been unable to contain it. The pavement outside
the low wall of the yard was always strewn with the detritus
of Hodgie's handiwork and I often stopped there to pick up
woodchips and shavings to take along to the burn to serve
as toy boats.

In my dream I saw myself stopping to speak to Hodgie
as usual. He was wearing his fisherman's black jersey, with
neck-buttons, kerchief and cap, and his thick brown kersey
trousers. Half bent he was, with his back to me, worrying
and whittling away at his wood as always. But the ground
on my side of the wall was swept strangely clean, so I asked
him for one of his odds and ends. He answered me with a
silence unusual for him, as if he hadn't heard me.

'Hodgie,' I said, 'don't you have a piece of wood for me
today?'

He paused in his planing and polishing. The back of his
skull was a closed door.

'No, not today,' he said, though still he never spoke, never
turned round.

'Why not today?' I asked.

He turned to face me, but with the same unspeaking
mouth. Then he lifted his arm, the other still holding the
plane, and pointed down the steep brae. Following his finger
I saw a small procession of figures at the foot of the hill. As
they came upwards and closer I made out six men dressed
in black and moving in single file.

'What are they coming for?' I whispered, afraid.

I knew what they were coming for.

Even yet Hodgie said nothing — but he stood aside from
the wall where he had been working, and it was then that I
saw what it was he'd been making all this time. He'd been
making it all his life. As have we all. Where had I seen that
box before, with its terrible solidity and smell?

The six men stood beside us, all in black. The leader spoke.
'Is it ready, Hodgie?'
'Aye,' said Hodgie, 'it's ready. I'm ready.'
Hodgie was dead within a week.

It was such a short journey from his house to the old kirkyard, just a few steps, that his brother said no hearse would be needed. He and five others carried Hodgie's coffin on their shoulders, out of the yard, past my spy-hole in the fence, and along to the graveside. Six pall-bearers, dressed in black. Nothing unusual about that.

If it was precognitive it was not a word I knew. I told my mother and she said it could be 'coincidence'. That was not a word I knew either. But I reminded her of her own dream of cousin Andrew, the airman who died, and she went quiet.

After Epp and Hodgie there were others, and King Death moved swiftly through the village like a character from a morality play, simple, stern, inexorable. The hearses and cars wound their way up the green mound of the sea-girt kirkyard, a shining soundless trail, distanced into ants. I spied on them from afar with a wary eye, or hid in the cornfield that swept down from our house.

When there was to be a funeral old Penman, the town crier and announcer of exits, strode slowly through the streets like a medieval leper, swinging his arm, ringing a huge deep-throated hand-bell, whose iron tongue accompanied his own, that told you the day, the time, the place. Only the hour-glass and the scythe were missing. Otherwise he was the ultimate bellman.

From the back of beyond it germinated, the distant clanging, before you were aware of it, like a summons, a pulse in the blood, a slow whisper from the sea. Conversation faltered as the tolling grew closer, louder, as if the church itself, steeple, bell and belfry, had risen from the rock, groaning on its foundations, and was grinding its way through the village to bid us remember our end. And the memorials marched along with it, the village dead, an army terrible with stone banners of epitaphs and texts: *Behold He Cometh, The Day Dawns, The Kingdom of God Is at Hand, We Shall Not All Sleep.* Mortality was on the move, hauling eternity in its wake.

'Do you hear that?' my grandmother whispered. 'Old Penman's ringing his bell. Somebody's dead.'

Her words hung in the air like a sudden pall, and just for a moment everything stopped. The uncles stopped clattering their dominoes on the bare wooden table; the girls' bubbling laughter burst in their mouths, leaving the air around their heads expectant and empty; Leebie paused in her patchwork, the Singer needle poised like a stuck sword – the whole family sat gorgonized, marble heads laved by the flames that lurched suddenly up the lum as the fire spat in the silence.

'Who is it, do you think?' asked Jenny. Her face had gone white under her black mane. 'Who can it be?'

'Just listen,' said grandmother, 'and we'll hear.'

The clanging filled our street now, and the accompanying announcement. The town crier had a voice like grating shingle, sucked backwards by the sea. The words broke over the stone heads like waves.

'The funeral of Charles Davidson Marr will take place at two o'clock this Wednesday, from No. 5 Elm Grove, and from there to the old kirkyard.'

The air sang with the sudden silence that surged back on this sentence, and we waited.

'Charles Davidson Marr died of a heart attack at seven o'clock this evening. Friends are welcome at Elm Grove between nine a.m. and seven p.m. tomorrow, when the last kisting will take place. The Lord is my shepherd. I shall not want. He maketh me to lie down in green pastures. He restoreth my soul . . .'

'That was a sudden call,' said grandfather.

'No, no,' grandmother said, 'he always had a bad heart, Chae Marr.'

'Does that mean he'll go to hell?' I asked.

Chae Marr's bad heart meant only one thing to me: infernal wickedness. Epp had often called me a bad-hearted boy who would burn in hell.

They told me to hold my tongue, but I asked what the last kisting was.

'It's when folk come to take their last leave of you,' said grandfather. 'After that they screw you down.'

'Good God Almighty, don't tell the boy stuff like that!'

'Why not? He has to learn sometime, doesn't he?'

'Sometime – not now, for God's sake.'

But the sometime had already passed, with Epp.

'That Penman ought to be put down,' grumbled uncle Alec. 'He rings that bloody bell before a body's had a chance to grow cold.'

'He'll be ringing it in your face next, if you as much as catch a cold,' said Billy. 'You'd better watch out, Kiffer!'

Grandfather stuck a thin strip of newspaper in the fire and relit his Woodbine.

'He's like a shark following a ship,' he said. 'Nobody welcomes the sight of him.'

So the bell-ringer became the death-bringer. And whenever I saw the sad eyes and sepulchral step after that, I avoided him, even if he wasn't carrying his bell. One look from him, I decided, could be enough to make my bad heart blacker – maybe even fatal. And old as he seemed when I first knew him, he lived on all through my childhood before finally succumbing himself to the common stroke. Even then he was not quite done with us. Some folk heard his bell the night he died, and on the following two nights, announcing his own funeral with slow and solemn tread, out in the deserted streets. My grandmother heard the story and pulled down the blinds and drew the curtains, utterly terrified until he was safely below the sod – as she put it.

But even with Penman off the streets death would always have been unavoidable – death and birth and all the business of the flesh. Only two doors along from the braehead house lived Liza Leslie, midwife and dresser of the dead, in a small house surrounded by a huge sloping garden, walled in from the sea. The spaciousness and seclusion were ironically appropriate, as she was always out and around, at all times, seasons and weathers, and yet spoke to no one, never answering a greeting, which few took the trouble to give, knowing her habit. And never wearing a coat either, but with her grey shawl and hair flying about her shoulders, her long black skirt flapping at her heels, bare-armed, head held high, eyes fixed dead ahead unblinking as she made her way to houses of mourning or mirth.

Not that mirth was up her street. 'Man that is born of woman hath but a short time to live,' she would say as she delivered a baby, 'and his days are full of sorrow.' That was about the extent of her conversation. She was another ancient, hailing from an age when men and women bred bleakly in the face of death, prepared for the loss of offspring and the waste of effort. We give birth astride a grave – the absurd dramatic image might have served as her motto. She simply arched our existence, a village rainbow, drained of colour, drained of hope, untouchable, elusive, spanning the polarities of crib and coffin, bearing the secrets of being and not-being in her hands. Speaking to nobody in particular, yet she held all of us when we came into the world and when we went out, washing away our first day's blood and our last day's sweat and tears, and ignoring us in between. She was the iron gates of life and death.

Honeybunch was another inhabitant of seclusion, but she would have benefited from the service Liza Leslie provided to the community as washer-down of bodies. Quite simply, Honeybunch would never wash. Her scent was her main claim to village fame, though that is not my abiding memory of her. Honeybunch was the first woman I saw naked.

'Poor lass, she's not right in the head,' my grandmother would say whenever Honeybunch passed by the house on her way down to the shore.

I asked what was wrong with Honeybunch's head.

'She lost her wits for love, they say, poor soul.'

Grandmother saw life outside the window in terms of Bett's library romances. But for me Honeybunch was the girl in the song that Georgina had brought from Yarmouth, the one that sat sighing by a sycamore tree. Down on the beach Honeybunch would gather stones and make the outlines of boats, their stone prows pointing out to sea. Then she'd sit inside them on their sandy decks – and cry. The fresh streams ran by her and murmured her moans. Her salt tears fell from her and softened the stones. Life into art and back again, the two coming together for me in a perfect enchantment.

Honeybunch must have been about forty, but she was willowy and wonderful to look at from the perspective of my half decade that didn't yet divide women into ages. In my teens I'd have dreamed of meeting such a woman in the meads and gone groaning to her grotto. I was under the spell of Keats. At five I'd never even heard of Keats. I'd heard of Honeybunch, though, as one of the wonders of the little world. Honey-haired, bee-footed and almond-eyed, she came down from the country, folk said, from some estate, a mad aristocrat, cast off by the upper crust, her mouth musical with a magnificent English, quite unlike my father's, in which she drooled and drawled all to herself.

In the long summer she sat whole days on the sands as the blue tides swished in and out, twelve hours at a time, touching her toes and withdrawing from her with slow courtesy. She pondered the pebbles which she picked up and held in her hands all day long, staring at them and saying nothing. She walked inland through woods and fields, children following her like trains of pages, and back again through long lines of surf, following the curving patterns on the beach, printing her footsteps with a child's care between the brown ribs of sand left by the ebb. She paddled in ditches, lay on piles of old nets at the back of the harbour, her bare feet among fish-heads and crabs' toes and rotting bait. She spent long hours at the rubbish-dump on the west braes, playing with the joyless jetsam of the community. She combed her hair with bones and broken combs. Then she wandered through open doors, sat down in shops and houses and asked for cups of tea. Or she appeared in church on Sundays, in the middle of the sermon, still barefooted and bedraggled, sitting down in the pews among the coffin-coloured fox-furs, the festooned and bird's-nested hats, exuding the smells of the waste places of the town rankly amid Presbyterian polish, moth-balls and pan-drops. She stank to high heaven. From six feet off you could have adored her: from three feet you could have died. Children accept smells as part of the universe. Church-going ladies scatter, their embroidered handker-chiefs clapped to their noses.

So Alec Fergusson, the old sexton who'd given me my salt-water baptism, was the man who performed the act of charity that not a single woman would have dreamed of doing – he washed her. Took her through his burnside cottage, out to the back garden and into his wash-house, stripped her bare buff, laid her down like a sleepy queen on a marble slab, and gave her a good soaping and rinsing before he let her go.

The Women's Guild complained to the minister. 'That mad madam with the marble in her mouth! Washes her down, back, belly and in between! It's got to come to a stop!'

Kinnear was no kitten and gave them his answer.

'Cleanliness is next to godliness. And if the godly ones around here aren't going to make her decent for the kirk, then either Alec does it or I'll damn well see to it myself!'

The old gravedigger went on attending to the bathing of Bathsheba.

Once I saw her come out of his front door, her hair spread out by the wind, her torn dress draped about her like a flag around a sun-bleached column. I stood and watched as she walked past me into the waves, laughing, and I imagined what it must have been like to have washed Honeybunch. Then I crept up the steps and looked over Alec's wall. He was still out there in his back garden, mending a puncture on his bicycle. Behind him the door to the wash-house was open and I could see the slab, soapy water still trickling from it. Less than five minutes ago Honeybunch had lain there stark naked and been washed from head to toe.

I don't think it was sex that reared its lovely head so soon, to make me look out for Honeybunch's washdays from then on. Curiosity, I suspect, plain old-fashioned childish wonder, that's all. I didn't have long to wait.

My uncle Billy had told me about Leebie's belief that if you walked three times round the Old Kirk 'widdershins', you'd meet the Devil on your completion of the third circuit. 'But you have to do it against the sun,' he insisted, taking great care to explain to me the anti-clockwise import of 'widdershins'. Otherwise, he assured me, it wouldn't work.

I asked him if he'd done it himself.

'Of course, lots of times.'

And met the Devil?

'Every time.'

And what did he look like?

A pause.

'A bit like Tom Tarvit.'

Another pause.

'Only with horns.'

Billy had been round the church at midnight, of course,

but he recommended I try it out on a nice sunny day, when it would be less scary and easier to run away. So it was perfect weather when I came down through the cornfield under a summer sun, early in the morning, making for the church. It was built on the west side of the burn and the only crossing was a great stone slab that had once been a tombstone. The skull carved at the top end had been worn by wind and wave and weather, though women still complained to Kinnear that their high heels got stuck in the eye-sockets if they crossed without care and attention. The minister explained that they were helping the soul of the departed. The stone came from the grave of an old aristocrat, up Abercrombie way. After lording it over ordinary people all his life, he'd settled down to an eternity of atonement. Being trampled by the common folk was an act of penitential restitution. So the church women were advised not to avoid the spot.

'Dig your heels in, ladies, and let the toff have it in the eye – it'll do you both good!'

On other stones the eyes were deep green. But here the moss had been winkled out by a succession of stilettos. I stuck my fingers into both sockets, dilly-dallying and shilly-shallying, as my teachers later complained of me, though on this occasion with heartfelt excuse. I was beginning to lose interest in seeing Tom Tarvit leap out at me with horns on his head. I went up the steps slowly and turned right, hugging the huge edifice, feeling its cold stones, reading the headstones as I went, and studying my faltering feet. Nothing. Only an old hose, lying in the grass, leading to the sexton's toolshed. I came round again on the sea side and did my second circuit, slower than the first time, then started on my third. This time there seemed to be more distractions than before – dandelion clocks to blow, butterflies to catch, a ladybird beetling its way across an inscription, scurrying as fast as its little legs could carry it but still taking ages to traverse even the first name of many: Alexandrina Peterina Johnston. Why did they give them such long names in those days?

It was while I was stopped in thought that I heard the sound of singing.

> *Rock of Ages, cleft for me,*
> *Let me hide myself in thee . . .*

It was an old man's voice, but he was singing lustily, as if it were a Sunday, though the hymn wasn't coming from inside the church but from the west side of it, the far side from the village. I still had to get round there before I could complete my final circuit. I stole among the memorials and, clasping one that was just my size and provided the perfect cover, peered round its flaky edge.

And there she was – Honeybunch without a stitch on. Alec had laid her lengthwise on one of those table-top tombstones with carved legs, and at first I thought that she was dead, and that Liza Leslie was on her way. A bucket of soapy water stood on the grass and Alec, wearing his yellow oilskin apron, was wielding a large scrubbing brush with washday vigour. The hose was turned on and the cold water was streaming over the naked form. I could see the goose-pimples standing out on its flanks and two curious strawberries standing out brightly on its chest. But Honeybunch's eyes were closed and there wasn't a movement from her to suggest that she felt a thing. Alec parted her thighs slightly and got busy with the soap again, following up swiftly with the hose. I was amazed to see the dark brown bush that grew between Honeybunch's legs. It was then that she turned her head with startling slowness, opened her eyes, and looked straight at me, unblinking and unsmiling. Alec continued to wash and to sing.

> *Nothing in my hand I bring,*
> *Simply to thy Cross I cling;*
> *Naked, come to thee for dress,*
> *Helpless, look to thee for grace,*

Foul, I to the fountain fly;
Wash me, Saviour, or I die.

I was running madly back through the headstones by
now, the holy words following me like retribution, when I
crashed straight into a big black coat and felt a pair of burly
arms about me. I looked up the row of buttons to the dog
collar and black hat, eclipsing the sun.

'Well now,' said Mr Kinnear, 'is it Kiffer or Kipper, I
wonder?'

I looked up at him – and over my shoulder to the singing
sexton, now hidden by the church. Kinnear grinned.

'Great old hymn, that one. Good voice too, old Alec. He's
in the choir, you know. Did you know?' I shook my head,
trying to get away.

'And what's he doing, singing round there now, at this
time of day? Shall we go round and see?'

I struggled like a fly in his fists.

'Did you see what he was doing? Did you see who he was
singing to?'

I shook my head.

'Didn't you see anything at all, Kiffer?'

I shook my head again.

The minister grinned wider and held me more gently.

'So you didn't see a naked woman?'

'No.'

'Ah, you've found your tongue! What an unruly member
the tongue is – always saying the wrong thing.'

He took his hands from my shoulders and tousled my
hair.

'You should always see what you see, Kiffer.'

I nodded and started to sidle away.

'That's two of God's good works you've just seen round
there – a beautiful woman and a clean-living man. There are
women with their clothes on who may be cleaner – but not
so pure. And there are other kinds of men.'

I was running down the steps by this time, and back over the burn. As I looked over my shoulder I saw the black hat beyond the churchyard wall.

'I didn't see *you* in Sunday school last Sunday – make sure you're there this week!'

I ran faster for the braehead.

'Or I'll have to get Alec to come and hose you out of bed!'

His laughter filled the churchyard.

When I came cautiously back that way the same afternoon the place was deserted. Honeybunch was a speck on the beach, west of the castle. I looked down from the huge drop and saw another boat taking shape. Slowly I came down and approached her, which I'd never done before. I lifted a large stone from the sands and placed it next to the one she'd just laid. She smiled and said nothing. And we carried on building. I'd come to know Honeybunch. We were bound by a secret neither of us could understand. A warm wave of pride flooded through me. We finished the boat, stepped on deck and sat there together, side by side, saying nothing, for what seemed like the longest time I'd ever known in the whole world.

Honeybunch was my first love – and it came to nothing. There were plenty of other females on the loose but they didn't have Honeybunch's fascination. She was *romantically* mad – they were simply mad. And they floated about the village as part of its moving scenery.

Bella Bonnysocks went to the shops with not a penny in her purse, selected a few simple items, enough to keep her from starvation, and said to the shopkeeper, 'Tom'll pay for it, when he gets back from the lines.' But bridegroom Tom was never coming back from the lines. The young man was lying where he had lain for forty years, at the bottom of the grey North Sea, caught in a deep-sea fishing line which had wound him like a bobbin out of her life, leaving the unworn wedding ring to lie empty on her display cabinet, a barren circle of gold for the rest of her days.

Kate the Kist walked into James Miller's boat-building office first thing every morning, lay down on his floor and demanded to be measured for her coffin. Exasperated, he eventually gave her one and sent it up to her house free of charge. But she was soon back on the floor again, claiming she'd shrunk. He sent up a second box but made her pay for it, as she insisted on keeping the first. In time she reappeared saying she'd grown again, and had grown out of the first one. Miller lost patience and informed her that from now on she would be treated like everyone else and would have to wait till she was dead before he would supply her with a coffin. She duly died. Miller and his assistant went up to her house, wondering if they'd have to 'go for a third'. They didn't – but they discovered the coffins sitting on the flagstones in her wash-house, crammed with pots of home-made jam. Kate fitted into the first and the jam was extracted in lieu of payment. The second load of jam was auctioned at the next church fair, complete with coffin, as Miller said he couldn't in all decency offer anyone a second-hand one.

It was bought, however, complete with jam, by Wilhelmina Well, who refused the new sink which the Council had installed in her cottage. She drove a pick-axe into the shiny porcelain and carried on drawing water from the old well at the foot of her garden. It had no bottom, she said, and so the water was purer than pure. Then one day Wilhelmina simply disappeared. They tried the well, of course, pumping it for hours, but when there was no sign that they were getting anywhere they gave up.

The coffin was then kept in storage for Mad Maria, whose suicidal urges came on her every winter. On freezing cold days she would walk gingerly down the slipway, wade into

the middle of the quarter-tide until she was up to her knees,
and start to wail like a stuck siren. Then she'd slither back
to shore, legs and feet caked in mud, shaking her head and
complaining that the water was much too cold today for
drowning herself and she'd have to wait for warmer weather.
But when summer tides cooled the hot green stones of the
slipway, poor Maria never felt the winter in her blood which
turned her old feet to the water's edge at the turn of every
year. One year Maria caught a chill and Kate's old coffin
finally saw service.

Another Kate was Candy Kate, who pushed a barrow
round the streets, from which she sold crystallized candy.
She also carried on her back an open pack of it, from which
boys would be detailed to pilfer. When she swung round
to box their ears she'd be sure to spill some of her wares
and we'd run to harvest them, while she went among us
delivering kicks and curses. Sometimes the sugar candy was
eaten between blooded lips and sweetened a singing skull.

Or we shadowed Jean Jeff. She was French and stone deaf
and her real name was Genevieve, which was impossible for
us to pronounce. So we settled for Jean Jeff, trooping right
behind her and bellowing at the tops of our voices, 'Jean
Jeff's stone deaf!' while she carried on walking, oblivious
to the trail of howlers in her wake, muttering quietly to
herself, sometimes arguing fiercely with whatever phantoms
peopled her shuttered mind. Sometimes we laughed at these
women, and teased them if we were bored, but mostly we
simply accepted them, weird old widows who walked among
us like a caste of priestesses, elevated or at least set aside
from normality by some special law.

Then there were the old men, men who had been
fishermen, many of them. But now with nothing left to
keep them active on the tide, they pottered about its edge,
and about the edges of their own existence, killing time and
frightening small boys.

There was the awful McCreevie who drowned unwanted

kittens. He just dropped them in a pail of water, sat on it and laughed. Once I watched, horrified, as the pink blind mouths mewed to the blue sky. There was no mercy in McCreevie's square, grinning head. He sat down on the pail again, tittering softly to himself. Then he sloshed them out on to the grass where they lay among the daisies like little grey gloves that had lain in the rain for a day. Yet they'd only been in the water for a minute or two. How could such things be and not be in such a short space of time? Their wet inertness was terrifying. Surely if they were just laid out in the sun for a while they would live again? But they stayed like that on the grass, sodden little fingerlengths of fur.

McCreevie saw me watching from over the wall, picked up the litter in one spawny fist and opened up his mouth like a well, making as if to eat them. He shook with laughter at my horror, leering at me through that black imbecilic hole in his face.

'You next,' he grinned. 'Only I'll cut your head off first.'

I ran screaming for my granny.

Sometimes McCreevie could be seen making for the harbour, carrying a sack which moved and mewed. Children followed him at a distance.

'What's in the bag, McCreevie?'

'Young ones – just like you. Coming to keep them company?'

But nobody wanted to watch McCreevie as he went over the harbour wall and out to the breakwater blocks, to hurl his bag into the dark cold water, where Miller's watch had long stopped. I didn't have to follow him. I knew what it was like out there, in the deep sea.

I preferred to join the bands of boys who tortured the Blind Man. He was so bad-tempered that he cursed and cuffed anyone who got in his way, lashing out with his rubber-stopped walking stick. We catcalled after him, ran rings round him, tugged at the stick, turned his cap the wrong way

round on his head, often at our peril, as he detected distances
and obstacles with lethal accuracy. Out for his constitutional
he paced along the piers with perfect precision, bringing
himself to a halt with not a step left between him and a
sudden drop to a dark drowning. Summer visitors would
shout out in alarm as they saw him tapping his way closer
to the water, only to be cursed for their concern and told
to mind their own bloody business. Sometimes we tried to
confuse him in his counting by shouting out our classroom
sums, but he refused to be put off, plodding on doggedly and
swinging the stick as he went, occasionally striking wide if
he sensed somebody within his range. Cracked heads and
shins were occasionally sustained.

Once, on an afternoon of freezing fog, I saw him
approaching me on the pier. In trying to give him a wide
berth I stumbled into a fishbox and he immediately interpreted this as a possible attack. He half bent, the blind head
shot forward for better scent and hearing, swaying from
side to side like a cobra preparing to strike, and he scythed
the air with his stick. I had no option but to retreat, tripping
over coils of rope and getting caught in bundles of nets,
obstacles that never seemed to trouble the man with no eyes.
Backing away from him, I came at last to the windy pier-
end, where the waves cracked like black whips. And still he
came on.

'I've got you now, you bad little brat! I can hear you and
I can smell you and you've nowhere to go! I'll break open
your head and feed your brains to the fish!'

My heart whacking, I slipped softly over the edge of the
pier and crept down the rusted iron rungs that allowed
access to boats. But there was no handy little boat moored
there that I might have slid into and under a tarpaulin, snug
and safe from the weather. I climbed all the way down until
the black water was slapping the soles of my shoes. And
waited. The Blind Man's face appeared above me out of the
fog and he struck the topmost rung with his stick.

'I know you're down there, fishbait! I've got all day!'

And he stood there in a grim silence throughout two terrible hours, at the end of which my feet were quivering, my fingers were blue claws, and my jaw was jabbering at my knees. When he finally left his post I made my way home jack-knifed with cold and cramp, an object of derision to hooting children.

Most of the weird old men pursued their own quiet trades, scarcely dimpling the surface of village life.

The Snailer combed the braes for the humble specimens which had given him his name. He brought them back to his garden in biscuit boxes for breeding. He had no success but he sold those he did find at a half-penny a dozen as his own cure for salt-water boils. And so he earned his tobacco and his weekly half pint. Not many of the fishermen bought them, but I knew that they worked. I suffered badly from boils and had one on my leg once that made the limb blow up to nearly twice its size. Limping along the braes to avoid one of Leebie's kaolin poultices, I was hailed by the Snailer, who refused to let me go until he'd rubbed one of his catches into the sore for almost an hour. Next morning the leg had gone down like a punctured balloon. After the treatment the snail was tossed aside into the grass.

I couldn't pay him but offered what I thought was the helpful suggestion that he might manage to sell some of his wares to Jean Jeff, as I'd heard they ate them in France. The Snailer turned purple.

'Bloody French!' he spat. 'Bloody Philistines! Eating me out of house and home if they could! Waste of good snails!'

Next day, as a pacifier, I brought him one of grandfather's screw-top beers, which I'd purloined from the pantry. He was profuse in his thanks and told me to come back any time for free treatment and to say goodbye to the kaolin poultice.

They were not all loners, but the dafter they were, the more solitary their lives. The Tanker could be seen most days occupying one of the larger rocks west of Newark. As you approached he'd grip his imaginary machine gun with both hands and let you have it – vocally and from juddering fists, following you all along the sands.

'Bastarding tanks! bastarding tanks! bastarding tanks!'

It was his only line.

Then he'd sing us a song of slaughter, high up on his turret, bow-legged and grinning, pointing at us in time to the music as if he were conducting:

> *If you want to see the old battalion*
> *We know where they are –*
> *They're hanging on the old barbed wire!*

'You're a useless shot, Tanker!' boys would shout back. 'You can't aim for peanuts! I should have been dead five minutes ago! Look – I'm still alive!'

And they'd pick up small boulders from the beach and lob their grenades at the machine-gun nest, inspiring the gunner to greater fire-power. We saw a loony on a rock, that was all. But from his pinnacle the Tanker saw much more – squadrons of war advancing all across the plains, their long gun barrels trained on him and flashing fire. Only a madman would think it was just a group of small boys.

The Jockey – on his imaginary stallion – was a more peaceful figure, though more liable to knock you flat coming round a corner. He'd rein in if he saw you coming, though, and pass the time of day. Sometimes an apple or a lump of sugar would be proffered and he took these on behalf of the horse.

'Did you ever win a race?' we'd ask him.

No, he'd never had any success as a jockey, he'd admit

ruefully, which was why he'd left Ireland. And what was the trouble, we inquired? The answer was always the same: 'Slow horses and fast women.'

Women, fast or slow, were the speciality of Pussy Starr, though he preferred them slow, Billy said, because then he could catch them. His nickname, however, was a mystery to me.

'Does he like cats?' I once asked. And the whole family laughed, even my father.

'Oh yes,' Jenny said, 'he likes cats, all right. But they don't like *him,* and they have to keep their claws out when Pussy's on the go!'

The Postie advertised his weakness for women in time-honoured fashion, unless he opted instead for the letter-box approach, hence his name. There was a fat mad lady called Nancy who lived up a lane, her front door looking down to the harbour. She had a habit of wandering out of the usually open door, wearing only her knickers – though these were mizzen-mast affairs, grandfather said, visible even from out at sea. A bench for the old men stood against the harbour wall, offering them a view of the lane all the way up to Nancy's door. Members of the Women's Guild kept moving this seat 'a few respectable steps to the west' but each morning the old men would move it back again, claiming it was closer to the harbour office, where they needed to 'keep in touch'. As soon as you heard the titterings and saw the pipes jabbing and the old men come to life, you knew Nancy was on parade. Usually we were chased away, but to us Nancy's ballooning breasts soon became just another part of the scenery, banal as the weather. Sometimes we'd wander up Petticoat Lane (as the old men called it), walk straight into her house and help ourselves to digestive biscuits and oatcakes which she kept in her sideboard drawers, while Nancy sat around chattering to no one in particular. Occasionally she'd ask us to run errands for her. Once she sent me to the chemist for six sticks of liquorice – 'so as I can have a really good clean-out,' she said. Mr Bett as usual looked at me with some suspicion. Even liquorice was lethal in his permanently worried and inflamed head.

'Who are they for?' he asked. 'Your granny?'

'No, Nancy sent me.'

He withdrew the sticks of liquorice and thought for a moment.

'Have you only just come from Nancy's?'

I nodded.

'And what was she wearing?'

'Only her knickers.'

Mr Bett smiled. I'd never seen the chemist smile before.

'I'll take them round myself,' he said.

He saw my face fall.

'What's wrong, lad?'

'She was going to give me a penny for going.'

Mr Bett looked worried again, but he went to the till and took out a penny.

'Mind the shop while I'm away. If anybody comes, tell them I'll be back in two minutes.'

As an afterthought he went to the liquorice jar and pulled out an extra stick.

'That's for you,' he said. 'One's enough. And for God's sake don't touch anything while I'm gone.'

When I reported this incident in the braehead house it split the family into two camps. The women all took the view that Mr Bett wanted to spare me another sight of Nancy's paps (as they called her breasts). The men saw it differently and grinned and stroked their chins, just like Mr Bett.

'Good for old Jockie – and him an elder of the kirk to boot.'

I didn't see what his boot had to do with it. But that was Nancy.

Of all her admirers the Postie was the most serious, but she took a dislike to him, unusual for her, so ingenuous and so mild to all, and would shut her door when she saw him coming up the lane. So the Postie earned his nickname in a flash. And caused hilarity in all but the Women's Guild. Even we children knew the story, though not its full significance, not in my ignorant case, at least.

The girls did the tutoring.

'He sticks his willy through her letter box!'

'Why should he do that?'

'Don't be stupid. And do you know what happens next?'

'No, tell me.'

'She runs to the fireside for the tongs – and snap, crackle and pop! She's branded him and she holds on tight and he's howling his head off on the other side of the door!'

And the girls ran screaming down the street. If they met the Postie they'd shout to him: 'Got any post for us today? Has it got a stamp on it?'

The Postie enjoyed their attention.

'I'll show you in a minute – I've got more than one in here. And they've all got stamps!'

And they ran screaming off again, their laughter silvering the sky.

Peter Cleek had a hook for his left hand. He pushed a big barrow through the streets, holding one of the shafts inside the hook and the other with his good hand. Usually he brought round herring, but in March, when the cod had huge roes in them, he'd shout along the street: 'Good cod roes! Good cod roes!' Then we'd shout back at him: 'Isn't there any herring in the firth today, Peter?' And he'd answer, 'Good God knows! Good God knows!'

George Young went after all the horses in the town, waiting patiently with sack and shovel for them to drop their cargoes of hot compost straight on to the street. The baker's big horse, the milk horse, the fruiterer's and the fisherman's, he followed on their rounds, and all the little horses that carted the gear to and from the boats and hauled the unloaded herring up to the station. Occasionally a bit of apple would be offered, or just a few words by way of encouragement. Not even waiting sometimes for the horses to move off, he reached between their hind legs with his spade and raked away the steaming loads, shovelling them into his sack, which he then swung on to his shoulder, marching off in search of more takings.

If the horse was wearing a nose-bag we'd shout, 'Hey, George, the bag's in the wrong place. Why don't you tie it to its backside?'

He'd do anything to fertilize his strawberry patch, where the berries grew like the food of the gods, and he sold the produce for high prices to those who could afford them – unless we'd got to his garden first.

'Geordie Young, the King of Dung!' we shouted after his back through our tightly held noses, marching after him and furiously fanning the air in his wake. He appeared to revel in the title, his red face lighting up like one of his own strawberries, his eyes crinkling as he silently nodded and laughed, winking and wagging his head.

Sometimes there were public spectacles. Mad Mansie was a ton of a man who, when drunk, became like Mad Maria. But unlike Maria he had no suicidal qualms. He took off all his clothes, folded them neatly on the pier, and threw himself into the harbour in a decorous sitting splash. It was only when hit by the cold sea that he experienced an instantaneous change of mind. Wallowing and wheezing whitely in the oily water, and unable to swim, he gasped and spluttered for help before disappearing. Once my uncle Alec dived in and saved him. Mansie was so fat, Alec said afterwards, that the wet oily naked flesh kept slipping through his fingers like blubber.

'It was like trying to life-save a bloody whale!' he said. 'I've told him next time to keep his clothes on – otherwise he'll bloody drown!'

Other characters were less dramatic but equally memorable. Philip the Philosopher had only one question.

'I'll prove to you that you're not really here,' he used to say to us, stopping us in the street.

'Go on then, Phil.'

'Right, then. Are you in Edinburgh?'

'No, Phil.'

'Are you in Glasgow?'

'No.'

'Are you in Aberdeen?'

'No.'

'Right then. If you're not in any of these places you must be somewhere else, then?'

'I suppose so.'

'Right! If you're somewhere else, then how can you be here?'

The Philosopher's bent logic straightened us out for one mind-boggling minute while he went on his way triumphant.

And there was the old cold gold-earringed sailor called Gowans, who drew me conspiratorially into the folds of his sea waistcoat, pointed his white buccaneering beard at me, and whispered the one which, of all the strange sentences of childhood, stands out sharpest.

'I've seen monsoons and typhoons and baboons – and teaspoons!'

Often they congregated in front of the harbour, these old men, maybe twelve of them at a time, bunched together like a dozen herring on a string, walking up and down a small stretch of Shore Street, no longer than the span of an average fishing boat from stem to stern. Twenty steps then turn, twenty steps then turn again, they made their old men's half-strides, walking backwards and forwards to keep out the cold, or taking the measure of the imaginary deck their feet had left long ago. Or they strolled to the end of the pier, blew their noses with their fingers into the wind, and sauntered back again, perambulating penguins with a communal instinct, with nothing left to do on a cold day but blow their beaks and spit.

The working fishermen, their hands hauling on sodden

nets, were too pressed to develop deep aberrations. All the same several of them quirkily proclaimed their individualities against the rough routine of a life of toil.

One of these was Star Jeems – a man of enormous size and strength, who scorned the use of hoist or barrow or horse when shifting his nets from boat to pier and from harbour to house. Jeems, like most of the fishermen, was called after the name of his boat, the *Morning Star*. On a Saturday morning crowds of boys would gather on the middle pier to watch it come into harbour. After all the fish were landed the great moment would arrive when Jeems would heave his share of the nets on to the pier wall using a single hand, straighten himself for a second among his massed admirers, then walk a quarter of a mile to his house, trailing a long tail of children and bearing a weight that would have bowed the legs of a rhinoceros. For good measure he would then walk up the steps of his own house all the way up to the garret. This was sheer bravado, for he then flung the nets back down into the yard for their Saturday washing. But he liked it to be seen that he had no need of the hoist and tackle that topped the garret window.

These so-called eccentrics, whom so-called progress has swept away, were victims of hard work, poverty, social isolation and much inbreeding. They were also victims of the slings and arrows of outrageous fortune, the thousand natural shocks that flesh is heir to – as somebody once famously said. But mostly they were victims of their place and time. Yet we children were never harmed, never molested, had no fear of abduction, murder or rape, or were even warned about them. We got through our childhood without a single casualty, though it was a place of open doors and lunatics on the loose.

4

The Dragons of Eden

Miss Shoes was the first. Hughes, as a matter of fact, but the regional pronunciation produced the word which had me immediately looking down at her feet, as if that was where her essence resided. Miss Boots would have been closer to the mark, I remember thinking at the time – dainty little dark brown things, with high heels, buttoned up the side and trimmed at the top with rabbit fur. The reason I recall them in this detail is that we sat cross-legged on the floor on our first day at school, Miss Hughes perched on a high chair in front of us. With her spinster's passion for method she had arranged us according to our height the moment we walked through the door, and because I was a small boy I was put in the first row, right in the centre. So my school life begins with Miss Hughes's boots, buttoned up the ankles, all the way to where her legs began. These were equally fascinating, encased as they were in thick brown woollen stockings with wavy patterns wiggling upwards to her knees, like the lines left by the tide on the beach, where Honeybunch loved to walk. Ah, but Honeybunch was poetry in motion. Miss Hughes was a stiff affair. Her stockings ended – or disappeared – beneath a dark green skirt that looked as if it might have been cut from Epp's velvet armchair, and the same buttons went up to her neck. She wore a loose smock over this, but it was unbuttoned, allowing us to view Miss Hughes in all her glory. And topping all was a fluffy white cloud of hair surrounding a patch of wrinkles and a pair of spectacles. Miss Hughes grew in front of us like a dandelion clock.

And faded as fast – blown by time before she had time to get to know us, or we her. 'Shoes is dead! Shoes is dead!' That was the playground cry that greeted me one morning to tell me that I'd never again see, except in memory, Miss Hughes's little buttoned-up feet pointing at me as I snipped and pasted bits of coloured paper on to strips of newspaper, intensely aware of the smell of glue, but with no idea as to why I was doing this or what in the world I was doing here in the first place. I recall no parental warning, no cushioning hints about going to school and saying goodbye to freedom. Probably there were none. People were less self-conscious in those days. Things simply happened.

School was one of them. I just woke up one morning and found myself there, surrounded by children. I'd never been so surrounded by children. They were all faces I'd known individually in passing, and in random groups, but never together and in such a small space. A crowd of shapes and scents and sounds that made no sense to me.

What are the pieces that remain, still standing out in relief, their definition undimmed by the passing years?

The smells.

Varnish is one of them. Our desks had been varnished for the start of the new term, but nothing could conceal their dismal oldness. Old oak they had been made from, older than Epp's coffin by far, perhaps as old as Epp herself, who may have sat at one of them when she was a little girl. Certainly our mothers and fathers (my father excepted) had occupied them, and even our grandmothers and grandfathers, and there were dragons who took delight in telling us, 'Your father and his father before him sat in that very desk where you're sitting now, and that's why you're there – it's a desk for dunderheads!'

Dunderheads or clever dicks, it made no difference. These solid slabs of oakwood were what held us, brutally banged together to form mantraps for boys and girls, to keep us sitting in rows, two by two, like the animals in the ark, sealed in from the great flood of ignorance that raged about our lives. So we sat there, heads upright, faces to the front, calves and torsos perpendicular, parallel to the walls, thighs aligned to the plane of the ceiling, shoes flat on the floor, feet together. We were told to sit like that, and that is how we sat, like crooked alphabets, for the next seven years. We sat and sat – and grew into the angles of our desks. And the wooden desks, dead coffinwood, grew into our souls.

The mind strikes match after match – ignited even then by the smell of varnish, though I never stopped long enough, in those dark little rooms in my head, to analyse the images as they exploded into light. Not at five years old. But Epp's box came floating back again into the haven of childhood, and the men wriggled like maggots in the ribs of their skeleton craft, high up in the boatshed. And old Hodgie Dickson worked and worked at his daily death. And Epp's mouth was closed by Liza Leslie, who bandaged the sneering jaw, placing a knot at the top of the white dead head, like the bow on the head of the beribboned girl in front of me. They came crazily at me, all of them, out of the grain of the wood, where they lurked in camouflage. Kate the Kist lay down on my desk and demanded to have her measurements taken.

> *One, two, three, four . . .*
> *Twelve inches one foot, three feet one yard.*
> *Six feet, how many inches?*
> *Six feet long, six feet deep.*
> *The days of our years are three score and ten.*

'Waken up there, boy! You're dreaming again! Write this down on your slate – with your chalk, boy, with your chalk!'

Chalk. The smell of it. Chalk dust trapped in the slanted sunbeams, clouds of it settling on the teachers' clothes and hair, powdering their smocks with its ghostly moss till they looked like faded old dusters.

'Stop chewing that chalk, boy, it's for your brain, not your belly!'

Down on to our slates went the first words, the first chalky cells of literacy that would combine and multiply and make scholars of us. Fish, star, starfish. Gull, sea, seagull. Verse and universe, satyr and Satan – Satan flying over the rooftops, over the shaky slates of the school on sooty pinions, the crumbs of sinners falling in flakes from his jaws, gouged gobbets of eyes falling like fish-heads into the waves. God is Love.

'Write it down, boy!'

God is love.

'Wrong again! Love with a capital, you turnip! Let that remind you!'

The first blow. And a fire burning on the side of my face where Miss McNeil's fist had found my ear, for love spelt with a small letter. Her hand rubbed out the offending character and replaced it with a rigid, right-angled Pythagorean capital. Her fingers were caked with chalk dust, like the white unringed fingers of old Epp as she gripped the poker in her rage. Flour like a dusting of chalk on Mrs Guthrie's wedding ring as Liza Leslie removed it before preparing Mrs Guthrie for the ground. Flour into chalk, bread into stones, a classroom killing, the end of infant life, the death of imagination.

And the strange smells of other bodies. Through the veils of chalk and varnish, the odours of antiseptic sinks, bottles of ink, strips of plasticine and pots of glue, there filtered the rich reek of the farm boys, creatures of dung, not of our tar-and-tangle element and therefore inferior to us. They came clumping in from the fields wearing muddy boots and question marks for faces. They slammed themselves into their desks and stared dazedly into space. None of them was ever able to answer any questions.

I sat near the bottom of the class myself, marked out by my inability, inhabiting the same desk as a farm boy called Bert Mackay.

'What do you call a young horse, Mackay?'

The silence started up at once, cruel as a knife. The teacher repeated the question. The silence persisted. I could feel Bert's head close to mine begin to blow up big and red with the effort to discover within itself a piece of information that simply wasn't there. The question-mark face contorted to almost comical proportions. But nobody laughed.

'Answer the question, boy! What do you call a young horse?'

I made to help him.

'Be quiet there! How dare you whisper! Do you imagine that if you were struggling with the plough he'd lift a finger to help you? How do you spell "plough", Mackay?'

Silence.

'How do you spell "foal", Mackay?'

Nothing.

'What is a foal, Mackay?'

Bert breathed like a horse, straining in the mud of his mind. The rich ripe earth smells steamed out of his carcass with the sheer fury of his thinking. He whimpered and groaned. But no answer came out of him.

'He's fit for carting dung, that's all!'

Geordie Young, the King of Dung.

'All right, then, we'll give him an easy one. What's a young cat called?'

'A kitten, miss.'

Blind pink mouths mewing for mercy to the blind blue sky and McCreevie's thick grinning head breaking open with laughter.

I'll break open your head and feed your brains to the fish!

'What did he say? Pay attention, boy!'
'McCreevie, miss.'
'What? Your drivelling dreams again? Supposed to be
helping him too! The blind leading the blind! This'll waken
you up! I'll make you see, all right!'

The heavy hand of Miss McNeil, beating away the dreams
of Eden, keeping them at bay, day by day.

The school day started with the unbridled anarchy of the
playground, where we wheeled and dived like gannets in the
gladiatorial amphitheatre of the sea.

On my first day I was prey rather than predator, before
I learned to attack. The trouble was that I never really
wanted to attack anybody. A pacific soul, I suppose, in my
dark green velvet shorts with the straps over the shoulders.
I let go my mother's hand and walked sullenly through
the iron gates, into the maelstrom. At once they zoomed
in on me. Arms spread stiffly like wings, they swooped and
soared, goggle-eyes stabbing as they advanced, clattering
tongues machine-gunning me dead with fear before they
closed. Even the Tanker couldn't have held them back. Dog-
faced dog-fighters, they struck, tore, bit, clung, punched and
kicked. They swung from the twin ends of the long scarf
that Leebie had knitted for me, till my face turned blue.
They knocked me breathless to the ground, faces jostling in
the sky like bunches of bruised fruits, busy hands rifling my
pockets for anything that could be eaten. Then they were
off and I was dazed but initiated. After that it was merely a
case of spreading your arms and contending for the honour
of being a Spitfire rather than a Messerschmitt. Messer-
schmitts were always brought down. Our re-enactments of

the Battle of Britain were instinctively patriotic and I was seldom a Spitfire. I came to have a sneaking sympathy for the Germans.

Boys like Bert Mackay who sat through most of their schooling like bemused beetroots were the ones who ruled and gloried in this element where mental life ceased to exist. Hacked and hounded by the teachers, they made up for their daily humiliation by hitting anything they could. If you were lucky it was a football. Heavy-booted feet that shuffled in misery beneath the desks now sent balls crashing like cannon shot into the school wall, occasionally missing the windows. Heads bent in toil and bowed in disgrace for most of the day tossed and butted like bulls. And ink-stained fat fingers that could scarcely hold a pen let alone form a letter, bunched themselves into fists, delivering punches with all the zest of beings goaded beyond their natural forbearance.

The girls, who simpered through the lessons in a smarter, soapier silence, carried on their demurer games in their own playground, separated from us by a high brick wall. Breaking school rules, we would scale the wall and watch them playing with their skipping-ropes, rhymes and roundelays.

> *Salt, pepper, vinegar, mustard,*
> *Miss McNeil's got a face like custard.*

Or at the risk of a thrashing, we dropped down on their side and were among them like commandos on a raid. Our mission – the Garter.

> *Heaven help me, I'm a martyr,*
> *Kiss me quick or I'll grab your garter.*

The kiss or the garter. Capitulation was unknown in that death-before-dishonour society. The snotty swotty

girls considered it beneath them to give a boy a kiss and
the coarser fishergirls preferred a fight. They were lithe
creatures with loose salty tongues and rough tumbling hair.
Fists and feet flew as we closed in on them and grabbed at
their legs. Long white thighs kicked against their deflow-
ering. Navy-blue knickers flashed above rumpled stockings
and flowered dresses, and shrill silvery screams rippled like
summer lightning. The Battle of the Garter was fought and
won. Willing hands hoisted us to safety over the wall, eager
to touch our glory. We pulled the garters like headbands
over our tousled brows and, whooping like braves who'd
taken their first scalps, war-danced round and round the
playground to the hysterical hootings of the jubilant male
tribe and the outrage over the wall.

Was there anything faintly sexual in it, I wonder? Not
one whiff, at least none that I remember.

The bell rang then, hammering us into submission.

'Line up!'

A hundred unruly tongues were stilled and the chaos of
bodies came miraculously together in two long lines, the
animals entering the ark. The girls were lining up at the
other end. We could see them through the open double
doors. It was a one-corridored building, seven rooms for
seven years. You entered at one end aged five, knowing
nothing, and emerged at the other aged twelve, knowing
the geography of Britain and the capital of France, but not
knowing that some of the girls now had periods – and pene-
tralia in which we would soon be interested. Not knowing
either that we could have even greater fun with our own
genitals than simply seeing who could pee highest up the
outside wall. All that lay ahead of us, seven years away, at
the end of that corridor, where the girls waited.

The headmaster blew his whistle like the guard at the
station, a sign to the teacher at the other end of the school
to let in the girls. Simultaneously he barked an order and in
we went, like mice beneath the hawkish nose and eye, the

sharp jaw, the bristling ginger moustache. Heads down, we stared in passing at his plus-fours, the shit-catchers, which all the fishermen said they wouldn't be seen dead in, and the term we gleefully applied to him. In the singular, it became his nickname.

We filed into our classrooms.

'Good morning, boys and girls.'

'Good morning, Miss McNeil.'

'All stand! Our Father . . .'

> *Which art in heffen*
> *Halloo pee thigh name*
> *Thigh kinktom come*
> *Thigh will pee ton*
> *On earth as it ish in heffen*
> *Kiff us this tay our taily prett . . .*

'And forgive us our *tits!*'

So the coarser girls would mimic her out of the classroom, winking and stabbing their chests with inward pointing fingers. And we'd double up, hysterical at the thought of Miss McNeil's earnest plea and supplication to God on high, every morning in life without fail. And the prayer would be trumpeted around the playground.

'Miss McNeil's dead!' screeched Golly Gowans as he bombed his way past me at battle speed across the playground, loosing off bullets at the Red Baron intruding from another world war, who went into a nose-dive and revealed himself as Peem Peattie fighting in flames at my feet.

Another one? Surely not. 'What do you mean?' I shouted after him.

Golly tilted his wings, banked dangerously, and came

bombing back up the playground to make sure the Red
Baron was dead.

'Miss McNeil's dead!' he screamed again.

He whizzed by on the second run, his hands juddering
on his guns.

'Died in her sleep last night.'

Dead. I said the word over to myself in the sudden silence
Golly had left in his wake. The Red Baron bundled his spilt
books back into his schoolbag and wandered off. How could
those thick hairy tweeds be dead? Someone had been inside
them all the time. A human being. Miss McNeil was gone now
to Liza Leslie to be washed, gone with Epp and Hodgie and
Miss Hughes into the back of beyond. This was becoming an
alarming habit. The dragons were so ancient they were keeling
over in front of us. I had not yet worked out from observation
that this is simply what people do. Die. But children expect
their teachers, like their parents, to be eternal.

Prayers were in order when we came to Miss Hughie, whom
we called Shuggie.

Shuggie was a religious maniac, a fundamentalist who
had weighed the Old Testament in one hand and the New in
the other and found the latter wanting, so she threw it away
and gave us Jehovah instead in all his glory.

A stuffed stork stood on one tireless leg in a long glass
case in the corner of her classroom. She directed our
attention at once to this bird, which she intended to use as a
visual aid to her own brand of sex education.

'Now children, there is a stupid superstition that babies
are brought to your parents' homes by the stork. That, of
course, is just an old wife's tale, nothing more. You can all
of you see this stork in the corner, can't you?'

We looked at it. We looked at it every day of our lives.

'Now does that bird look remotely capable of bringing a baby boy or girl safely down your chimney? I ask you.'

We had to admit it seemed improbable. Not that we had ever believed it in the first place. Or even thought about it.

'So where do baby boys and girls come from then?'

My hand shot up.

'Liza Leslie, miss.'

'Don't be so stupid!'

A crestfallen silence, and then I remembered. Of course. 'Please, miss.'

'Well?'

'Boys from the Bass and girls from the May.'

The class collapsed while Shuggie raged. 'I've had enough of you for one day, you blasphemous brat! Go and stand in the corner!'

I stood in the corner while Shuggie explained that the child comes from God and that human life is his gift. In Shuggie's class lessons all came to the same thing.

History: *In the beginning God created the heaven and the earth.*
Art: *And God saw everything that He had made, and behold it was very good.*
Biology: *And out of the rib which the Lord God had taken from man, made He a woman.*
Geography: *And He placed at the east of the garden of Eden a cherubim and a flaming sword.*
Arithmetic: *Six days shalt thou labour and do all thy work.*

All the humanities she gave us in one sentence: *For dust thou art and unto dust thou shalt return.*

So Shuggie kept us in the wilderness. We never came to Canaan. But a retiral in the next class up brought a new teacher to the village, and Miss Balsilbie came like one of the daughters of Zion to show us the promised land.

When she swept through the pale green door of Room Five at the start of the new session, I felt my toes tingle and my tongue cleave to the roof of my mouth. Miss Balsilbie's blouses were white roses that fluffed and fell as she breathed, and an infant's breath might have blown them clean off her back, sending all those soft and snow-crimped trimmings fluttering to the floor.

I held my breath.

Miss Balsilbie carried her white roses all round the room, visiting each desk in turn and sitting down beside us, which the dragons had never done. I waited my turn in a state of breathless excitement. But when she came to me I was beating my head against the blind brutal wall of my sums. My jotter was a mass of errors and erasions, filthy with ignorance. My sleeves were ragged, fingers ink-stained, nails bitten down, shoes unpolished, bare legs grimy from playground games. How could she bear to sit near me? The roses brushed my cheek, whispered something to the lid of my desk. I held my breath as tightly as I could. Miss Balsilbie extended her swansnecked, swansdowned arm and her hand touched my exercise book. She held in her fingers a long, beautifully sharpened red pencil. Her nails were strawberry moons. The pale-blue veins showed up like dim far-off rivers.

'No, no, dear,' she drawled, 'you don't know how to divide, do you? Here, let me show you.'

She squeezed herself into the desk beside me, her skirt rustling mysteriously like water falling over my knees, making me shiver.

'Goodness me, child, you're shaking. What in the world is the matter with you?'

She placed her pencil on my desk and put her arm around me. 'You don't have to be frightened of me now, dear, do you? Even though you can't divide.'

Her laughter tinkled as she hugged me tighter, drew me so closely into the roses that I was afraid to breathe. I'd never been this near to a teacher, could never have imagined such softness. The roses fell – and swelled again. My heart was cold as ice. It belonged to Miss Balsilbie, now my snow queen, who taught me how to divide, where all the others had failed.

Miss Balsilbie read us poetry.

> *Have you seen but a bright Lillie grow*
> *Before rude hands have touched it?*
> *Ha' you mark'd but the fall o' the Snow*
> *Before the soil hath smutch'd it?*
> *Ha' you felt the wooll o' the Bever?*
> *Or Swans Downe ever?*
> *Or have smelt the Bud o' the Brier?*
> *Or the Nard in the fire?*
> *Or have tasted the bag of the bee?*
> *O so white! O so soft! O so sweet is she!*

'Does that poem remind you of anyone, boys and girls?'
We gaped.

'Doesn't it make you think of someone? Anyone you know?'

My heart beat hotly in its case of ice. I wanted to tell her. The voice continued to woo us.

'Is there no one in the world like this? Or is it just a dream?'

My hand rose shakily. 'Please miss, it's you.'

The roses fluffed and fell again and she blushed.

'Me? Why, gracious me! Why does it remind you of me, I wonder?'

Words failed me.

At bible-reading time she recited portions of the Song of Solomon:

> *I am the rose of Sharon and the lily of the valleys.*
> *I am dark but comely, O ye daughters of Jerusalem.*

*Stay me with flagons, comfort me with apples: for
I am sick of love.*

She was the goddess of the hour, the heroine of the Old
Testament. And if she was the apple of her own eye, she was
of ours too.

It couldn't last. The Women's Guild? The raging
Shuggie? Or just a child's chance remark? Whatever the
reason, the charge and the verdict were the same. We heard
it vaguely whispered that Miss Balsilbie had been considered 'unsuitable'. And so Miss Balsilbie was exiled from
Eden and a Miss Quinney, an Englishwoman, came in her
place. She was horrified by our local dialect and barbaric
accent, and left at the end of session, breathing fire. But
by that time the fiercest dragon of them all was waiting
for us.

Miss Sangster was a long frozen leek of a woman, standing
straight and hard as an undriven nail. From her coat-hanger
shoulders her smock hung like a faded flag, covering her
bony crêpe-stockinged shanks almost down to her ankle
boots. Even on her own head she had no mercy – as if to ask
us how we could expect any ourselves. The thin grey hair
lay like ash on the pink skull. She parted it simply, scorning
her womanhood, shearing it just above the ears and leaving
bare the reptilian nape of the neck. The eyes were glittering
pin-pricks under the glasses, the lips pursed prunes. Vinegar
veins and chalk arteries, she blew on the embers of numbers
and words, covering forgotten dates with her dusty breath,
warming cold fingers before the tired fires of life. These
fingers of hers were always ringed with plasters and little
bandages covering a multitude of warts. They were the
broken hands of a loveless lady, the sex within her denied

and defeated long ago. But with these hands Miss Sangster beat us into daily submission.

A panoply of punishments stacked her armoury. The warty fingers closed on an ear, a nose, a tuft of hair, and for minutes at a stretch she would be tweaking and tugging and twisting for an answer. She slapped our faces, banged our heads against the wall, beat us on the backs of our bare legs if we did our sums wrong. She jammed our foreheads down on to the lids of our desks until our flesh took on the grain of the oak, and we wore it in our faces for the rest of the day.

Knuckle-jabs were her speciality, delivered with a hissing insult. Taut as a tiger, she crept up on an unsuspecting idler, bending one warty forefinger until the bone shone whitely through the parchment skin, drew back her elbow and let fly. The arm shot like a piston, dug deeply into a sleeping back. She had three treasured body blows: she attacked the spine itself, or the flesh just beneath the ribs, or the kidneys. Rabbit-punches she threw out ten a minute, striking either with the heel or with the battle-axe edge of her hand, sharply across the napes of our bowed necks.

It never occurred to us to consider the moral or educational implications of any of this. It was her teaching method and an intrinsic part of the lesson. Questions and answers were punctuated by the punches she landed, the smart slaps of the ruler, the stinging whiplash of her tongue. *Eleven sevens are seventy-seven*, whacked across the knuckles. *Darnley died at Kirk o' Fields*, dented upon our heads. *Sheffield gives us steel*, hammered out on our hides. Miss Sangster was fists and fingers and feet.

But her most feared instrument of torture was the belt. At school, belts or straps or tawses acquired the mythical status of Notungs and Excaliburs, and the teachers who wielded them became legends in their lifetimes. Personal styles were compared, annual belting averages calculated, record punishments of individual offenders committed to memory. Mothers, fathers, aunts and uncles – all stripped their sleeves and showed their scars. Uncle Billy flaunted his with alacrity, sustained at Miss Sangster's hands, ignoring grandfather's kindly assurances to me that these were recent abrasions caused by hauling on the nets, and nothing more. But present fears were worsened by the horrible imaginings which continued to colour the truth, long after it was plain and clear.

Legend had it that Miss Sangster's belt was at least six yards long, the length, perhaps, of the average dragon's tail, from which it was cut, still hard with agony. Yet all of us could see that it was no more than twenty-four inches. It had nine tails, apparently, like the notorious cat used on the *Marship*, whereas it was plain to see that the leathery lizard's tongue had no more than two tails. The whole world knew that Miss Sangster kept her belt steeping overnight in a stone jar full of vinegar, just for the purpose of increasing its bite. But when I looked into that notorious stone jar on the window-shelf, I saw that it contained nothing more than a jumble of broken coloured chalks.

In any event the belt never left her person, because she wore it under the frayed flowers of her smock, draped across the shoulder and down her back. It was thus within easy reach, and when stung to an anger that could not be assuaged by the application of a finger-jab or a punch, she shot her hand between the two loose buttons of her smock and whipped out the belt as if she were pulling a gun. Then she let fly.

So in many a playground battle where tense gunfighters faced one another for the draw, the imaginary weapon turned out to be Miss Sangster's belt, and instead of a scenario cruel with cordite fumes and the whang of bullets, we watched the last scenes of such dramas turn to farce. Wyatt Earp and Buffalo Bill held out their hands in mock misery and each flogged the other to within an inch of his life, wielding a belt of the mind, created out of our common suffering. The heroes then thrashed the air wildly with their palms, or tucked them tightly into armpits and groin while they moaned and intoned:

> *Davy Crockett married Sangster,*
> *Got the belt, became a gangster.*

In her application of the belt Miss Sangster's dedication and experimentation knew no limits. A girl would normally be let off with a straightforward licking on the open palm, executed without frill or flourish. The boys enjoyed no such maimed rites. For us she retained a repertoire of tricks which and to which she was always refining and adding.

She made us put both hands together but place one beneath the other so that even the unbelted palm underneath would get the benefit of the blow. The hands were then switched so that the bottom one could come on top and receive its proper due, having already foretasted the pain. Sometimes she told us to place our hands on the hard slabs of our desk lids, knuckles against the wood, palms upwards. Then she slammed down on us with all her strength.

She had developed a way of flicking the belt so that it curled around the victim's wrist and arm, leaving long red snaky weals. We swung our arms aloft like flaming windmills, desperately trying to cool the burning, and because we could not hold our pens properly afterwards, she thumped our heads with dictionaries, complaining bitterly about our inability to write, even with the benefit of a good belting behind us. According to uncle Billy, however, she had mellowed since his day – all of seven years ago. As he had been unable to put pencil to paper to her satisfaction, she had offered him some encouragement. She jammed his pencil crossways between his fingers, the pencil resting on little finger and forefinger and held fast by the two middle fingers. Then she thrashed and thrashed until the pencil broke.

'How many strokes did it take?' I asked Billy.

'I lost count,' he said. 'Over a hundred, certainly.'

'A hundred!'

'That's nothing. She said the pencil was too thin. Next time she used a joiner's one – and a thousand lashes later the pencil still hadn't broken.'

He reached into a nearby drawer. 'Here it is, the very same pencil.'

I took it carefully and held it in both hands, breathless with veneration and dread.

Sometimes a boy would jerk his outstretched hand away just as the belt was coming down for the fifth or sixth time. If the belt then struck her on thigh or knee, she reacted like a threshing-machine gone mad. She lashed out with her leather at legs, arms, body, backside, head and ears, anything that could be reached, chasing the wrong-doer round and round the free-standing blackboard until he was caught and beaten or ran right out of the classroom door, down the corridor and into the fields, not to reappear until her white-hot wrath had died down once more to its slow constant smoulder.

One day the blackboard that had been the centre of so many circular pursuits became the focus of activity of an unexpected sort. Miss Sangster was hard at it, hammering facts like nails into our resistant skulls, when the door opened quietly. Mr Gourlay, the headmaster, entered solemnly and waved us back down in our seats as we made to stand. He motioned to Miss Sangster that he would like to speak to her, and it was clear that his sign language indicated 'behind the blackboard'. The two of them then disappeared from sight, except for their legs. They were not only on view but the only source of interest and amusement on offer in Room Five at that moment. The headmaster talked in whispers and had scarcely begun when we saw the two pairs of legs, the crêpe stockings and the plus-fours, draw quickly together until they were touching, almost interlocked. Miss

Sangster's legs seemed to go limp and we heard her produce a little moan. We looked around wildly at one another. This was unbelievable. Shit-catcher was kissing Sangster and she had collapsed with passion in his arms.

Our jubilation, however, proved to be as brief as the moment itself. The legs parted, said goodbye, and Mr Gourlay left as quickly as he'd come. Miss Sangster then re-emerged from behind the blackboard, faced us with glistening eyes and said in a voice we had never heard from her before: 'Class, you are dismissed for the rest of the day. Our King, George the Sixth, is dead.'

At the time we had no notion of the date. Some of us could scarcely have given the correct year, if asked. But now I know, of course, that the day when we thought, with a wild surmise, that the plus-fours and the crêpe stockings had fallen madly in love must have been 6 February 1952.

What do I really remember from her? What are the roots that clutch out of the stony rubbish that she gave me? What fragments to shore against my ruins? Nothing from T. S. Eliot, that's for certain. A few spellings? A few capitals and kings?

Open your sum books at the end. Put your hands behind your heads. What is the capital of Norway? Tell me the time on the clock. Tell me the date of the Battle of Culloden. Tell me the sixth commandment.

Poor, lonely, unloved, unmanned, unwomanned, suffering Miss Sangster, who wept at the king's death, who taught me compassion years too late – what was the point of your time spent in the classroom, beating banalities into us by the sweat of your brow, by the denial of your sex, by six of the best, by all that was uncouth, unholy and utterly uneducating? Dear, dreadful, sweet and sour Miss Sangster, you passed on, out of Room Five, out of our lives, out of your own life, into the classless coffin-desked kirkyard that swallowed up your answers as of no account and left behind you only one eternal question.

Miss Sangster did not die in office but retired as soon as she'd educated us, as if the effort had exhausted her. Uncle Billy, however, assured me that she'd been drafted on to the *Marship* to quell a mutiny by the bilge boys, and had approved so much of the regime of floggings and torments that she'd decided to stay on board for the rest of her life as cat-o'-nine-tailer in chief and able-bodied spinster.

But I was beginning to suspect Billy's stories. He lectured me on our submissiveness to our teachers and reminisced about his schoolday adventures in the notorious One-Gallus Gang. Galluses were the braces we all wore in those days if we were unlucky enough not to be the owner of a striped, elasticated belt with a snake clasp. Members of the One-Gallus Gang made a virtue of necessity and proclaimed their individuality by snipping off one of the two front straps of their braces and pulling the single remaining strap crosswise down their chests to meet buttons that had been shifted to the middle of the trousers. This simple sartorial alteration lent them an air of stubborn disreputability, which they studied to deserve.

Members of the One-Gallus Gang did no homework, brought no books, gave no quarter. When they came to school, which they did only when they chose, they beat up the headmaster and held the teachers hostage in the outside toilets. They turned on taps, redrew the map of the world and drank ink through straws. Most of their time they spent well away from school, avoiding the feared Whipper-In, the School Attendance Officer, employed to ascertain that absences were legitimate and illnesses genuine.

One day they lay in wait for him as he pursued his rounds up in the country. They ambushed him near Balcaskie, sank him up to his head in a dungpit, tied him up, and brought him back to the village in triumph and a wheelbarrow. They tied his shoelaces together and tossed him into the harbour at low tide. Then they returned to raid the school gardens. In broad daylight they dug up every furrow of potatoes planted by Primary Four, pelting the teachers with clods when they tried to prevent this spoliation. The headmaster called the policeman, who arrived with a dripping Whipper-In on the back of his bike. As it was wartime the Home Guard was called in and Billy and his bandits found themselves facing reinforcements, eager for some sort of action. They beat them off and within half an hour Dad's Army was in full retreat. Then the headmaster went to a special telephone, a red one in a locked cupboard, and rang Field Marshal Montgomery . . .

The One-Gallus Gang fought a valiant rearguard action all the way. They bore off the precious potatoes in the school wheelbarrow and built a huge beacon on the beach which burned for three days and three nights, and there they roasted every last potato, consuming the entire school harvest of that year. They crowned this feast with bars of burnt chocolate salvaged from a low-flying off-course Messerschmitt which they'd brought down simply by firing some of the potatoes into the propeller as it went over their heads. The pilot surrendered and so the gang avoided the *Marship* and were decorated instead.

'This is one of my medals,' Billy said, reaching casually into the drawer and pulling out an award which grandfather had said he'd won in the Dardanelles.

'He did,' said Billy. 'We both won the same medal, awarded for valour. Mine should have been a Victoria Cross but they'd run out by then and they simply took what they could get for the ceremony.'

But all that was nothing, he said, compared to the exploits of the One-Gallus Gang in old George's day. Great-grandfather had been a founding member. In those days they cut off dogs' heads for fun, crucified cats, played football with hedgehogs and roasted them along with the potatoes. They dug up the bones of buried teachers who had belted their great-grandfathers, and they drank rum out of their skulls, washing down their three-day banquets with contraband spirit, seized from the excise officers. The One-Gallus Gang was a regiment with a long and illustrious history – and all I had to do to belong to it was to cut off one of my braces, said uncle Billy, reaching into the drawer again and taking out the scissors.

'Here you are, it's simple, only you have to do it yourself – it's no good if somebody does it for you.'

I held on to both braces, and the following year took them both off proudly to wear my first striped elastic belt with a silver snake clasp.

Another of Billy's stories was that the headmaster was really a woman dressed up and that the plus-fours allowed her to wear her long ankle-length bloomers without being rumbled. Women were unlikely to land headteachers' jobs, he explained. Six out of seven were sex-starved spinsters but the seventh was always a man. Mr Gourlay was the proud possessor of a pair of tits, kept secretly pressed beneath his – or rather *her* – checked waistcoat. And underneath the bloomers – well, we won't go into that, said Billy, grinning and winking and tapping the side of his nose.

'But what about going to the bathroom?' I asked.

'Women don't go together.'

'But what about Mr Gourlay's – I mean *Miss* Gourlay's – wife? He's married. I've seen her. She comes to prize-giving.'

It was another clever deception, all part of the plan. Mrs Gourlay was also a dissembler, a man dressed as a woman. They were all what were called bohemians . . .

And so it went on. There were genes for fiction in our family. I inherited some of them. I wish I'd inherited a few more. Did such stories merely spring from the delight in fantasy, I wonder? Or were they a subconscious escape from the daily misery of school life for boys who were either unacademic or highly imaginative? The regime suited neither and the imagination continued to work underground.

And me? I found refuge in – of all things – a pig, drawn

to it by Miss Sangster's assurances that I was pig-ignorant.
The walk to school each morning was a glum business. I
avoided the cracks in the pavement, tightrope-walked the
kerb, picked a leaf from a hedge every ninth step – and
tapped my head furtively against a certain wall seven times
to ensure my mother would not be dead when I got back
home at the end of the school day. I invented rituals endlessly,
designed, I think, to keep me safe from the dragons.

The last stop before school was a house with a large
garden which had been turned into a smallholding. Hens
clucked about. Pigeons murmured in a loft. Potatoes, carrots,
radishes and leeks grew in ranks – and giant golden onions
heaved themselves out of the ground like Russian churches,
buried up to their domes. The coping stone was missing
from a single section of the low wall and this enabled me to
lean over and scratch the pig as he gruntled about his sty. I
envied him his pastoral torpor, the king of illiteracy, innu-
meracy, ill manners, and at the same time encouraged him
to wallow in it, scratching his back every morning till he
grinned sleepily at me and fell ecstatically on his ample side
into the mire. How far away he was from the bewildering
world of sums and the banalities of Birmingham: where
was it situated, how many people lived there, and what did
they do? Whatever they did, they didn't scratch this pig
– which was as dumb as me and just as wise. Between us a
bond grew up. When I approached the smallholding each
morning he ran to me and sidled smilingly up to the wall,
waiting to be scratched and tickled. We grinned together in
the sun, united in ignorance. Then I went into school, every
morning, every year.

So we were passed on from Miss to Miss, season by season;
booted and balaclava'ed, coughing and cod-liver-oiled in
the winter, shirt-sleeved and sweating in the summer; hare-
lipped, stuttering, gap-toothed, warted and all. We threw up
our bean-bags and caught them on our heads. We sloped our
writing towards the door. We chanted our tables, touched

our toes, calculated the price of carrots, parsed our nouns, prayed for our king, suffered under Miss Sangster and came out into the light at the end of that dreary tunnel relatively unchanged. We had grown skins, perhaps, to make us insensitive to dreariness without vision. In the coarse curriculum that we followed, there had been little to awake the sleeping imagination, and those bunned and bespectacled old battle-axes who belted us about the bare legs were hired assassins, paid to kill creativity and keep the Gradgrind mills turning. Ramrods without breasts (except in Mr Gourlay's case), steam hammers somebody must have cared for once, they themselves knew nothing of love and all their lives were rehearsing for death.

5

The Next World

The Holy City – that was what they called us in the East Neuk of Fife. People booked early for church-yard plots that ran east–west rather than north–south, so that when you stood up at the last trumpet, you'd be facing Jerusalem – just in case you'd lost your sense of direction after an eternity in the earth. Resurrection was nothing if not literal in those days. Meanwhile, until the old Jerusalem passed away and the New Jerusalem rose out of the Apocalypse, East Neukers could always come along to St Monans if they wanted a whiff of the temporal alternative to the Holy City. Here ten churches catered for the spiritual needs and zealous propensities of a thousand souls; and at an early age, when ten was the awesome numerate ceiling which I just managed to touch, by standing on mental tiptoe, that was impressive. The churches were as many as the many-tided sea, against which they were individually etched. Religion was the rock on which our fishing township was founded, and the varieties of religion it practised, with acrimonious exclusiveness, were the rocks on which true religion foundered. But nobody saw it that way, least of all the fishermen, who relied on the Rock of Ages to keep them from the literal reefs.

Among us there were Roman Catholics and straight Presbyterians and Congregationalists; there were Open Brethren, Closed Brethren, Fergusson's Brethren and Duff's Brethren – any Brethren at all that cared to construct

an entire theological alphabet out of one undotted iota or
jot or tittle of the law; there were Pilgrims who, like the
Brethren, did not believe in salaried ministers (Jesus having
been without a stipend), but who, unlike everyone else, did
not believe in churches either, except in the figurative sense,
and so brought God under the fabric of one another's roofs;
there were Baptists and Evangelists and Jehovah's Witnesses
round the doors – except old George's. And there was the
Salvation Army, terrible with banners and brass. They hell-
fired at you in the streets one and all and summoned you to
judgement through your letter box. They spilled out on to
the piers, where the setting sun turned the tranquil harbour
to a lake of fire. This was if you did not come to church.

And if you did come to church they made it even worse
for you. They leaned over their pulpits and pleaded with you
to come forward and be saved till their faces turned purple
and the veins broke out on their brows, under the storm-
tossed wrath of their raging white hair, so that they looked
like something from the world of *Moby Dick*. Religion in the
Holy City was not offered to you as a polite cup of tea – they
shot it through you like a dose of salts.

This next-world sentience was not confined to – or by
– any particular time or place. It was built into your genes,
felt in the heart, inhaled and exhaled, heard, smelt, seen and
felt, dreamed, drunk, sweated and bled. You couldn't even
ask the butcher for a pound of mince without remembering
God. Geordie Grant, with his cloud of white hair and a spare
rib in one hand, had the smell of Genesis on him.

Most of the shopkeepers were church elders, or sweet-
sucking spinsters who could see out a sermon the length
of a Polish winter. Some of them doubled as Sunday school
teachers and your penny sherbet also cost you an interroga-
tion on last week's text. '*For God so loved the world* . . . Right
now, finish it off for me, chapter and verse, and earn your
sweeties like a good boy.' It was puzzling to have goodness
demanded of you while being assured with every second

breath that you were a vile sinner through and through, and could do nothing about it except pray for God's forgiveness and grace. The other puzzle was trying to remember what precisely these vile sins were that you had committed. Murder and adultery were not on your personal list, that much was certain. You didn't even know the meaning of adultery, let alone commit it, although it was one of the big *shalt-nots* that was hammered into you every Sunday without fail.

Sunday mornings were always the same. You knew it was Sunday the second you woke. It wasn't just the cessation of the sound of drudgery, it was the quality of the silence, a seventh-seal quality, like in the Book of Revelation, when the Lamb opened the final seal – *and there was silence in heaven about the space of half an hour.* My ideas about heaven were understandably confused during my first decade, but I was in no doubt about one thing: it was a big place. It had to be, to accommodate all the souls, even just the tiny percentage of saved ones, of all the people who had ever lived since the beginning of the world. Furthermore, heaven was the place where we'd all meet again, after death, and folk meeting up with their families after an unimaginable length of separation were hardly likely to sit around in a sort of polite Sunday silence. Not the families I knew. Though nobody would actually spit or shout or make rude noises, there would be quite a buzz, there was no question about that. So for all that multi-global gossip suddenly to cease for half an hour – the idea simply took my breath away.

I used to lie still at first light on Sundays, my nose and ears just above the blankets, assessing the air for information – of the eternal sort. What would God's broadcast be about this morning, in the ether, in the heart? Because we were told that just as God could hear your thoughts, whether you were addressing him or not, so you could hear his words, if you only listened.

I listened. To begin with the sea and the seagulls were the

only things that moved – blue whisperings on the shingle and white circlings over the chimney tops. And webs of sunlight winking on the green weed-grown walls of the quiet piers. Even the boats seemed to behave themselves on Sundays – none of that rowdy jostling and bobbing and creaking.

After an hour or so the village started to shake itself into wakefulness. I could see in my head what was happening. At first it was just the fringes of the tapestry that fluttered and stirred – the old folk who never properly slept and were always up at the crack of dawn. Slippered old wives shuffled across their doorsteps, scrubbed sparkling white or gleaming with Cardinal polish, scattering the crumbs of their frugal breakfasts over their front dykes for the sparrows in the street. An old man tottered to the end of the farthest pier, lit his pipe and smoked in silence, staring across the blue stretches of the firth, remembering.

After that the scrollwork from the village chimneys appeared on the sky and the Sunday morning smells of sausages, bacon and eggs, and fried tomatoes came curling out of open doors to mingle with the scents of the sea. Down in Gerrard's emporium the reprobates were already buying the *News of the World*, and their kids were loading up with lollipops and bags of caramels to take back to their godless sitting-rooms. And the Peatties and the Sharkeys and the Dohertys had already taken the bus to the chapel in Pittenweem for early morning mass. Only those who walked in darkness would dream of waking God up at such an ungodly hour, or of worshipping in such a pagan place. The Pittenweemers were torn-arses and scum. All who were not St Monansers were torn-arses and scum. Everybody knew that – in St Monans at any rate. But all along the windowed streets Calvin's children, God's various elect, were wending their way to the appointed places.

The main parade was put on by the members of the Old Kirk. Under its sea-splashed walls came banker and bankrupt, spinster and strumpet, schoolteacher and fisherman. From all points of the compass they came in tributaries of black and navy blue, in which the hats of the women bobbed like brightly coloured corks in a stream. Along the nave and into the white arms of the transepts they spread. And the kirk took them all in, under its lichened slates, just as its green graveyard eventually accepted the whole spectrum of the town.

The Old Kirk stood to the west of the village, reachable only by that skull-and-crossboned bridge over the stream. It was a square and squat-steepled crucifix of an edifice, the spire indicating the eternity from which the houses tailed away in a curving line to the east. On Sundays the hymns floated backwards like celestial breezes over the red roofs.

> *Holy, holy, holy, Lord God Almighty!*
> *Early in the morning our song shall rise to thee.*

And one by one, in the holy places, they struck up their songs of praise.

From the Braehead Church:

> *Yield not to temptation, for yielding is sin,*
> *Each victory will help you some other to win.*

From the Gospel Hall:

> *This is my story, this is my song,*
> *Praising my Saviour all the day long.*

From the Meeting Place:

> *Blessed assurance, Jesus is mine;*
> *O what a foretaste of glory divine!*

From the Mission:

Rise up, O men of God:
Have done with lesser things.

From a converted fish-shed with a rusted tin roof and an
accompaniment of drips and draughts:

We love the place, O God,
Wherein thine honour dwells.

Through the chinks and cracks in its old wooden boards
I stared once, round-eyed, at the benched bent breathings
and the deep holy silences of its congregation. Amazingly,
I couldn't recognize a single soul. Who were they? Where
did they live during the week? Was working for a living
also sinful, like the music of the organ which, to the glory
of God, never once sounded its trumpet blast against the
Jericho of these damp and rotten walls?

And from the Pilgrims on the pier:

Who would true valour see
Let him come hither.

In the middle of the divine din the Salvation Army burst
from their hall and swung through the streets to fight the
good fight and stand up for Jesus like soldiers of the cross.
A brazen battalion, clad in scarlet and black, and wearing
the helmets of salvation, the breastplates of righteousness,
the shields of faith and the swords of the spirit, they went
marching as to war, and if Sundays in St Monans felt like a
competition about who could shout to God the loudest, the
Sally Ally won hands down. As to what God thought of it
all, heaven knows. The noise in itself was deafening, and he
must have despaired at the conflicting babble of faiths. None
of them could find any room for doubt, and with nothing
else to unite them, they were divided by their convictions
and turned the little town into a Babel without a tower.

Babylon the Great had fallen but a new one had risen in its place, biblical history repeating itself. God sighed and pulled the clouds over his head.

For some it was the music of the organ that was the wind of sin. Others couldn't suffer the practice of paying a man a salary to preach to his flock. The narrowest and most fanatical of the sects had been known to wreck the radios of their sinning offspring, throw the works of Shakespeare into the harbour along with the Sunday newspapers, and divide the damned from the saved in their own kitchens, putting up partitions so as to fulfil the biblical injunction not to take meat with sinners. One, a joiner by trade, built a sliding screen which came neatly over the table so that the family could sit down and eat – together but divided.

What began with Epp was carried on at Sunday school where, in spite of God's wrath – or more likely because of it – we learned to sing to him with cheerful voices, raising the braehead roof, or sometimes grouped at the water's edge on a warm summer's day, adding our raucous offering to the chorus of village praise. But that was rare. Normally we left the sunlight behind us and went into the gloomy stained-glass presence of the Lord, where they suffered little children to come unto him – and those who did not come regularly would suffer. Not now – but on that terrible day. So while the doomed stayed at home listening to Max Bygraves on the wireless, we came along to sing-along-a-Jesus and let the damned follow Max into the flames. The best plan was simply to bawl it out, whether you believed in it or not. After all, God would surely award marks for trying, wouldn't he?

But God was no respecter of persons and he was no respecter of years. Even the sins of our tender decades and half-decades would be sufficient unto the Day of Judgement to ensure that we burned – in the fire that needed no coal or kindling or scrumpled-up copies of the *Sunday Express* to keep it flaming every day. God was the captain, Satan the stoker, sin the spark and human flesh the fuel that ensured the eternal inferno.

> *Give me oil in my lamp, keep me burning,*
> *Give me oil in my lamp, I pray,*
> *Give me oil in my lamp, keep me burning,*
> *Keep me burning till the break of day.*

That's what we sang, and even as I sang I sweated. The image came too close to home and crackled with damnation.

> *You will go to hell! You will go the burning fire!*

The Sunday school teachers confirmed Epp's gospel of doom and put flesh on her still furious bones.

Look in the face the fact that you are bad, that you are a cracked vessel, leaking sin, that you have done wrong.

You do wrong every day of your life, from eye-opening to eye-shutting. You did wrong from the first breath that you took, O thou child of weak-willed Adam and foolish Eve. You did wrong to be born at all, thou offspring of original sin.

Conceived in sin and born in sorrow, you are an error, a living wrong, a perversion of the creation.

God sees everything that you do, everything that you think and feel he hears and senses. He hears every lie told, every wicked whisper of the heart, every impulse in your idle hands, your fingers and feet, your immortal soul. An empty seat in Sunday school, a vacant pew in church, where you ought to have been – every absence is a witness against Christ the Son, every negative a positive assault, carried out by you. He who is not for him is against him, and God the Father will not be mocked in the person of his Son. A text unlearned is a failure to love him. A crude word is another nail hammered into his crucified hands. And a refusal to believe in Him is the sure and certain road to eternal damnation.

The bible is God's revelation to man. Church and conscience are of no avail in themselves, good works are useless, a kind and caring heartbeat is unheard in heaven, and a gracious life already dead in God's eyes, unless these things are accompanied by prayer, by scripture and by belief. Belief in the bible is the cornerstone of faith in God. You must know your bible then, better than you know yourself, for you will never truly know yourself until you know your bible: every book of it, every chapter of it, every verse of it, every sentence of it, every word of it, every syllable of it – which is the inspired word of God.

The bible is your sword of salvation. To defend yourself against the Adversary and attack the armies of the ungodly, you must first know the length and breadth of your sword, from point to hilt and from edge to edge. Now let Satan see that you can wield the whole sword effectively. Are you ready now? The books of the bible by heart. Off you go! *Genesis, Exodus, Leviticus, Numbers, Deuteronomy, Joshua, Judges, Ruth* . . . All the way from the Creation to the Armageddon, right down to Revelation.

Now you must know all the vital strokes and how to deliver them with precision and speed against the enemy, the eternal enemy of man. Put your swords under your armpits, and when I say, 'Draw your swords', find the following texts as fast as you can. Remember that whoever is slow with his sword and uncertain with his thrust is a prey to Satan, who is swift as a tiger and strikes like a snake. Are you ready then, soldiers?

John, chapter three, verse sixteen. Draw your swords!

For God so loved the world that he gave his only begotten Son, that whosoever believeth in him should not perish, but have everlasting life.

Mark, chapter sixteen, verse sixteen. Draw your swords!

He that believeth and is baptized shall be saved, but he that believeth not shall be damned.

First Epistle of John, chapter one, verse eight. Draw your swords!

If we say that we have no sin we deceive ourselves and the truth is not in us.

Revelation, chapter twenty, verse fifteen. Draw your swords!

And whosoever was not found written in the book of life was cast into the lake of fire.

So with our swords in our hands we were equipped for the fight against principalities and powers of evil.

But the white-headed men who peered over the pulpit counted my blessings, totted up my sins, lamented my fall, demanded my faith and put a sword in my hand with which I never felt properly at ease. Eventually it rusted in its sheath and I took up a pen instead.

Still at one time I succeeded in drawing my sword better than the best of them. One summer the evangelists descended on us. We had no idea where they came from or where they disappeared to, but we knew very well why they were there: to spend every day of the seven-week school holidays luring us away from our play and whipping us up into a frenzy of self-loathing and love of Jesus. If there were men among them I remember none. All I recall is a bevy of red-lipped, blazered and straw-bonneted young girls wearing cotton print dresses and with bare sandalled feet. They blazed into our midst and sent the minister and the Sunday school spinsters packing. They opened the double doors and let the sunlight and the sound of seagulls come breezing in to break up the stained-glass silence and the dim religious light. They marched us down to the sands and sent us into the waves to be cleansed and born again to cries of Hallelujah. The firth had become the Jordan. And if those clear-eyed, honey-haired girls were not exactly a band of angels, they were their beautiful assistants, coming for to carry us home, and carrying accordions instead of harps.

One of them in particular I remember. She was in charge of our bible education and was determined to make us faster on the draw and more accurate with the chapter-and-verse thrust. As an incentive she carried in the inside pocket of her scarlet blazer a stack of bookmarks, all bearing coloured illustrations of scenes from the bible, and all done in lurid Victorian detail, sentimental or apocalyptic. The first to whip the bible from under the armpit, locate the given text and rattle it out, became the owner of one of these bookmarks. They served no functional purpose for me as I had no books to put them in, but suddenly all my collections of carefully accumulated cards from the cigarette packets gone through by grandfather and my uncles lost their appeal. The trains, the aeroplanes, the clipper ships – their glamour had gone and all I wanted was to win these biblical bookmarks. Not for myself but for the sake of the beautiful evangelist. Even the cigarette packets themselves seemed tawdry now. I went home and looked at them in their secret drawer: Four Square, Three Castles, Black Sobranie, Turf, Wild Woodbine and the Players packets with the red-bearded sailor on the front, the kindly seaman who stood in for my father, I would have swapped all of them for one bookmark. So I became a demon with my sword, a little soldier impressing his lady, the tall young girl who kissed me with her red lips a dozen times a week as I went up to collect my bookmark. The summer went on and I never missed a meeting.

Ah, but summers end. And so do games. After the very last gospel meeting she went down on her knees in front of me, her spotless cotton dress touching the ground. She took both my grimy hands in her clean ones, looked earnestly into my eyes, and asked me the question I had dreaded.

'Christopher, are you saved?'

The game was up. It was about more than collecting coloured cards and impressing an angel. I shuffled an embarrassed 'no' with my scuffed shoes and a shake of the head, but the pain was so delicate on her pale brow, so exquisitely sweet on her sad red lips, that I allowed her to save me. It was a multiple conversion. Bert Mackay was saved along with me – and a girl called Cynthia. But it was Bert she used as an example to reinforce the enormity of what we had just done.

'Bert comes from a farm,' she said, looking at us with sweet solemnity. 'He that putteth his hand to the plough and then looks backward is not fit for the kingdom of heaven. Remember that, all of you, for Jesus' sake.'

'What did she mean?' I asked Bert afterwards.

It was Bert's turn to educate me.

'You shouldn't look back when you're ploughing,' he said. 'If you do, your line won't be straight. You have to fix your eye on a point in the distance and never take it off. That way your line will be perfect.'

I was not yet ten years old. Next morning she left with the band of hope in the big bright van in which they'd come seven weeks before. She blew me a kiss and I went back to the dragons. All my former queens were dead or disappeared, Mrs Guthrie, Miss Balsilbie, Honeybunch. Now the beautiful evangelist was my angel queen and the sweet chariot was taking her away. My lip trembled. But it was not just because I knew I'd never see her again. It was because I knew I'd never plough that straight unswerving furrow. I was a Judas, a nine-year-old Iscariot. And she was betrayed.

I was left with a guilty secret, an uneasy relationship with God – who knew very well that my salvation had been a charade – and a collection of bookmarks. With no books to put them in, I laid them in the drawer beside the cut-out fronts of the packets of Players and Woodbine, till I decided that Jesus and the bearded sailor, though not dissimilar to look at, made uneasy bedfellows, one advertising tobacco and the other eternal life. Eventually I offered the bookmarks to old George, who frowned and pursed his lips at such fripperies but was pleased to hear how I had acquired them. He paid me the tribute of actually using them and I felt a faint gladness when I saw them sticking out of his pulpit bible, marking his favourite texts.

The absence of books from our house did not mean any lack of stimulation. Epp had thundered forth her heroic poetry, Georgina's songs spoke of doomed lovers from another culture and hinted wistfully at their sad stories. The old folk told me countless tales. But other than these, and the scraps of stories chiselled on the kirkyard slabs, it was the bible that was my first sustained contact with a narrative masterpiece in the form of printed literature.

Adam and Eve were creatures of dust and bone, Adam composed first out of the dreary dust of the ground, to which he was bound back, and when he slept, God the butcher broke open his body, ripping out a rib, exposing it like the ribs of the ships in the boatshed – and so Eve was made. Dust and bone with the smell of death on them, they were a grim couple, Sunday school teachers without their clothes, the merest shades of people, inhabiting a garden where there was no sound or smell of the sea, and where a serpent slid, subtler than any conger eel, a cold-blooded killer with a brain in its sharp little skull. It knew all about the apples of desire.

And so they yielded, and knew at once the sinful nakedness of Honeybunch, walking cool as she liked through Alec Fergusson's cucumbers as he mended his bicycle in the garden, walking bare buff and beautiful into the waves, never to come out again. Then the dreadful disembodied voice of the Lord God was heard walking in the garden in the cool of the day, a walking voice, spying into their sin, telling them that they were found out.

The serpent was punished, as grandfather once punished a conger eel on the pier, writhing and snapping at his heel till his heavy boot crushed its skull into a pulpy silence. But Adam would have to butter his bread with the sweat of his brow, and at his life's end he would have to go back to the ground from which he'd been taken, back to the old kirkyard with the rest of the town. For dust thou art, and unto dust shalt thou return. And Eve would conceive and bear in sorrow.

So out they went, like bad boys and girls, a flaming sword at the school gates forbidding them any second chance. They were a dreary desolate couple and they had let us all down. The whole history of the world proclaimed their failure. They had spoiled things for the rest of us, for the rest of our lives. And yet I felt a crushing sorrow for them as they were sent out, the same sorrow as I felt for Cain, who stood in a field and denied his brother's murder to God's own face, blustering, brazening it out. Am I my brother's keeper? I know nothing about it, honest!

Yet even as Cain fibbed, his brother's blood came bubbling up from the ground like a red tongue, telling all, tolling out the truth. What hast thou done? What hast thou done? And so Cain too was cut off from God and driven out from community and kin, an exile to the end of his days. And his punishment was greater than I could bear.

But Cain knew his wife and she conceived. Strange words. Of course he knew his wife! What did it mean? And what did it mean that the sons of God *came in unto* the daughters of men? Words hung up like underclothes around the images they never quite created, hiding the man and the woman and what it was that they did. What was it that lay behind the winks and grins and sudden silences in those interrupted adult conversations, taken up again in low voices after I had left the room?

'She didn't, did she? Oh, tell me she didn't!'

'She did, she did, the first time in Balcaskie, the second time in Peter Hughes's barley, and then she even did it in the ice shed. And do you know what happened?'

'What, what . . . ?'

Jenny and Georgina crouched so close by the fireside, bare toes touching on the fender, that their breaths met to seal the conclusion with a kiss.

'Oh, God sakes, I don't believe it!'

'It's true!'

The tinkling music of their laughter and low voices, stirred to pinkness in their long white nightgowns, lured me into the room.

'Tell me, tell me . . . '

'It's not for young ears to hear. Away you go now, cockie.'

'Geordie's looking for you. Go and learn your bible.'

I went and learned my bible. And nothing was ever normal again.

Joseph haunted me from Egypt, where he lay like Epp, embalmed in a coffin. Before that, in prison, he had interpreted the dreams of Pharaoh's butler and baker. The butler had a good dream and was released, but the baker's dream was bad. I knew all about bad dreams.

Mr Guthrie came out of the bakery with the baking trays on his head as he always did, right up to that last Sunday morning. Three white baskets on the chief baker's head, the bible said, and in the topmost basket Pharaoh's bakemeats, which the birds of the air came and ate. The three white baskets were three days, and in three days, Joseph told him, Pharaoh would have him hanged, and the birds would eat his flesh. And so it came to pass.

Mr Guthrie hanged himself from the beams of the bake-house in the small hours of a Sunday morning, locking the door behind him. Nobody knew why. One of the bakers had to smash the window to get at him and was sick when he saw what he saw – Mr Guthrie hanging high from a hawser, with his head wrenched to the side and his haddock's mouth bursting a black grape of a tongue. And the seabirds breaking open his skull with their beaks and feeding on his brains. Poor Mr Guthrie.

I felt sorry too for Lazarus the beggar, Lazarus full of sores, lying at the rich man's gate as he fared sumptuously every day, while the dogs came and licked his sores. But I felt even sorrier for the rich man, because Lazarus went to heaven, but the rich man went to hell, where nobody licked his wounds, or gave him a single drop of water to cool his burning tongue. I knew what it would be like to hear a voice tell you that this was for ever, with no resurrection except to eternal torment. *And not one drop of water will you get!*

Was I deprived? Abused? Did I miss out somehow on Sleeping Beauty? Would I have been better off with Snow White and the Seven Dwarfs? Rhetorical questions, I think. The bible was black gold and I was rich beyond the dreams of literary avarice – give or take a little scarring of the soul. In the end it is the Book of Job I remember best. A difficult story for a child to read for himself, especially in the language of King James, but old George cracked it open for me and never tired of telling it. I even asked for it, knocking on the blistered door, and he always obliged. He never read it from the page, though, telling the story instead in his rough distinctive way, which I can still remember, word for word.

This is how he told it.

Job, you see, was a real toff, because he was a very well-off man, but he was also a man of God, and he had a heart of gold.

One day, when God was holding forth, Satan turned up.

'And what have you been up to?' God asked.

'Wandering round the compass,' Satan answered. 'North, south, east, west, on land and sea. You know how I like to travel.'

'Have you heard tell of my servant, Job?' God asked. 'Did you see any sign of him? Now there's a man of faith for you! He's what you call a pillar of the kirk.'

'Och, him!' scoffed Satan. 'Aye, I came across him all right, but he's nothing special. He's got every cause to be religious. Just look at how you've feathered his nest all these years. Cupboard love, that's his religion.'

God took that a bit hard. 'Right,' he said. 'Do just what you like with his gear, but no harm to the man himself, mind.'

Satan went away rubbing his hands.

Next thing you know, Job was tucking in as usual, when one after another the messages started coming in.

Bandits have raided your cattle and murdered your men – I'm the only survivor!

Lightning has struck your sheep and their shepherds – I'm the only survivor!

Fierce tribesmen have carted off your camels and done their drivers to death – I'm the only survivor!

A whirlwind from the wilderness has smashed your son's house to smithereens, and all the young folk have lost their lives in the ruin – I'm the only survivor!'

These were some punches. But Job took them like a man, right on the jaw, and this is what he said:

*Naked came I out of my mother's womb, and naked shall I
return thither: the Lord gave and the Lord hath taken away:
blessed be the name of the Lord.*

And he never said a word against God.

Next time God was holding forth at the bench, Satan
turned up to put in his needleful.

'So,' said God, 'where have you been stravaiging to this
time?'

'Oh, the usual,' said Satan. 'Boxing the compass, round
and about. North, south, east, west. You know how I like
to travel.'

'And what have you to say about Job now? He's still the
godfearing body he always was. Even though you made me
wreck him, he didn't crack, did he?'

'Skin for skin, as they say,' Satan answered. 'Hit him in the
flesh itself, right into the very bone, and he'll soon squeal.'

'All right,' said God, grim-faced. 'He's all yours, but don't
make it fatal.'

Satan took a bearing on the earth and went for Job like a
gannet. He struck him with saltwater boils, blistering him
from the soles of his feet to the crown of his head, and Job
sat in agony in the ash-hole, itching uncontrollably and
scraping himself with shards of shattered earthenware.

'What about your precious God now?' asked his wife.

'You're havering like an old fishwife,' said Job. 'You've
got to take in torn nets some time or other. It's God's will
that matters.'

But then his three cronies came and made things worse
by trying to comfort him. They sat down and wept salt
scalding tears, and that just made him see how bad a state
he was in. So he opened his mouth and cursed the day he
was born.

'I wish I'd died in my mother's belly and never sucked at
her breasts. I'd rather be lying right now, a stillborn bairn
in the old kirkyard, with kings and counsellors of the earth,

dead in their tombs, dumb as the gold and silver they piled up for nothing, for other folk to spend.

'Why are folk born at all to be burdened and bitter souls, their only comfort to yearn for a death that never comes, their only treasure the tomb, their only gladness the grave?

'You try to live a good life and you see what you get for your trouble.'

But God answered Job out of the storm-wind.

'Who's this darkening my door with debate, blethering like a daftie? Get a grip on yourself, man.

'Where were you when I sank the foundations of the earth and threw it up in six days? When I poured out the sea and tethered the tides and all the morning stars struck up a song?

'Ever tried telling the sun to rise? Go on, have a go, make the morning come if you can, take hold of the horizon and shake down the stars, keep the pole-star pointing to the north and tell the Plough not to rust. See if they listen to you.

'Ever seen what lies on the sea-bed, have you? Or behind the gates of death? Or gone into a snowflake or a hailstorm? Are you the father of frost and rain and ice and dew? Could you freeze the sea to stone, do you think? Could you tie up the Pleiades or loose Orion's belt, tame the Bear or dim Arcturus?'

Job was quiet through all this, but he never agreed.

Then God tried one last shot.

'You know how to fish, I suppose? You use a hook and line. Now try it with a whale. Can you get a hook through his snout or bore through that jawbone with a thorn?

'How do you think you'd get on? I'll tell you. You can hurt him with harpoons, stick him full of spears, butcher him with barbed irons – all that's straw and stubble to him. You'll piss your breeks in the process! His teeth are like marlin spikes, his eyes like harbour lamps, his nostrils like funnels, belching smoke and fire. His heart's like a millstone, his sides like a battleship, his brow like a boulder. His spout's a tornado, his tail a typhoon. A whale is made of whinstone, my man – and I made him what he is!'

After that Job saw the point.

'I don't know what came over me,' he said. 'I'm just a bag of wind, a pierhead blether. I can see how small I am – worse than nothing. From now on I'll keep my hatches battened.'

And God gave everything back to Job – as a matter of fact he doubled his fortune.

So keep your mouth shut, and let God do the talking.

In his most scripturalist phase, before he failed, George taught me the bible in the direct and vivid style of an old whaler, only occasionally referring to the big book itself. He also liked to combine seamanship and religion in the spirit of his generation and grandfather's.

There were no ornaments in George's room. But on one of the walls he had hung a large painting of a ship, which he called the Gospel Ship. It was not a full-rigged vessel – it had twenty-four sails – but on every sail and key part of the ship there was an apt quotation from the bible. He made me learn the names of the sails and parts of the ship, and with my eyes shut I had to tell him the quotations, chapter and verse, together with the references, on every part, and on any part that he might pick out at random. This went on for many Sundays for many years. There were fifty references altogether and I can still do this behind closed eyes.

The ship was guided by the morning star, shown blazing in the sky, with Revelation 2.28 printed underneath. *And I will give him the morning star.* At its stern a lighthouse revealed the rocks it had come safely through, and round the white tower was written the reference Psalm 119.105, *Thy word is a lamp unto my feet and a light unto my path.* A flock of seabirds followed the ship, carrying a message from Ecclesiastes 10:20, *A bird of the air shall carry the voice.*

Every one of the twenty-four sails and each of the masts bore its text, and every working part of the vessel was appropriately inscribed, as were each of the ship's flags. Along the hull of the ship were written the words, *Though billows encompass my way, yet shall I fear not.* And at the very bottom of the picture was a little couplet:

> *Jesus, Saviour, pilot me,*
> *Over life's tempestuous sea.*

The sea in the painting was suitably stormy, to fit the caption, and it wore an ominous frown that reminded me of the second verse of Genesis, known to me before I even knew myself, describing the primordial chaos that reigned before God took the universe in hand. Darkness was upon the face of the deep. And the spirit of God moved upon the face of the waters. God was invisible but the sea revealed something of his angry expression, and it was those broken masts and spars that frightened me more than anything else in the entire religious scheme of things. *How shall we escape if we neglect so great salvation?* It equated damnation with drowning – and for the impressionable child who just happened to live surrounded by sea, it represented an ever-present threat.

Emerging from one of the church services, from Sunday school, or from bible-reading either with George or by myself, was like coming out of the picture houses in Anstruther or Pittenweem. The technicolour stayed in my head and projected itself on to the blues and greens of fields and sea, staining and splashing them with nightmare and blood.

Everything was unreal. The preaching was still going on from end to end of the village, from pier to pier, the holy words whipped up on the four winds, howls and hosannahs offering pre-echoes of heaven and hell. The clouds looked strange and unfamiliar, as if they might fracture at the next fraction of recorded time, to reveal the whole biblical chronology of things from the first day to doomsday. And in the huge hole that would open up in the already darkening day, the village and its people, its works and ways, the safe steady ropes of its traditions, its fishing and farming, so changeless and sure, would snap, and in a twinkling we'd all disappear down the dark crack of doom.

When the storm did break at last, I was standing outside the Congregational church, high up on the braehead, the last chords of the organ voluntary drum-rolling at my back.

'Sky's too blue over by the Bass,' an old man said, and he pointed shakily with his stick.

'There's going to be thunder.'

Down below us the firth took on an ominous flat calm and there was a terrible quietness. The only sign that the tide was flowing was an uneasy rippling like a whisper on the water. But the purplish grey-blue clouds were massing like anvils on the skyline, all the way along from east to south, showing the direction from which the hammers would soon come crashing. Far above them the whiter clouds dazzled, their edges unnaturally bright. God's furious face was just behind them and his wrathful glower was what was causing the glare. Without the protection of the clouds his glance would fall on us like an atom bomb. The sea changed from mercury to molten lead and from lead into a black brooding oil. Then the wind sprang up from the south-east, the thunderheads racing in the opposite direction, travelling against the stream of air, and with a flash of lightning across the firth, the storm burst. The Bass roared like a blue bear gone berserk, its deep growls cracking open the sky's theatre of war.

But I knew as I ran screaming for my mother and the smothering blankets that the storm was not a mad bear at all but something much worse, because Epp had told me long ago that the thunder was God speaking to the wicked, and I knew there was no one more wicked than myself. My unbelief was abominable and my hypocrisy was an affront to God. I had lied to please the pretty evangelist. I loved her more than Jesus. Bert Mackay would plough a straight furrow but I couldn't even do that. I'd never make it to the kingdom of heaven.

A thousand other sins clamoured against me, raging with the thunder and the hissing rain that fell like fire into the firth: Mrs Guthrie's apples, the extra cream cookie smuggled once into the paper bag when she left the counter, the roses in Miss Balsilbie's bosom and the white shock of Honeybunch's flesh, the burning bush, the tree of knowledge that grew between her thighs.

Everything I had done was a sin, smashed down now on the anvils of the sky to deafen me to mercy and drown out the songs of praise from the Holy City. Every wrongful thought, every playground profanity, the peeing up the wall, the garters round the head, the Blind Man with his stick knocked away from him, Honeybunch spreadeagled and shining on the tombstone. All the crystallized candy stolen from Kate, the taunts at deaf Jean Jeff, the times without number I'd refused to go for messages or told my mother the shop was shut, shufflings and grumblings and lies, lies, lies . . . ! And Miller's lost watch, lying somewhere out at sea, where I sometimes wished my father to lie after a thrashing, not forgiving him as I should have done, but wishing him stopped like that watch, a thought for which I'd surely be punished in kind, as happened in sleep often enough, falling down again into the cold dark depths where the whale waited with the face of Tom Tarvit to swallow me like Jonah into the everlasting stench of the bilge, along with the *Marship* boys.

Howling, I tore off the bedclothes and ran out into the street. Scores of boys were down at the harbour, turning fear into fun in the middle of the thunder by braving the storm on the Blocks.

6

Winter Drifting and Spring Lines

The Blocks were as far as you could venture out to sea if you weren't a fisherman and kept your feet on terra firma. Not that they felt all that firm underfoot. Green sleet coated the crumbling surfaces of the concrete megaliths that zigzagged out from the back wall of the east pier and took you into deep water and the heavy swell of the open ocean – ocean enough for me, at any rate. But the petrified forked-lightning formation of the breakwater was the long arm of the law, science's law, that protected the town and its harbour from the pitiless laws of nature.

And yet the natural world was in itself a protection of a sort, a skin that stretched between you and the next-world terrors of the evangelists. All year round the skin was there, enveloping and enthralling, keeping you in that state of nature, reminding you of how simple things might have stayed, if only Adam and Eve hadn't gone the way of their nature. Their disobedience meant we were destined either for the dust or the deep blue sea. We'd come up again as flowers or foam, recycled. All flesh was grass. And what wasn't – was the curl of a wave, the wishless swing of seaweed in the bay, the mother-of-pearl film on a twist of shell, the glint of what had once been life. Or it was a white flash of wings over the water. Grandfather said that the souls of drowned fishermen became seabirds. So they still hunted for fish and never left the sea, but their spirits soared high above it now, freed from bondage to wind and wheel and tide. And their wailing was for the life they'd left on shore, calling to their loved ones. Grandfather was no churchgoer either. He said that the sun was god.

'Gone to glory? Gone to graveyards more like.'

That was about as far as he would be drawn on the subject of religion. Instead he drew a perfect circle with a pencil stub round his old shilling and asked if I could show him where it started and where it finished. And when I couldn't he said that nature went round and round just like that, endlessly, and we'd go with it when we were dead, and that was our eternity.

'So you might as well start getting used to it now, lad. Take my tip, follow the wheel of the year. You'll learn a lot and you won't put a foot wrong.'

It wasn't difficult. Our lives were bound to that wheel and we turned with it, grandfather marking its revolutions in his own eccentric way. We stood on the braehead on the first day of the year at nine o'clock in the evening. The snow was glistening on the south side of the firth, the lights of Edinburgh, where I'd never been, like fallen stars all along the skyline; and at nine exactly where his hand pointed, Regulus rose out of the sea, the first sign of spring. Grandfather had discarded the conventional calendar long ago. He followed his own clock, telling the time from everything that went on around us: the fieldfares arriving in large numbers after the snow, the robin singing in the small hours, the snowdrops spearing the earth – brave wee troopers, he called them – dandelions bursting, the woods full of young green nettles, dry mud floating on the flood tide. But as well as the usual signs, he taught me to recognize the sound of spring in the peculiar quietness of the air at sunset, as if the whole earth was holding its breath, waiting for the huge surge of sound and colour, the clamour of returning life.

Crabs spawned among the rocks, brittle starfish appeared in the shallows, and whelks bejewelled the bottoms of the rock pools. Gannets flew over the firth again, and massive flocks of oystercatchers, and west of the town the bay was flecked with purple sandpipers. All these things were the numbers on the clock.

At the start of the year, if he couldn't fish and was tired of mending nets, grandfather went out whelk-gathering, dipping his brown hands into the clear icy water that turned them weirdly white. Usually he refused to take me along because of the cold.

'The whelks is a miserable wet job in January,' he said. 'A depressing month for melancholy folk, and bad enough for me.'

But he always had a rhyming alternative.

> *January is wondrous good*
> *To lop trees or fell wood*

And as he could never sit down for long, he took me by the hand, slung his axe and sack across his shoulder, and we started off for Balcaskie.

There was a thin wind. Fieldfares fluffed their feathers in the leafless hedges, ignoring the withered berries that shivered there like black widows. Not a hip or haw was to be seen, but the robins were lighting up their braziers in the bare hawthorn bushes and the whins were sending out yellow sparks from the hills.

We waited until Peter Hughes, the farmer, had gone over the road past Balcaskie. He was carting dung to the fields. Lumps of it lay among the frosted grasses where the gulls were stabbing at them alongside jackdaws and rooks.

'Poor wee buggers,' said grandfather, 'doddering about up here with these landlubber birds – they should be out at sea looking for herring.' He looked over his shoulder across the already darkening fields to where a few boats were etched on the firth. 'And so should we.'

He leaned over the fence, pulled off his cap, and set it back on his head in exactly the same position.

'Ach, no we shouldn't. When you see these seabirds ferreting for a beetle in a bit of cow-dung, you know there's not a herring to be had in the whole firth.'

The cap came off and on again, as if confirming the observation.

'So why waste time taking the *Venus* out? A herring gull's got more sense behind its beak than all those fellows out on the firth right now. They need their heads flushed out.'

Peter Hughes passed us again with his rich dark load, his horse breathing like a steam engine. His sheep were shivering over their frozen turnips. The cattle stood in a black huddle around the frozen water trough.

'Let's give the poor beasts a drink.'

Grandfather broke the seal of ice with his axe and watched with satisfaction as the pink tongues shot into the water like hot melting pokers.

'A man like that,' he said, 'who can't even see to it that beasts can get their drink. He works for the nobs in Balcaskie, so he doesn't give a damn.'

We went over the fence.

'We won't let him or the nobs see what we're up to, though. Do you want to taste the sun?'

He snapped off the withered skull of a cow parsnip and put one of the seeds into my mouth.

'What do you taste?'

'Earth,' I said, spitting.

'That's the sun in the earth, and that seed holds it locked up all through the winter. It's not the earth you're tasting, it's the sun. Eat it – it's solar energy.'

A natural presenter, that was grandfather. He knew things about things. His dream was that I would go to university one day and do the things he might have done. Except that what he did, he did perfectly, and neither asked for nor expected more.

In the wood we found a fallen tree. He hacked and sawed and sweated while I poked about among its litter of dead leaves. A bunch of snails lay buried deep in the pile, fastened together in the frost, sealed up in sleep and slime for the winter.

'Don't separate them, they'll be warmer together.'

I tried to stick back the one I'd snapped from the cluster.

'You'd better hide them again – the Snailer might sniff them out, all the way from the town.'

Do worms eat snails or do snails eat worms, I wondered. Grandfather laughed. 'Neither. But you won't find any worms around here right now. They've delved deep and all the moles have gone after them.'

His old eye spotted something lying among the scattered leaves and branches. 'Acorns,' he said, 'still lying there nice and dry from the autumn. Let's gather a few.'

He came out of the wood like January itself, my grandfather, white-haired, bright and bearded, a sea-god on shore leave, blowing on his fingers, his bag of logs on his back. By this time the heavy sky had fallen like lead on the top of Kellie Law, but he hurried me up the hill with him to cut a branch of whinflowers for my grandmother.

'She can't get out now – and they remind her of how she ran about the hill as a young thing. Burning the whins was always a great affair.'

I tried hard to see grandmother as a girl, dancing round bonfires on a hilltop. It was easier to picture grandfather sailing to the Dardanelles – like sheep to Churchill's slaughterhouse, he said, recalling it as ever at the oddest moments.

We could see the wild glare from Jamieson's forge long
before we reached home, a frown on the water, like a blood-
stained moon. We put the whins in a jam-jar and set it
on the sideboard. Their yellow lamps were still dimmed
by dark-green shades, but soon the buds would burst and
they'd be brightening the corner and bringing a smile to
grandmother's eyes.

Grandfather nodded at them. 'If I ever do retire I'm going
to keep bees. You can help me with the hives and I'll get you
the sweetest honey that there's to be had from these flowers.
We'll call it Golden Gorse.'

Then he remembered his acorns. He brought them out
of his baggy blue pocket and laid them on the grate. One by
one he crushed them with the end of the poker and tipped
them into his old blue tea-clipper mug. After that came
water and a screw of sugar.

'There you are,' he said. 'That'll do me better than Camp
any day, since there's no tea in the house. Will you go down
for some later?'

Agnes Meldrum's Camp Coffee – chicory essence – was
the closest we ever came to coffee, till Nescafé flavoured the
'50s with its magic brown dust and nobody needed coupons
any more.

He put the steaming brew to my lips. I shook my head,
then watched as he sipped his own special brand of Balcaskie
coffee.

'Golden Gorse and Balcaskie Brew – maybe we'll open a
shop, once I'm done fishing.'

Then he was asleep.

A strange man, my grandfather.

No, not strange at all. He was very ordinary. That was
the strange thing. He showed me the small short-spined

sea-scorpions appearing in the water in early February, and the porcelain and thornback crabs in the rock pools. The whelks had left the pools now and ventured out on to the rocks and skerries. As early as the first day of February the fulmars were flying offshore and the skylarks singing loudly over the fields. Hundreds of gulls fluttered along the newly ploughed furrows in long white bridal trains, behind tractors that looked like busy red-cheeked farm girls coming over the shoulder of the land. But by the third week of the month the fieldfares and redwings were getting ready to leave, and eider ducks were cooing on the tide. Aconites buttered the woods and Dog's Mercury gold-dusted the ditches. On clear frosty nights Rigel and Aldebaran glittered over the firth, lamps above Edinburgh.

'And Edinburgh would frizzle up in a second in one of those sparklers. The whole world would go out like a moth.'

I followed his pointing finger south at ten o'clock to where stars were being born in Orion's sword even as we spoke – out of time.

'There's no ten o'clock or anything o'clock in Orion.' So he liked to say.

When grandfather wasn't entertaining me, my own first attempts at self-amusement were snatched from the rolling wheel of the seasons as it whirred past our windows. I played on the beach among the tangles after a sea-cat gale in February, and saw the dead sea-cats in among the giant weeds, their slippery corpses not yet stiffened, voiceless things of the sea, which I pulled out by their tails, whirling them round my head and loosing them like unchained comets to land with a thud on the bouldery shore. The old folk and the poor used to eat these sea-cats. Nobody looked twice at them now, not even the niggards who would go out and kill for a coupon. But old George took a different view. After a wintry gale he would ask me to go down to the shore to look for them. 'As long as you can see blood coming from them, they'll make a good enough eating.'

He examined each one I brought him, slashed with my penknife to check for blood, and trundled all the way up the brae in my miniature wheelbarrow. The sea-cats, he told me, were so stupid that they deserved to be eaten. During the deep storms they clung to the big stalks of the tangles, not letting go even though their holdfasts were uprooted from the seabed, and so they came ashore, still clinging to the washed-up weeds, to take their last journey, a funeral procession in my little blue barrow all the way up to old George's dinner table.

Some he kept, others he returned to me to throw back into the water. Down on the beach again, I sorted through the tangles for a fair-sized root which grandfather cut out for me in the shape of a pistol. So my first wars were bruited behind the boat-building shed with a rubbery gun that had come out of the sea. A gun like this would last for several weeks before it shrivelled and stank, but while it was battle-worthy it allowed me to stretch my arm in conquest over the Philistines, and I walked among the corpses of the sea-cats like Samson, setting my foot on their necks and praising God for my victory, bellowing out the words to let George hear them from his window. I was a giant over my foes, the sole survivor of an unsung epic, the battle for the east sands.

Or on Saturday afternoons during the winter herring I'd go down to the pier to see if there were any spare fish. If a boat had landed a big catch, the last herring out of the vessel that wouldn't make up a marketable quantity were sometimes thrown to waiting boys to sell for pocket money to the cadgers, who then hawked them around the village, or up at the farms, where the fishermen seldom went.

One year there was a Flanders frost in February. That was the name the old folk gave to a south-east gale that brought in the fiercest of frosts, and ice as hard as armour.

Many of the smaller craft hadn't put to sea for more than a week. But uncle Alec had married a girl from Cellardyke, and his father-in-law, known as the Dyker, had a motor-yawl called the *Jonathan*. During the Flanders frost the pipes froze in the school and we were sent home. From the braehead I saw the *Jonathan* coming into harbour. I raced down to the pier to see if they would have anything left over, but every fish was used up. The cold had nailed my boots to the edge of the pier and I was shivering.

'Hang on a minute!' Alec shouted as I turned to go.

The yawl had an old-fashioned pump beside the mizzen mast, but it had a brand-new one too, for pumping bilge-water over the side. He pulled a few times on the handle of the new pump. Nothing happened.

'Hold on!' shouted the Dyker, taking Alec's place and heaving like a hero at the shining new handle.

After a minute's effort, in a sudden spurt up came exactly one dozen herring, every one of them as stiff as a board. They rattled on to the deck like dead lead soldiers.

'There's twelve apostles for you,' laughed the Dyker. 'They wouldn't be looked at in Cellardyke, I can tell you. See if you can find faith great enough in St Monans to believe in them!'

I must have lost my innocence by this stage. Instinct told me that a cadger would see them for the false apostles that they were. And in my wickedness I sold them to a widow at her door and asked ninepence for them, which I was given without haggling. A fearful guilt kept me from spending this money for several days. Then, when Penman's bell stayed silent and there were no reports of an agonized death in King David Street, I made my way to Agnes Meldrum's and came away laden with liquorice and sherbet, two bars of Highland toffee, and a roundshot of gobstoppers clashing in my pockets. Just to be on the safe side, I passed along King David Street. Horrified, I heard the old widow sobbing behind her hedge, telling the neighbours that her cat had

died. The anguish started up immediately, the guilt. I ran
back to the braehead. Over the roofs and all along the
coast as far as Anstruther, I could see the spires pointing
to heaven, directing my attention to the endless blue air,
tinkling with frost, where grim-faced angels, eagle-eyed,
scouted for God, swooping down on any signs of nonsense.
One minute an empty innocent sky – the next they were
in your head, breaking through the flimsy protective skin.
That's how it was – nature was not proof against original sin.
Self-disgust and fear sent me flying out to the Blocks, from
which I threw all my sweets into the cold heavy swell, the
handful of gobstoppers hitting the waves like cannonballs,
sending up explosive little splashes before sinking down to
where Miller's watch still kept the time of the earliest crime,
stopped at the very moment. On the way back I heard that
the widow's cat had been left out all night in the frost and
had died. Relief and fury drove me mad and I ran along to
the braeheads again, where in the gathering darkness the
Dyker and grandfather were trying to extract leeks from
the garden using hammers and chisels.

  In the worst of the south-east gales, when grandfather had
stayed on shore, I sometimes went with him to collect West
Anstruther clay, to fill up the holes in the back of George's
crumbling fireplace. A long period of south-easters sucked
out the sand from the beach, exposing boulders standing
on a deep-concealed bed of bluish-grey clay. This was the
stuff old George liked us to bring, because when it dried he
said it went harder than the heart of old Pharaoh, way down
in Egypt's land, when he wouldn't let Moses go. The local
saying was 'as hard as West Anstruther clay' but George
used to say that that was not as hard as the hearts of the
West Anstruther folk themselves, heathens who made even
Pharaoh look like a softie.

  Grandfather had seven men in his crew including himself.
Each man brought with him six nets, making a fleet of
forty-two nets for the boat. The white winter nets were

preserved with alum, which drew in the mouth like lemon. Each man also brought six of the big floats called pallets. The old ones lying among the lumber in George's house were made of sheep's hide but the newer ones were canvas, due to disappear in their turn. They were tarred inside with two pints of Archangel tar from the ship chandler's, and painted with one pint of linseed oil on the outside.

I saw all the preparations, but never the mystery of the catch, because grandfather went out in the dark and the drifters worked during the night. But sometimes in the freezing darkness I rose to look out through frosted glass on a winter firth that looked like another city bobbing on the waves, rivalling Edinburgh. Probably there were only a dozen or so boats, not the hundreds that had filled the firth in grandfather's much-remembered day – but imagination filled the gaps. The East Neuk fleet were hunting the herring.

They shot their nets before the wind, stopped their engines and put up their mizzen sails. This put each boat's head into the wind, and the wind kept the nets in line. They shot them down off Crail, drifting away up past the Earlsferry before the tide turned and they came down again. And a whole week on the night tides might earn the boat ten pounds, a single pound for every man, two for the skipper and two for the boat. There were tales of fishermen elsewhere earning fortunes, but grandfather never did, and he shook his head at such stories. Sometimes they came in like the sons of Zebedee, according to George, having toiled all night and caught nothing – a biblical backing for the dignity of labour and the misery of empty pockets. Often only a few shillings tumbled out of grandfather's handkerchief, as he brought home his earnings in the old-fashioned way he followed till he died. I listened to the old-timers on the benches, talking about the old days when the Fifers caught thousands of cran before the first war, with dozens of English merchants coming from as far as Penzance for twenty years. And I was

told about the *annus mirabilis* of 1913, when the boats fishing
out of Yarmouth alone brought in nearly a thousand million
herring, my grandfather's boat among them, before he went
to the Dardanelles.

I was told many stories, but sometimes now I wonder
if I didn't dream them all, as the oil-rigs straddle the firth,
grandfather lies in his grave, and the white ghost of the
winter herring haunts the harbour of my mind.

So February passed, with its frosted flag-rushes by the burn
that bled my hands like the blades of fiery-tipped swords,
its raw thaws, its needling rains and misty glooms. And
its roof-rattling gales. Yet the very gales were a stir of life,
blowing red-hot sparks from Jamieson's smithy right across
the harbour in dancing constellations, baring the cold red
arms of the country folk as they burned their weeds, drying
the sodden clods in the earth. The long silences of the
fields were breaking to the high jingle of horse-gear, the
early morning cawing in the tall elms. With a wild roar
of freedom the burn was unlocked, and twigs and straw
continued a journey to the sea that had been arrested for
weeks. Days came when in spite of everything winter sowed
snow among the spring corn, the fields were white as flour
again, and the young year seemed to be turning back to age.
But the furrows appeared again like strong dark waves on
the earth, giving the fields their inevitable shape, while out
on the waves of the firth the winter drifting went on.

It was the spawning season. The herring gathered in dense
shoals in the region of a mysterious triangle whose points
were Elie Ness, Fife Ness and the May. Locked each year
within these lines, proclaimed by nature, precise as Euclid,
inexorable as death, the herring teemed with the milkiness
of life, pouring it out into the sea. In early winter the men

avoided these parts of the firth, fishing in the softer grounds in the middle, or round the Fidra, or off Kirkcaldy. But as February went on, the fish went up the horns of the firth on the south side and came down the north side. They were looking for their favourite birth-beds, between Anstruther and Kellie Law, around the May, off Dunbar, or in the stormy Hirst that lay between Crail and Fife Ness, where many a fisherman's drowning mouth had closed, on the coarse and rocky ground that the herring loved. The spent herring swam off then, scudding away to deep waters, but where after that nobody knew. Nor could I fathom where at that time I was making for myself. Even now, as I return in spirit to my own spawning place, throwing out the net of words, hoping to catch something of my beginning and my end, I am little wiser. Even my grandfather, who hunted something much more tangible than truth, was never sure of a catch.

'But there are two things you can always be sure of,' he said.

Birds and stars. These he swore by, saying that if he fell asleep for a hundred years and woke up at home, before a minute was up he'd be able to tell you the date to within a day or two. Spica appeared above the May at nine o'clock on the first day of March, and soon Arcturus would be over the island, adding its brightness to the lighthouse. The night-flying moths had come now, soft little sparks of light, flickering in the dark, the parachute spiders tickled your face, and in the evenings the hares were boxing in the first faint steam of the fields.

And yet the gales blew harder still, scattering hundreds of herring gulls high and low, setting them adrift above splintering seas, tearing the water into white strips, drying out the winter woodpiles, so that up in the country Peter Hughes started to look at his fences. Then the farmers started ploughing in earnest, turning up the clods in wet black shining waves, which quickly dried and were soon blowing dust into our eyes and teeth.

'When you bite the dust,' grandfather said, 'don't worry, you're the opposite of dead – you know the spring has come.'

The spring dust hit us in the face – and Bert Mackay stayed off school to help with the sowing, envied by the rest of us, who couldn't go to sea with the men. The older farmers, Bert said, would wait till the moon was waxing before they sowed a single seed of barley or oats. In Balcaskie and the burn woods the rooks and crows opened for business, their requiem voices cracked and harsh, but sounding brisker and more affirmative now as the nest building got under way.

> *On the first day of March*
> *The crow begins to search*

So Leebie would say, stopping her sewing for a few seconds to listen to the distinct cawing. On the other hand, she added, no self-respecting rook would dream of building till the third Sunday in the month.

> *On God's third the rook*
> *Bestirs himself to look*

The Dog's Mercury that had dressed the ditches was now out in the woods, pussywillows appeared, dozens of daffodils, the lesser celandines and coltsfoot were in flower and the cowslips in bud. Primroses sprinkled the braes, like pale young girls who'd spent winter in bed and come out for company, to die unmarried and give their fragrance to the winds. Sometimes a daffodil trumpeted to an early swallow, or a violet fluttered in the sea-breeze. The small tortoise-shell butterfly and the first dive-bombing bee droning low over the ground made me stop dead in my tracks and listen, suddenly remembering summer. Grandfather pointed to a honeybee settling on a late snowdrop.

'Look at that,' he said, 'two seasons having a quick natter together.'

Spring and winter, meeting briefly, parting, a murmur of summer.

'Can you plant your foot on nine daisies at one go?' Leebie liked to say. 'If you can't, then don't tell me that the spring has come.'

But I was looking for tadpoles, not daisies. The frogs that had lain like blotched stones, sunk under layers of mud, rose now like bog kings from their own spawn, the black jelly floating among the reeds and grasses, to be eaten by anything that moved. Whatever was not eaten, spawned, so that soon last summer's jam-jars were alive with tadpoles, not one of which ever performed for me the miraculous metamorphosis but stayed as they were, ugly black shooting stars that became quarter-comets at best, wandering aimlessly about the neutral curved space of their glassy cosmos to no apparent purpose.

The vernal equinox passed, with daylight now strong in the sky at teatime, the stars of Orion bestriding the Bass at sunset – and along with the equinox the terrible storms that had grandmother and Leebie up at the windows the whole day, and my mother and aunts wide awake in their beds, their minds tossing on the firth, where grandfather and his boys bobbed like human corks with just several spars of wood between them and a raging lion, shaking its white mane.

During the winter fishing the men sailed in and out of the harbour every morning and I saw grandfather most days between drifts. He took little food with him in the winter, preferring to eat when he got back to the house. But I sometimes ran along to Lizzie Reekie's better-stocked little shop on the braehead, closer and quicker than Agnes's, to buy a last-minute round of stores for the night-fishing. Eggs at a penny each if they were pickled, sevenpence for a dozen, and eightpence or ninepence a pound for steak. Once, when grandfather was too busy to come ashore, I took the box of stores down into the boat, and he took time off to fry me an egg. He cleaned the cast-iron frying-pan with steam from the boiler, banged it down on the black lacquered stove, and cooked me my first meal at sea, though the boat was only two inches from the pier and barely afloat on an ebb tide.

But as the shoals moved eastwards along the shore, everyone knew that the winter herring was coming to an end. Old George, standing at his window, watched the fleet coming home one day at the end of March.

'Here come the Ishmaelites,' he said. 'They never died a winter yet, God be praised.'

Some knack of knowing told him that the winter fishing was over, and that when next the men went out to sea, they would be taking with them the spring lines for the deep-diving cod that moved invisibly in their cold soundless shoals.

Down on the shore in the quieter weather the tide was creeping up the dry stones of the beach. The water, which had been wintrily muddy in the evenings, in the mornings became clear as glass all along the coast, and scum could be seen now floating on the flood tide. Then the first green water of the year appeared whenever there was a fresh wind blowing from the north-west. The sea turned a living blue, with further out the long lanes of deep emerald green that could never be seen in winter. In the shrimp-filled rock pools, where the baby porcelain crabs scuttled like loose thumb-nails, the green sleet started to grow and the whelks to gather in larger numbers, wet black ruby clusters. At low tide the broad blades of the oar-weed tangles were exposed, lapping listlessly above the water like aimless eels, indicating that the tides were going further and further back. Far out on the firth the gannets were ploughing round the Bass.

And the birds were threading past each other in the great tapestry of migration, the fieldfares flying back to Norway while the settling shelducks closed their wings for the first time on the coast, their arrival established.

But I knew for sure that spring had come when grandfather came in after the last haul of winter herring and took me along to the shallow waters west of the old castle to look for the sticklebacks that swam into the bay on the big March tides. He called them 'troonts' – sticklebacks was the English name – and the females were called 'baggies', perhaps because of their distended bellies full of eggs about to spawn. Always they died during the night, unless we threw them further out, and if we came back that way early next morning, we found them lying lifeless for lack of oxygen in the water, their big upturned bellies like floating graveyards under the blue sky. But the males, called 'doctors', with their red fronts, usually survived, so we took them home to be kept in jars of fresh water in the house, often for many months, and always outliving my tadpoles.

Butterfish and grannyfish came coasting in, and the lumpsuckers which grandfather called 'paddles'. Sometimes they came inshore in the middle of February and cast their skins and prepared for spawning in the lamb-like days of late March, or early April's calm glassy weather. Grandfather showed me their eggs once in a crack between two rocks, guarded by a male fish, which lunged at his pointing hand like a living Lilliputian blade. But when caught on rocks between tides by the suckers on their bellies, they showed no interest at all in Gulliver and his shipboy, their only audience, and we left them there to wait for the next sea.

Back at home I felt sudden rising surges of desire to get outdoors again at once. A terrific feeling of well-being, and yet a craving for some undefined something, drove me up clothes-poles to hang there for as long as I could, hugging them tightly between my legs, a silent fire in my groin, a silent scream issuing from my wide-open mouth, grinning at the sky. The same feeling sent me racing back down to the sea again, where I ducked my bursting skull into the waves, tore it out at last, gasping madly for air, and shook it wildly, laughing like a lark, scattering the stinging barbs of brine from nostrils and eyes and tongue.

April brought the first bird's-egg-blue skies under which the trees and hedges were misted with green. By the end of the month it would be a gathering wave, and in answer to the annual urge the birds flew by, busily ignoring us, their beaks stuffed with nesting materials. The wheatears appeared, and at sea the eiders and gannets were joined by cormorants and terns. Young flounders and eels swam into the harbour and we looked out our fishing lines, brushing off the cobwebs, inspecting the hooks and making the first idle surveys for bait along the shore, where the sea anemones and urchins were appearing in the clearer water. As the insects arrived and the ladybirds started to show themselves off on the opening ash and birch leaves, the year got out its paint-box, ready for the wildflowering of wood anemones, dog daisies in the frog-filled ditches, red dead nettle and heartsease up at Balcaskie. Bluebells began to flower there, the burn at the kirk brimmed with marsh marigolds all the way down to the sea, and the graves were dusted with speedwell and forget-me-nots.

From the kirkyard hill I looked out on an intensely dark blue sea, the skyline sharp as a razor, and a breathless clearness like an unheard music filling the air. Bats brushed my hair briefly as I came home from the braehead late at night. The hedgehogs were beginning to brave the roads, though the roads were quiet enough in those days under the first faint traces of the afterglow in Cassiopeia. Vega, the torchbearer of summer, blazed out again, and by the end of the month a miniature airforce was breaking up the skies. The swallows were with us once more.

When the spring madness entered the blood, some of the bolder boys played truant. Echoing the older traditions, a few yawls were still hauled up the brae and into the field opposite the school ready for tarring. They offered hiding places for the day-long playing of cards and the smoking of cigarettes, three shalt-nots in one. None of them actually featured in the Ten Commandments but it had been hammered into our heads that there were hundreds of unwritten sub-sections for which God had simply not had the space on those primitive stone tablets which Moses had been given on the mountain. So I erred on the safe side and refused to join Peem and Golly and Bert as they slipped out of the school gates instead of answering the headmaster's whistle.

But once, after an early morning thrashing from my father, I committed the dreadful crime alone, following my shadow out of the playground and into the field. The yawls, cratered with barnacles and slimy with weed, were raised high up on trestles like wooden horses – Leebie had been telling me all about Troy. Sidling round to the starboard side, where I couldn't be seen from the school, I clambered up the rough ladder, pulling it after me, slid under the tarpaulin and curled up in the belly of the boat. Bert and his gang had left enough evidence to damn them, cigarette ends stubbed out on crushed treacle sandwiches, crisps and crusts littering the clinker-built boards. And a picture magazine in which the women wore no clothes at all but went about their household chores like Eve, doing the dishes and seeing to the hoovering completely naked, as if they'd had no time to dress, or had simply forgotten.

I tossed the magazine aside, lay back and looked up at the single blue eye of sky, then closed my own and waited for the day to pass and night to fall, when I and my mind's companions would make the horse-boat give birth. We'd drop out of her belly in a wicked litter, swing open the school gates, scale the drainpipes up to the shaky slates, and signal to the sails waiting out there in the firth under cover of darkness. Then they'd glide inshore, dark sharks' fins, piloted by Poseidon, bearded like grandfather, and the village would fall in flaming ruin. Sangster would be ravished, whatever that was, along with all the old maids who taught us, including the headmaster, who'd lose his plus-fours and also his mock wife, who'd be made into a male eunuch, whatever *that* was. But I'd be paying no attention to any of this. With the steps of Achilles and my hair aflame, my sword before me, I'd be making straight for the palace, for the king my father, the cock of the midden, to lop his limbs like Geordie Grant and wreak the vengeance that should have been the Lord's.

When old George asked what I was learning these days and I told him it was about Troy, he grunted and spat.

'Pagan trash – but you can learn one thing from it.'

That was when he quoted the only verse I ever heard from him that hadn't come out of scripture.

> *The walls are down of old Troy town,*
> *Her maids are maids no more.*
> *Her sons are dead, they should have wed –*
> *All lost for one great whore.*

When I asked what a whore was, he referred me to the Book of Revelation and the Great Whore of Babylon – 'A first-class whore if ever there was one.'

Whether the pagan intrusion or the spring weather was to blame, George suddenly took it into his head that I was to have a day off school while he took me in hand and cleared my mind of what he called 'unnecessary nonsense'. I imagined a day spent sitting on his sea-chest, spouting chapter and verse, or a long voyage on the Gospel Ship. To my surprise he got out his walking stick and told me to get ready for a long walk up country.

Out by Elm Grove we went, past Chae Marr's elms that were chequering the sky, green and blue, and on to the old Black Road to Balcaskie. It was lined with ash trees, their sooty seeds rattling in black bunches, keys to a year that had been shut away and forgotten. But the new leaves were springing open, unlocked by light, and the limes were lighting up the sky. Up in the woods the oak buds were bursting like drops of blood, while the silver birches stood like sea gods swept by their own waves, golden flowers that they showered back into the ground.

But we went further afield than Balcaskie – I'd never been this far before – more than a mile from the village, and then another mile, to Balcormo Den, where George stopped at a kingly beech, spread out easily across two centuries. There were no leaves on it yet, but the strong smooth bark was engraved with dates and initials, bound by arrow-pierced hearts. Old George pointed with his stick at one of the emblems.

There they were, his own initials with those of my great-grandmother, Bridget Burk, and the date of their great passion. Out of that passion had come my grandfather, and my mother, and now, George said, myself. But soon enough I'd just be a notch on a tree, for all my passion, nothing more. Or a chiselling on a kirkyard slab.

'Who remembers Bridget Burk now?' asked George, jabbing at the initials in the bark. 'Your grandfather and me, that's who. And when we're gone, maybe you'll remember her name. But once you're gone, there will be nobody to remember even that much. She'll be these initials and nothing else, till this tree falls – and after that nothing at all.'

He turned from the tree to face me, pointing his stick into the blue sky.

'There is only one abiding entity. Love the Lord, the One that endureth for ever. And remember this above all – love no flesh, and trust no flesh!'

And there ended the lesson.

Even then George didn't stop. We walked on and on, inland and upland, till we came to Carnbee, a country parish high in the air and miles from the village. From there, the firth that had always seemed so huge an expanse of ocean now looked like a little blue lane between fields and sky. And high up in Carnbee kirkyard he pointed at a grave and said that this was the dust from which one of the great writers of all time had sprung – Herman Melville, creator of *Moby Dick*. George had met him before he died. I asked when it was, but George couldn't recall. Sometime around 1890, he reckoned. He'd stopped paying much attention to man's time a long time ago.

And so we came back from our field trip.

Antares now started coming out of the water like an old drowned friend, his sea-lamp still lit, shining east of the Bass; and in the early fluttering night-time, flecked with pipistrelle bats, Leo was already sinking into Kellie Law, the lion dying on the hill. Sudden explosions of swifts took place by the burnside, over grasses speckled with fragments of hatched starlings' eggs. On the shore jellyfish littered the sands and the first shore crabs cast their shells. The jellyfish were helpless on shore, but once, swimming early in the year, I came under their ugly purple whiplashes and was stung to a frenzied retreat to land, where I took my revenge on those that were stranded, whipping them to shivers with one of the long rubbery-rooted tangles, a wholesale slaughter without a single drop of blood.

Close inshore, squadrons of gannets were dive-bombing the water, sending up white smoky plumes of sea. Huge flocks of them left the Bass in the mornings to feed in the North Sea, the long white files always returning each evening to their rocky sanctuary. Baby mallards whooed along the shore in the twilight and shelduck and eider babies were bobbing on the waves by the end of the month.

With the glass high on old George's wall and easterly winds coming in from the firth, the thick weather now swept along the shore. But instead of the brooding banks of greyness that lingered in winter, the fogs of April were white and patchy, with bays of clear weather between the horns of mist. Under the strong winds the sea turned dark blue and the skyline turned sharp as a sword.

Early in the month a hazy purplish-brown streak like thin smoke would form itself into a line just above the horizon's edge and the cold became cutting, so that the old men sought the shelter of the dykes and the thick harbour walls to carry on their conversations. All during the hours that this haar lasted there was a splendid clearness. George took down his telescope, opened his window and pointed the glass at the May, its cliffs rising like blue icebergs out of the choppy sea. The lighthouse-keeper was standing at his cottage and his shadow was sharp and black on the whitewashed wall.

'In this sort of weather you can see the shadow of a seabird on the water thirteen miles away,' said George.

One morning I was standing in the yard with grandfather just as he was getting ready to go off to the lines. It was the first day of the Easter holidays, just before nine o'clock. I realized that I was not at school and started to whoop for joy.

'Ssh!' whispered grandfather, suddenly gripping my arm. 'Listen!'

A second later there was a very slight splash from the rocks a hundred yards away.

'It's the tide-cry,' he said. 'That's the first time I've heard it this year. And that's the tide I'm going on.'

When there was low water and a big tide and the sea was flat, the silence would be broken in this way by the rustle of a small wave moving the tangle blades or running up the slope of a skerry to fall back over the steep landward edge of the rock. This was the tide-wave's first arrival as the ebb changed through slack water to flow. That split second in which the tide turned could never be heard in winter. My grandfather had heard it in his blood a single second before it happened.

In the early days, before Easter came round, there were no fishermen at home, and my mother took me along to the braes west of the castle to roll my egg, which she had boiled in very strong tea until it had gone a golden brown. We sent it spinning along like an old cracked sun through the paler galaxies of primroses now bewildering the braes. It stopped on the sea-bleached boulders at the bottom of the field, where the violets grew. After I had sat munching my egg among ladybirds and straw-gathering sparrows, there would be a bar of Highland toffee and a bottle of lemonade.

I ran down to the rock pools before going home, eyeing the cold clear water for shrimps and blennies. We took home a bunch of bladderwrack, so that Jenny and Georgina, separating the buds, could lay them on the embers of the fire late at night to see if they would pop when the names of their true loves were whispered to the dying flames, unheard by the rest of us. A silent hissing consumption by the fire, with smoke and steam drifting dismally up the chimney, was a sad affair. A sudden explosion was greeted with gales of laughter, and there was talk of wedding bells.

As the fire settled into a dead white ash, old Leebie

quietened everybody by telling us that it was St Mark's Eve, and that if we were to enter the old kirkyard and keep watch there all night, we would see the apparitions of all who were to be buried there in the coming year. Anybody with nerves of steel had only to go along and wait. But it would be a long haul till dawn, and you could breathe again only if your own spirit-double – your 'fetch', as Leebie called it – had failed to show up and join the line of doomed villagers that passed among the graves. I shivered and wished my grandfather were at home, to tell me in his sensible kind way what stupid nonsense these old women talked.

But by that time grandfather had been three weeks at the lines.

It all started with a line – and a hook let down into the blue water. Barbaric flint and bone, sharply shaven, and shards of wood, barbed, baited and hung beneath the waves from lengths of gut – a hook in the water was the oldest symbol of the fisherman's faith. When grandfather was away at the line fishing, I cycled along the coast to Cellardyke to see the Dyker. He had the burgh coat-of-arms painted brightly on the side of the *Jonathan*. It showed a man in a boat with an enormous hook let down over one side, and the motto underneath in golden lettering, following the curve of the wave – *Semper tibi pendeat hamus*: may you always have a hook in the water.

For me it started with Leebie's needles and pins, stolen from the brass box by the sewing machine. I stuffed my pockets with some of the strong pack-thread that she used to make sleeping-shrouds for the men – thick sea-blankets stitched tightly together – and stole down to the slipway to try my toddler's luck for the tiniest fish in the harbour. A whitened wave-worn stick for a rod and some bait were then all I needed. The scrapings of flesh from an old crab's hairy pincer, a shrivelled segment of lugworm, a single fish-scale through which I could see the sun, it scarcely mattered that the bait failed to meet its own definition. For the catching of a particular fish was not what was important in that first May when boys brought out their rods and lines, making them out of the debris and detritus of house and harbour. To have a hook in the water – that was what the sudden bleeping in the blood demanded after the long winter.

So I lay down on the tarry, sweet sun-warmed stones of the slipway and looked into the sea. It was high tide, and the water was calm and clear and green. Ignoring the alien reflection of my own face, I studied the stabbing, dagger-thin fish as they slashed the water without a scar, gliding away among cool boulders and weeds which just a few feet of sea made so mysterious. I let down my harmless hook into the green element and, holding my breath, entered the world of the hunter.

Growing up was going further out to fish, stage by stage, year by year, from slipway to pier, from pier to pierhead, to the breezy point of the Blocks, and eventually out to the furthest ledges of rock, where the rock cod swam invisibly, like silver mines on the move, glittering far beneath our feet. There the surface of the sea was a blurred black ripple of chords, and whatever came to the hook would snap out of the dark unseen. When it happened to me for the first time the sudden tug sent a shuddering up my arm and lit a fire in my groin, the urgent dark excitement of the huntsman, feeling the flick of life, and taking the strain as it turned into a bloody struggle. I was secretly glad they were hidden, these blind dumb shrugging mouths that couldn't see the sky, couldn't cry for mercy, couldn't look into my eye as I hauled and hauled at the live umbilical, my finger aflame.

I watched the other boys disengage the taut rubbery mouth from the hook, smash the soft head twice on the square stones of the pier, wrench it with an expert twist of the wrist and hurl it bloodily to the swooping gulls. Never destined to be a fisherman, I always threw my fish back into the water. But the boys who became fishermen went on from there to throw out bigger and bigger lines, further and further from shore. Offshore fishermen used harlins or handlines, baited with crab, or if they were drifting instead of lying at anchor, they used sprools or jigs, unbaited hooks that relied on the shininess of the scraped metal and the jerking motions of the lines to attract the instinctive snapping jaws. Leaving the shore well behind, they used the strangely named small lines, each fifty fathoms long and carrying a hundred and twenty hooks, until they graduated to the highest class of all and threw out the gartlins or great lines. These could be shot in the firth but were often taken out in the spring up to two hundred miles away, to what the old folk called 'the far-aways', or even as far off as the Faroes, and there they went down over four hundred fathoms into the sea, searching for cod.

From a bent pin at the slipway, dangling in four feet of water, to a hundred-hooked line four hundred miles away, sweeping the bottom of the world – it was a long progress from boy to man, and some of us never made it. But the hook in the water was what counted.

Grandfather always went to the spring lines with something of a shrug. 'I'm a net man, not a line man,' he would say.

Herring would never take bait, he said – they were too fine a fish to be deceived by this primitive device. They were taken by the drift-net, by night-time and moonlight. So he thought nobly of the fish he killed and often sang about them.

> *Of all the fish that swim in the sea*
> *The herring it is the fish for me.*

But he praised the Dyker and his fellow villagers as being

the most intrepid great-line fishermen on the east coast.
Some of the crew of the *Venus* would even quote the Cellardyke motto when the nets were being shot for the first time
in a new herring season, as if the driftermen acknowledged
the sharper reality of the hook as the badge of the fisherman's calling. *Semper tibi pendeat hamus.*

I saw little of grandfather in April and May when he was at
the great lines, too far from the firth to come home for more
than a sore night's sleeping in between the long hard hauls.
But before he left he insisted on the spring cleaning of the
Venus and all her gear. My head high among chimney-pots
and blue sunlit breezes, I perched on a mountain of white
nets that were bumped along by horse and cart to the mouth
of the burn. There they were spread out in the clear fresh
water to wash away the weed and scum and salt of a winter
at sea. Then they were wheeled up the brae to the backyard
for boiling and mending. The boat's boiler was cleaned out
and overhauled, the stove lacquered, the cabin revarnished
and its roof white-enamelled. New ballast was taken on and
the *Venus* was tarred and left to dry, while the white winter
nets were stowed away in the garret and the narrowest bait
nets brought out for setting down on board. These would
trap the smaller herring to be used as bait for the lines that
would in turn catch the cod. We dragged the lines in stiff
heavy coils from underneath the benches, where they were
stacked for ten months in the year. Grandfather examined
every coil before they were hoisted down to the yard for
mending and carrying to the boat.

A great line was no thicker than the pencils we used at
school but was made of Spanish hemp. It consisted of six
strings, each seventy-five fathoms long, which meant that
the whole line reached four hundred and fifty fathoms into

the sea. Each man carried with him five lines to the boat.
And so, with a crew of seven on board, grandfather's boat
had over fifteen thousand fathoms of great line to be paid
out.

Each of the main six lengths had twenty snoods – finer
sections of hemp with hooks attached by pieces of cotton
tippin. The entire line carried a hundred and twenty hooks
three and a half fathoms apart. So each man brought six
hundred hooks to the boat, and over four thousand hooks
were let down into deep water every time they shot.

The hooks themselves were a ferocious four inches long.
Tying them on by whipping the hook to the tippin was a
monotonous job carried out in the week before grandfather
went away. That week always brought to the braehead house
a musty dark circle of old men, all of them long retired from
the sea. They used to come up to the house sometimes on
their slow quiet walks to see George, and now they came to
earn themselves an even slower ounce of tobacco, mending
the nets and hooking up the lines on which their hands
were now too old to take the strain. But their tongues were
still supple enough, and as they worked they talked, telling
stories of sea and sail. The old remembering hands saw
giant cod on the newly fitted hooks, felt the shuddering
strength of the huge halibut hammering on the line, the
long hauling on the Spanish hemp, sodden and heavy from
the grey North Sea.

'You see this gartlin hook?'

One of the old ones laid in my hand the four inches of
iron he was about to whip on. It was longer than my palm.

'How big a fish do you think it can hold?'

I shook my head.

'I once caught a halibut of sixteen stones on a hook like
that.'

I held the hook between my finger and thumb and tried
to imagine the terrible thrashing torment of the thing.

'That's more than three times your weight, I'll be bound.

What would happen, do you think, if you bit on this hook now, and I started hauling you up four hundred fathoms? Do you think your gums would hold?'

The old one spread his lips in a grin. There wasn't a tooth in his head. He looked as if he himself might have come up through four hundred fathoms.

'Do you think you'd be lippy enough to hold on?'

'Stop frightening the boy,' said grandfather.

The old one persisted.

'I think your jaw would come off – and you'd go back down to the sharks.'

I handed him back the hook, my jaw dropping.

'Leave the boy alone.'

George had come down the transe and into the yard behind us.

'There's worse things than sharks,' he said.

'Not for my money,' said the old man. 'But I've never seen anything fight like that halibut. Sixteen stones if it was an ounce. It was the last hook on the line. We were so close in to Peterhead we trailed it behind the boat, and it was sold alive on the scales, still twitching.'

'George will have seen greater sights than that at the whales,' said another of the circle.

George seldom opened out – unlike the black book in which he spent his days. But sometimes the breath of talk would stir one of his pages.

'The greatest sight I ever saw was not at the whales,' he said. 'I was just a fisherman on a small sailing boat, and it was the turbot that impressed me most of all.'

'I've never heard of one that took the scales at sixteen stone.'

'It wasn't their size,' George said quietly, 'it was their faithfulness.'

And he told the story I had already heard from grandfather, about how they lived in loyal pairs – just the way God had ordained it, added George – and how the free partner always followed the one on the hook all the way up, breaking the surface even as the great line was coming out of the water, so that the man hauling could sometimes scoop up the loose one, if he was fast enough, when it swam up into the blue air beside its doomed companion.

'Yes, they were like Saul and Jonathan, these fish,' said George. 'Lovely and pleasant in their lives. And in their deaths they were not divided.' And he walked back upstairs to his bible.

I knew what happened next. The great lead-weighted club called the gowking stick hammered them into stillness as they came struggling on to the wet slippery deck. It was easy to see a youthful George as the cold killer who'd gone on to wrestle with leviathan in his age. It was harder to picture grandfather slaughtering such faithful fish. Couldn't he have thrown them back into the waves just for the beauty of their love?

But he was a fisherman. 'We live by the sea,' he said.

And I was secretly glad that sometimes the fish died together, and that one partner was not left to live out its life alone in those cold lonely depths.

Once ready, the lines were looped into the sculls, separated by layers of dried grass so that they would uncoil cleanly, and the hooks were arranged with great care round the borders of the baskets. Everything had to be lugged through the transe and out on to the braehead, where uncle Alec was waiting with a horse and cart to take the gear down to the boat. The bait nets and the lines were loaded first, carefully, and the rest of the equipment piled in after them, dahns and lamps and tins of paraffin, and on top of the heap the big bundles of corks used as floats. I carried down from the garret the terrible gowking stick, shivering at the thought of sixteen

stones of living silver being first stunned, then clubbed to a
brutal stillness as it drowned in the bright blue air.

On the Saturday before grandfather was due to leave, I
went with him to Gerrard the fish merchant to collect two
tons of ice. Gerrard's cold store was like the North Pole,
only it was reachable without sledges and huskies and berg-
breaking ships. The ice lay stacked in huge blocks as high as
the mizzen masts of the drifters, and they smouldered cold
emerald in the green sunlight that leaked through the thick
dim windows. Gerrard's men attacked the ice with picks and
sledgehammers as if they were fighting polar bears on giant
floes. Crushed and sparkling, it was shovelled into boxes,
swung into the cart and jogged down to the boat.

Some of the crew were waiting to load the boxes into
the hold, where they were covered with a layer of coarse
salt and stacked neatly away. I stood for a second or two
in that frozen space, shivering and staring into the empty
wings. There the fish would be buried in ice after they had
been caught and gutted, a dense dead shoal that had lost its
lustre, freed from the flux and flow of tides. They were all
lying there – Epp and Hodgie, Chae Marr and Miss McNeil,
they all swam out at me again from their black fathom – and
Shuggie too, breastless and gutted and packed in ice, to be
kept fresh for roasting in hell. And we would all have to join
them on one tide or the next. Grandfather took my arm and
brought me up into the blue heavens.

After that we went to Agnes Meldrum's and Lizzie
Reekie's for the stores. Tea, tinned milk, tatties, ox-tongue,
beef, mutton, pork, flour, butter, raisins, suet – and dozens
and dozens of eggs. The outby boats went off to distant
waters, taking on much more ice and stores. But by the time I
was born, grandfather was an inby man, staying at sea for no
more than eight or nine days at a time. He was too old now,
he said, for the Faroes, and he never left for the far-aways.

But it seemed far enough to me that they were going as
I stood on the pier watching the black-and-yellow funnel of

the *Venus* bobbing and ducking in the choppy waves of the firth, the boat soon diminishing to a speck in the distance. I could see it long after it disappeared, saw it from all the remembered stories round the fire or heard at the head of the pier, which was as far as the feet of the old men went when they headed for the sea.

So grandfather quickly cleared the brisk fluctuations of the firth and reached the deeper northern water with its longer slower swell. Then he waited patiently for the light southerly which he knew always provided them with plenty of bait.

'A cold east wind is no good at all. I've gone back to harbour in an east wind after casting nets all night long – and I've never shot a single line.'

The lines were baited with one whole and one half herring time about, and shot across the wind from the quarter starboard deck. When fully shot they stretched for twelve or thirteen miles, each man paying out nearly two miles of great line in a curving zigzag. It would take them six hours or more to haul them back in. With the wrong wind or weather a fleet of lines might take a whole day. Sometimes the wind would change to dead ahead for days at a stretch and become thick with rain, the boat sliding through endless curtains of wetness and not a single fish on the lines, so that the shooting had to be done all over again, and maybe again and again and again.

'It got to the stage you couldn't shut your fingers. Us old ones had to steep our hands in hot water to help the blisters. And the younger ones sometimes cried with the pain.'

Even in good times, grandfather said, their hands could be blistered with the greater strain of bringing in a bumper crop.

'A herring in every mesh – that's a myth. A haul that size would sink your boat. But a fish on every hook I've seen with my own eyes. A hundred and twenty fish on a line and not a hook missed out.'

And sometimes every single great line on the boat grew a
shoal of its own, coming up heavy with the harvest, not just
cod but haddock and ling, turbot and halibut and skate and
the big eels – all kinds of eating. In that way they fished the
North Sea all through the spring, coming into harbour on
an ebb tide and landing their catches at Shields, Aberdeen,
Newhaven and Dundee.

Often when grandfather was away at the lines the thick cold
weather came in again from the sea, the east coast curse of
hot air meeting cold, and we were plagued by May mists,
with strong easterlies and drizzling rains that made the
cattle stand still and quiver in the fields. The farmers called
it the 'coo-quawk' but even the lugubrious Leebie managed
to see the positive side of it.

> *A misty May and a leaky June*
> *Brings the corn home soon.*

I quoted this to the Dyker one May morning when he
and his older brother took me fishing with them in the
Jonathan, anchored just offshore. The two of them spent the
whole day arguing about the meaning of the word 'leaky'.
Did it mean a wet June or a June so hot that the staves of
the old water barrels would shrink, if not made by a first-
class cooper, and the water leak out between the joins? Two
bleached old statues sat murmuring about this, deep into
their graven beards, as the boat bobbed softly on the swell.
There was nothing the Dyker loved better than this, to be
talking the day away while hauling his creels or trying the
handlines off Cellardyke or the Billowness, with the sea like
blue silk and the sun standing still in the sky.

So for all its blights, May remained the Dyker's favourite

month, and he always blessed the first fish he caught at this season with another of those sayings that have gone the way of the people who said them, and the skills they knew.

> *One drink of the May flood*
> *Makes all the fish in the sea good.*

After the mists the intense heat always returned and the country burst in an explosion of colour and noise and light. Crab apples flowered, hawthorns were thick with scented snow, the woods misty with bluebells, the ditches rouged with campion, and the first poignant smell of foliage and cut grass lingered over the damp evening fields and gardens. Thistles took the field again, wild roses and raspberries were in leaf along the liquid green lanes. The hum of insects was loud at noon.

It was the time of year when we were able to tear off our socks and shoes and go barefoot and blissful in the clear rock pools.

The first thing we looked for was a 'pellan'. These were the shore crabs just about to cast their shells, and at this stage in their lives they provided the best possible bait. We grabbed them from behind and snapped off the small joint of one of the large claws, telling ourselves that crabs not only felt no pain but grew their limbs right back on again. When the jointed claw was snipped and the nipper came away cleanly, the crab was useless as bait, but if the flesh stuck out like firm white velvet, then it was pronounced a pellan – and this was a death sentence. Killing it between two stones, we scooped it out of its armour and cut it into segments, keeping the flesh of the toes for the finest bait. Crabs that had just lost their shells we called 'bubbles'. After that they became 'softies', till they grew their suits again, and we spared them, as they brought no fish to the hook.

Once found, pellans were easy prey, as they were quiet and

comatose when the shell was about to go, and never nipped
our nervous fingers, unlike the large bally crabs that would
bite us at every opportunity, giving crabs a bad name among
boys. The most ruthless of us punished them by relieving
them of all their pincers, giving boys a bad name among
crabs. In their quiet condition the female pellans were especially easy prey for the rampaging male ballies that scuttled
about the shore, like black knights searching for half-
drugged damsels in distress. Rape, not rescue, was the name
of the game. They clasped them to their jointed breastplates
and mated with them mercilessly. During mating the ballies
carried their prize pellans around with them like spoils of
war. As soon as we saw this double-act we knew that one
of the crabs was potential bait and our penknives became
sword-sticks of chastity driven between the two. Then we
hurled the frustrated rapist into the sea and set upon the
poor female, giving her death before dishonour.

Grandfather had his own expression for that glorious
time of year. 'It's Tammie Limie time,' he used to say.

Tammie Limie had a small sailing yawl called the *Fisher
Lass*. His wife Jess ran a draper's shop in the basement of a
huge house in East Shore Street. Her constant complaint to
her customers, rolled out regularly across the dark wooden
counter with the bales of linen, was that the awful spouse,
as she called him, would never wash his feet.

And as the year wore into winter, and Tammie dived out
of one pair of stiff sweaty sea-stockings and into the next,
shrinking from the merest glimmer of water in between,
and never going to bed without his socks on, poor Jess's
song of wifely suffering rose in plangency till the customers
held their noses in sympathy.

'Sleeping next to him is the cross I've to bear nightly,' she
sighed as she snipped and measured, nimble as a mouse, with
precise white fingers and tight little tremblings of her neatly
parted head. 'And the ones he wears are full of holes.'

At this point she would burst into tears, indicating with

fluttering hand the shelf-full of stacked sea-stockings behind her, waiting to be purchased.

'He can take his pick, as you can see – but he won't. And he'll not even wear slippers in the house.'

But when spring burst over the coast, all became bright again in the dark little draper's shop where Jess lived among neat clean fabrics and filthy feet.

'Never mind, Jess,' Tammie would say to his long-suffering wife, 'it'll not be long now, lass. It'll soon be the time for the pellans again – and clean feet in the month of May!'

Tammie Limie time. Brought up on the expression, as on hundreds of others, I assumed him to be as mythical a hero as Hephaistos the limper, Ulysses of the boar-gored thigh, one-sandalled Jason and Achilles of the heel, all those whose extremities had been part of their fame. The corn came up like Persephone and the shore crabs' shells came off like Tammie Limie's socks. Even Hermes, who played his part in the earth's awakening, had wings on his sandals. Feet found fame and were all the rage in May. It was a long time till I discovered that this was a modern myth, that a man's feet had succeeded in making him a legend in his own lifetime and giving a local expression to a time of year.

Tammie Limie time brought to our shores all the summer migrants – the willow warbler, the wood warbler, the chiff-chaff and the blackcap. Swifts and swallows flashed about the town like painted paper aeroplanes, whizzing between cobblestones and chimney-pots, zooming under the old men's benches, where they sat stiff-legged and sleeping or smoking in a statuary haze. The weird whooings on the water, the seaweed whispering as the tide drew back to let it steam in the morning sun – they were the music of another planet, and I stepped out on the altered shore like an alien on an undiscovered planet. Even the sea urchins seemed eerie. Grandfather called them Hairy Hutchins, but once I had scraped off the spines, they fitted the Dyker's chillier description of Dead Men's Crowns – as bald and brittle as the skulls of Chae and Hodgie stranded up there in the kirkyard in their single black fathom of earth. Sometimes they broke as I gathered them, scooping out the tough soggy insides – strange to see what life was made of in other forms, in those sea-heads without bodies – and I threw the cracked skulls to the birds and fish, to feed on the stuff of existence.

Break open your head . . .

Only whispers in the wind now, the Blind Man's death threats, in those calm innocent hours, with summer stealing on.

The first lightning flickered over the firth, where the gannets now gathered in even longer files, flying out to feed in even deeper waters. Mornings and evenings I watched them through George's powerful spyglass. He allowed me to rest the telescope on his shoulder while he sat at his bible, and I saw how their route never varied. They described a great arc out from the Bass in the morning, and so back in the evening. Always on the way out to their feeding grounds they passed to the north and east between the shore and the May, and always they came back again on the other side, the two arcs from sunrise to sunset forming an invisible ellipse, geometrically perfect. In January and February the sky was unbroken by a single bird, but in March and April the first flakes began to drift, and from May onward the Bass was a blizzard of birds, snowing hard all through the summer months until October thinned them out and November and December were quiet again.

Standing at George's window, wide open now for the summer, or on the green vantage point of the braehead, I could see the long files coming from far-off Fife Ness, flying low over the waves. It was best watching for them when there was a hard south-east gale blowing along with dull gloomy weather. Then they showed up a vivid white against the purplish-blue water – 'like white-clad sea-bound pilgrims', George used to say, raising his eyes briefly from the page – and as they flew they disappeared from moment to moment in the deep troughs between the rough snow-crested mountains of sea, rising again on wave-wet wings to head for their haven, the great rock out in the firth.

'But a far cry from the Rock of Ages! That's where we're headed for – and we must have eyes keener than gannets!'

Even bird-watching was glossed by scripture, and somehow George's running commentary was both appropriate and enhancing. The cormorants and shags rose high into the air when passing over land, but the gannets in their great beauty kept to the sea, flying right round the jutting jaw of the ness, rather than cross the land as the crow flies.

'What do you expect?' George spat. 'Crows are black devils. It's the gannets you want to watch, and learn from. They're God's own birds.'

The Bass Rock alone was the land they deigned to light on, he said. It was their temple, their firth-girt castle, and they left it only to pass over the blue ploughlands of the sea. So they remained the lords of the waves, the keepers of the rock, bright beings of distance and air. That's how I remember them, seen through George's spyglass and clothed in his imagery.

Shuggie used to make us sing a hymn, 'My soul, there is a country'.

> *My soul, there is a country*
> *Far beyond the stars,*
> *Where stands a wingèd Sentry*
> *All skilful in the wars.*
>
> *There, above noise and danger,*
> *Sweet peace sits, crowned with smiles,*
> *And One born in a manger*
> *Commands the beauteous files.*

I had no appreciation at the time of the beauty of the words, composed by a great English poet, but genuine poetry communicates before it is understood, and the imagery entered my unconscious mind, waiting for sleep to play on it, using the wordplay of dreams. The beauteous files became the long flying files of gannets, George's white-clad pilgrims, voyaging across the sea of eternity, avoiding the bank and shoal of time. And the Bass was the kingdom of heaven, from which I had been brought but to which I could never return. So sleep made some sense of the words we had sung for Shuggie without a flicker of understanding. It was not altogether comforting, but the overall impression was of the beauty of those white birds, winging their way in single file to heaven, like the souls of fishermen, freed at last from their toil.

But the hymn didn't end there. It went on, including this verse:

> *If thou canst get but thither,*
> *There grows the flower of peace,*
> *The rose that cannot wither,*
> *Thy fortress and thy ease.*

There was the Bass again, a fortress in its time masquerading as the kingdom of heaven, or was it the other way round? It didn't seem to matter much. The problem was how to get there – and grasp the rose. In a second dream, sometimes forming part of the first, the incorruptible rose became the dense flock of gannets that I sometimes saw feeding closer in to shore. The huge white flower, fluttering out in the firth as the birds hovered and dived, turned magically into Miss Balsilbie's blouse, and as I joined them on the wings of sleep, the blossoms brushed my face as I approached, before springing apart and drifting down into the waves – and out bobbed Miss Balsilbie's breasts. Or were they Honeybunch's? And so the dream went on, the snowy rose opening and shutting, the blossoms rising and falling in a milky fountain, speaking to my wide-awake spirit while my body lay asleep, of that unknown country far beyond the stars. A dream that remains, a month to remember.

But most memorable in May was the quality of its light. On a sunlit morning when I looked at the new leaves and plants and grasses, they exuded an unearthly luminosity, as if the light were all liquid. And this film of brilliance on the moist fresh foliage was like a clear green voice, a crystal song in the air, sad because so beautiful, and yet so brief.

It was the quality of the light that led my spell-bound feet up from the shore and into the country, where the uddered cows stood over their hooves in buttercups, lowing soft and swollen and veined in the rich golden sea, flecked with daisies and clumps of purple clover. Blue vetch berivered the ditches, the leaves of the raspberries and wild roses running wilder now by the roadsides, and the thistle strongholds were running up their butterfly pennants, Red Admirals fluttering among the green spires and towers. The thrumming of the insects threatened fields and sky with the coming of some kind of midsummer madness. But in cool Balcaskie, where I sheltered from a shower, the bluebells out-rang the rain in their dim and misty silence. Coming back out of the trees, even the hawthorn blossoms seemed to be singing to me, scent becoming sound, filling my head with the memories of all the Mays that ever were. On the way home I broke some of them off in sprays for grandmother to put in jars and fill the old house with the fragrance of her youth.

So the month moved us into that magical period that grand-father always referred to as the start of Milner time. Like

George, grandfather too had his bible, though it was a secular one, Milner's *Gallery of Nature*, compiled by one of those Victorian divines who were inspired by the creation rather than the creator, and who wrote about it with encyclopaedic ecstasy. Grandfather read it avidly and often pointed to the page where Milner stated that between 21 May and 21 July there was no astronomical night, and the sun swung like a dimmed lamp only a few degrees beneath the horizon. I stuck my head high out of the skylight window of the braehead house and saw Milner's afterglow hanging like a mist of hawthorn flower, over the red and green harbour lights, powdering the sky to the west. I knew then that the time was near when grandfather would be bringing back his lines and taking down the black nets from the garret, to get ready for the summer herring.

When he did come home at the end of May he littered the piers with hundreds of cod. They were arranged in scores on the bare stones, each score divided into fives: four with their heads up, and every fifth fish with its head down, tail pointing to the boat. They lay there like legions of lead soldiers, exhumed from the ice-cold hold of the *Venus*, to be stripped of their armour and turned to fodder under the June sun.

Some of the new steel drifters flung out their lines all through the windless blistering days, but the older wooden drifters like the *Venus* headed for the herring again and the summer drave. Some of them sailed to Shetland, following the shoals southwards through June and July, but grandfather had seen enough of Shetland and settled for Peterhead, closer to home, most of the St Monans fleet going along with him. All through the summer months they fished up and down the northern half of Scotland, landing their catches at Peterhead and Aberdeen, and returning to the firth in August.

But there would be the space of a week, maybe ten days, while the gear was being prepared for the drave, during which grandfather stayed at home and took me out in the *Jonathan* with the Dyker, some days fishing out of St Monans, others out of Cellardyke, depending on how their luck was running. They shot creels for crabs, sprooled for whiting and cod, went out with the harlins for haddock, or gave the herring jigs a go when grandfather would say, 'I'm gone in a day or so, let's start thinking herring.'

As the fish seldom moved much in the middle of the day, and were mainly caught in the early morning and the evening cool, they were able to take me along with them before and after school.

That's when I learned about 'meids'.

'Meids' was the word they used to describe their way of establishing their position at sea when they were not far from the land, and the commonest question I heard asked on the pier when a fisherman had just brought in a good catch was: 'What meids were you on?' It was a bearing on the land, enabling them to keep returning to the same patch of sea where they knew they were sure of a good shot. At the drift-net fishing, the sprools or the jigs, an exact meids did not matter so much. But when they anchored nets, laid lines or shot messenger creels, the meids had to be precise so that they could haul hours or days later.

Grandfather and the Dyker were dead-eyed demons at the meids, and their method was simple. For an informal meids they took any large object on land and steered the *Jonathan* until it was lined up with it in conjunction with a second object in front of it. The East Neuk countryside was mostly flat farmland, and for the St Monans men and the Cellardykers its one high green point was Kellie Law. It was well up in the country, beyond Balcaskie, beyond Balcormo, by the Carnbee loch.

After Kellie Law the kirk steeples of the villages offered the most obvious landmarks, some of them needle-sharp spires, others rising like distant pyramids in the blue deserts of space. When we were well out towards the May from

Cellardyke, the Dyker showed me how Kellie Law loomed over Anstruther Easter kirk and Chalmers Memorial kirk in one perfectly straight line. 'Kellie on the kirk', was his term.

But for a more accurate cross-bearing on the land, they used what they called a sharp meids. For this they took two pairs of objects, waiting until the known four were lined up, two and two. When the boat arrived at the apex of the imaginary triangle, they let go the anchor and started to fish.

When they were taking a sharp meids their favourite objects were the chimneys of certain houses or any of the bigger buildings they could fix on. Looking for lobsters, the Dyker's favoured meids was: Watson's oilskin factory chimney over Tom Melville's kippering kiln *plus* the big lum of the gasworks in line with his own cottage chimney, which he had painted bright orange, right down on the shore. He called this meids 'oilskins, kippers and gas', and it brought us to the hard rocky ground where the lobsters were caught. But if we wanted crabs on the sandier ground, he took the *Jonathan* a mile out from this meids, and instead of his own chimney, used the steeple of St Adrian's. He called this 'the back of the kiln', and it was there we caught partan crabs.

Grandfather's lobster meids was a simpler one. He lined up both sets of the chimneys of Darsie's Lodge with the kirk steeple, and called it 'Darsie on the kirk'. For the partans he used the lums on either end of Tammie Limie's house and took them in conjunction with the ones on the lodge. He called this 'Darsie and Limie' but sometimes referred to it as 'Limie's lums ringing'.

Out there at sea in the early summer hours I saw for the first time all the burghs from a distance, spread out along the coast, the red clutter of roofs smudging the hazy tracts of countryside, and above them the spires and steeples that were landmarks to grandfather but fingers to me, beckoning from the green fists of the graveyards, where all my people lay.

Other mornings we came so close in to shore that we were able to talk to the old men who fished there at the edge of the rocks. They cast their crab-baited handlines into a gap among the tangles, waiting till the corks jerked and sank before hauling in their red codlings and taking them off to fry up for breakfast or supper. We were close enough to see the grins on their faces and to congratulate them on the catch.

Blue days at sea. They came to an end when it was time at last for the summer drave.

Grandfather followed the old traditions. When he went to the early drave he used his oldest nets which the years of barking had made narrower, and which caught the younger, smaller herring. As the hunt wore on, the herring grew bigger and the spawn began to form, so he brought ashore his old nets and set down on board the widest and best that hadn't seen so many seasons of immersion in the barking boilers.

Barking the nets, though it narrowed them down over the years, lengthened their lives by preserving them from the corrosive action of the salt sea and all its weed and scum, especially bothersome at the height of summer. So the great lines and bait nets were pushed back beneath the benches in the garret and the black summer nets were pulled out and hoisted down into the yard.

George usually left his bible and came down for the barking.

'There's no substitute for the bark of the oak,' he would say. 'Melt that down and you've got the best solution for a herring net.'

Grandfather asked him how many of the Balcaskie trees he thought he could strip of their bark before he was caught and prosecuted. But he did his best by his nets, stretching them out dripping hot to dry in the wind and sun.

Few driftermen took the trouble at the end of the '40s to bark their mizzen sails. But even in the age of the steam boiler grandfather wheeled his canvas in a large barrow to his brother-in-law in Elm Grove. Great-uncle Jimmy had been a sailmaker and still had a barking pan in his back garden.

Jimmy harked back to the days of the Fifies and the Zulus – the sailing boats that had preceded the steam drifters. Barking the sails for boats like these, he said, was not something that could be accomplished in a back garden. There were three hundred and fifty yards of foresail weighing nearly a ton when dripping wet, and two hundred and fifty yards of summer mizzen sail. At the end of the line fishing the winter mizzen mast and sail were taken down and the mast was hauled up the brae by horses and rollers to the rough moorland opposite the school, where the women spread out their white washing on a yellow blaze of whins. Here the summer mizzen mast had lain all winter like a fallen tree.

Gallons of water were hosed into the barking pan, the fires crackled, the sail-broth bubbled and the steam rose into the sun.

'I was sent running down the brae to the butcher,' said Jimmy, 'to ask for seven pounds of solid sticky white fat for chucking in. One of the old men wondered whether they should chuck me in as well, just to enjoy a good mouthful of soup before the rest of the ingredients made it uneatable!'

Instead they poured in twenty-one pounds of tannin and fourteen pounds of oakum, and everything melted together and was stirred with a huge stick. The sails were spread wide on the coarse grass and the liquid brushed well in, like thick old brown wine. Then they dried in the midday sun and were turned over for the same treatment on the other side. Grandfather said that the *Venus*'s mizzen sail was like a woman's handkerchief compared to the giant canvases of the old masterpieces. All the same he took care of it and restored it every year.

Apart from the Gospel Ship George had hung one other painting in his room on the wall opposite his window. It was a study of the sea-view from that very window, painted when he was a boy. In the painting it was blowing a full gale from the west. The whole firth was a single white sheet of spray and scores of sailing boats were battling up from the east. Their huge foresails were reefed right down, with only the smallest bit of the mizzen sail unfurled. One of the boats had caught the full weight of wind and was heeling over on the crest of a sickening second of fear, perpetuated in paint, her gunwales and lee deck dipped into the churning sea right up to the commons, the white waves licking like fire at the main hold. To the west of her a bunch of tiny wild faces was staring from another boat at the whole exposed length of their comrades' keel, as if in some critical surgical operation someone's entire backbone were on show. Their features were too small to be made out, but the sheer horror of the moment was written into the rigid thrust of their shoulders and heads.

A flood tide was running. But the sea was not so heavy close inshore, as if the artist had felt the merciful grip of the wind on the land – the jutting tip of Elie Ness always allowing that small benefit to St Monans harbour when there were westerly winds. So some of the boats had already made the weather side of the harbour, and with both sails lowered, down before the wind they were driving fast, their bare masts of magnificent stiff pitch pine growing like trees again out of the blossoming white breakers, while further out, the supple yards of knotless larch were bending to the set of sail as the skippers took their chances, hurrying into harbour through the eye and teeth of the storm.

I stood in front of this picture countless times, and George often told me that he had stood on the braehead as a boy and

counted three hundred ships like that sailing up the firth.
So when the thick theatre-curtains of sleep swished open
on my dreams, the three-score sailing boats of the painting
multiplied into the three hundred of George's boyhood.
The paint melted and moved, flowed like the sea, the ships
rolled and rose and fell, and flying like a gull again in my
sleep, I was sailing before the wind into the flung froth of
the clouds, the spray roses bursting in my face like Miss
Balsilbie's blouse . . .

Struggling out of the spun yarn of dreams one early
summer morning, I looked out from the window and saw
an empty harbour. The fleet had sailed north, leaving a
population of old men and boys to be threaded into the lives
of women, and I wouldn't see grandfather now until some
weekend in August, when all the men in the town would
reappear.

By June all boys were to be found among the rocks at
weekends and after school, combing the shore for what was
to be found. We raked between the skerries for greatline
hooks, new nails and lumps of lead and copper to sell to the
boatbuilder for a penny if the weight was good; we hunted
for the little glass balls from old lemonade bottles, to use as
marbles; we sailed paper boats made out of old school jotters,
using sand as ballast, and if there was a westerly wind and a
jabble on the sea, we watched them sail out of sight or become
waterlogged and sink; we rodded for whiting or rock cod,
not killing them but keeping them alive in pools, throwing
them back into the sea if nobody needed cat-meat – we had
no use for them ourselves but were afflicted by a feverish
need to fish after the long winter, when the perennial June
question was, 'Are there any in yet?' Sometimes the village
effluence obscured the water in the region of the sewage

pipe, and if not breaking pellan pincers or cutting wriggling segments of lugworm, we'd bite off pieces of limpet in our mouths to make them small enough for bait. The practice, not having killed us, must have immunized us against every infectious disease known to man.

Or we made our tinny fires.

My preferred container for this was the larger size tin of Lyle's Golden Syrup. Grandmother kept her empties for me, always leaving a generous coating of syrup in the bottom for me to scoop out, Pooh Bear style, then she washed them and put them on the sink for me to take down to the shore. A clasp knife and a flat stone were used to punch a neat hole like a little door, one inch square, out of the vertical curved surface of the tin, sometimes enlarging it with a piece of strong iron hooping from a broken barrel. This sucked the draught through the fire, which we built inside the tin, with the lid off, the hole being placed to face the prevailing wind. Our fuel consisted of brittle bits of stick from the remains of old herring baskets, crumbs of cork, small nuggets of sea-coal. The poker was a greatline hook heated in the fire until it was a red-hot worm, then hammered into a crinkly straightness between two stones.

The Lyle's empty interior glowed again, not with syrup but with flames. On it we then placed a smaller tin as the cooking pot. In this we cooked our first bachelor meals – potatoes and peas from the fields later in the year, but during June and July mussels and whelks. When these were scarce, or the jealous gatherers chased us away, we kicked the limpets from the barnacled rocks and roasted them three at a time on the upturned lid of a tin of Cherry Blossom shoe polish. Their unappetizing saltiness was not enhanced by their daily availability.

Mussels on the other hand seemed to me too good a morsel for a haddock or a cod, even though thousands of them used to be shelled as fishbait for the lines. In grandfather's day the horse-drawn carts had brought home huge blue mountains

of them from the mussel beds in the River Eden coming into
St Andrews, and the fishing crews had put them in stone
circles between the skerries to keep them alive and fresh
for bait. Nets were laid over them to stop them spreading
and to keep out the oyster catchers, the birds grandfather
always called 'mussel-pickers'. The remains of these old
artificial beds could still be found among the rocks west of
the kirk. We called them the mussel scoops and if we went
scooping for mussels for our tinny fires, one of us always
took along a bottle of Grimble's Malt Vinegar, plundered
from somebody's larder. And so we Robinson-Crusoed our
way through June and the summer months.

In bad times whelk-gathering became a matter of bare
necessity, the black seasons when the fishing failed and
some poor fisherman would be found strung up among his
nets in the loft, or staring up from the harbour bed, open-
eyed in his endless sleep. Once, the train stopped when it
ran over something laid on the line in the darkness – and a
head was picked up in the morning. It was hard to imagine,
grandfather said, the crazy despair that had been locked up
in that head, now empty of any emotion.

Grandfather called them the black seas, the ones that
yielded not a single fish but sent men and women alike out
on to the rocks, lifting every available stone along the coast,
searching for whelks for sheer poverty. In better times
we gathered them just for a few coppers to rattle in our
pockets, to spend on Lucky Bags and liquorice and sherbet
dabs. In freezing wet weather the whelks clung together,
and gathering them was a dismal business. In the spring
and summer months it was a blue and golden time out on
the rocks, but then the whelks scattered, and bringing them
together in a pail or a sack was slow work, unless there was
a summer mist, which brought them all out like snails in
the rain.

When he had a day or two to spare before going off to
the summer herring, grandfather took me up to Kellie Law

under a soft blue sky in which stray clouds floated in silvery wisps. The warm silk of the south-west breezes stroked the fields, scarcely stirring the still green corn. The barley was just beginning to brighten. By the sides of the hot bright roads stone-crop, with its Midas touch, was turning the tops of the lichened dykes to bright gold. Poppies, not yet sprayed out of existence, stained the fields, over which masses of thistledown floated in ghostly galaxies and drifted across the footpaths, where deep green mosses softened the fallen stones. The hedgerows were lit by wild roses, dog roses and hips, and elderflowers hung in big white sweet piercing blossoms. All along the night roads the thick fragrant dampness of honeysuckle could be breathed in like crumbs of cake. But right now the ditches were cracked and dry, and in the purple noon the electric blue threads of dragonflies hovered over the burns, down to the last trickle, but yellow and straggly with aspiring irises and mantled with green cress.

On the high slopes of Kellie Law we sat and stared at the landscape stretched out beneath our feet. On the sprinkled farms and cottages we could see tiny people, seemingly unmoving, embroidered like the characters on some vast green sampler. Some were scattered at their work, others were in some kind of procession. One was strung out like a trail of bright flowers, sprinkled from the kirk at Carnbee. The other was a long narrow black column. But except for the colours of their clothes, one black and the other bright, there was no telling whether the distant files were marrying or burying parties – no sound or movement came up from below, and their imagined laughter or tears were rendered suddenly irrelevant, surrounded as they were by the sheer simplicity of green. It was at that moment that the packed patchwork of people's lives frightened me for the first time. These fields had taken thousands of folk who had tilled them over the centuries, and had spread over them like a great green bedcover. Those who worked the fields today would be ploughed under before they saw the oaks look any older.

'The country boys are seeing to their brides and their burials,' said grandfather.

We sat and looked at the procession of people printed on the landscape.

'One way or another there's always ploughing to be done.'

Fisherfolk marriages used to be left till later in the year, body clocks and social calendars ticking according to the cycle of work. I recalled a snatch of one of old Leebie's sayings.

> *Marry in March and you'll bend like the larch*
> *Marry in Lent and you'll surely repent*
> *Marry in May there's the Devil to pay*

'Any time's a good time for marrying,' said grandfather, 'if you're in the mood – but I've never heard of a good time for dying.'

Grandfather called the culmination of the year Milner's peak time, when Altair, his favourite summer star, was a dewdrop in the south-east, reigning over the firth, and the afterglow so strong that the sea was a silver glimmer all through the dusky night. He told me that George claimed to have sat on the summit of an Orkney hill at midnight on the solstice, one of a rum-filled ring of wild young men, and seen the sun's upper rim flaming just beneath the skyline. Nobody else saw it, but George was a full head higher than the rest of them and that extra head gave him the edge.

The green sleet was arriving now at its fullest growth in the sea, turning the rocks into whalebacks of slipperiness, but we prided ourselves on being able to skim like birds along the shore without a stumble, while a bad bruising or a soaking was the lot of the visitor boys from Glasgow who came at the end of June and whose feet went sliding from under them on our rocky coast.

At low tide in the mornings the steam rose from the tangles in a warm gentle mist, the whelks crawled out on to the rocks, and the pools lay like broken mirrors among the black crags. Now the eiders had stopped their whooing. Only the hissings and whisperings from the laminaria broke the silence of the shore, depopulated of its waves, as the tide held its blue inaudible distance. The rest of the seabirds too fell quiet for a space, as if they could sense that summer was tilting. There were fewer shelducks now and the wheatears had left the coast. The black-headed gull was shedding its executioner's hood and the winter white cap was coming on in its place. The cormorant was starting to lose the white thigh-patch on its black-green glossy feathers. The Great Square was already looming out of the sea late at night, a sure sign of autumn, and by midnight Pegasus was prancing between the May and the Bass.

Only a narrow and a quiet eye could see these things, the wintry decline of life beginning even at the height of summer, death stirring in the midst of life. Summer seemed, in fact, to grow stronger still for a space, the orchestral chatter of insects increasing as the birdsong declined, the bluebottles sunning themselves on the sunny side of the dykes, the invisible point of life expanding.

I made my way in slow motion to the harbour.

In the tar-and-tangle of the afternoon the old remaining boats creaked on the still tide, their dancing days done, and as I lay on my belly on the warm pier, the moored mind kept time with them, rubbing and bobbing against the sleeping moss-grown stones. The June sun beat like a golden gong in the sky. Opening my eyes again, my head hanging over the edge, I watched the flatfish flapping slowly in and out of the harbour mouth, taking the sun on the sandgreen seabed, where the seagulled sky was superimposed like a dream, birds and fish mingling in an impossible element. Around

me drifted the tall tobacco tales piping blue and easy from
the after-dinner daze of the old salts, who sat with their
backs to the stones, caps shading their eyes as they gazed
into the sea's golden drench, into the insubstantial air.

But I had no ear for their stories today. I shut my eyes
again. The smell of centuries was all around me, dark as a
drug, and the rocking voices of the old men, smelling of
sun and salt, made my head sink slowly into the deep green
mirror far below. Summer was outstretched in a blue stupor
on the pier. In the bright darkness of the old afternoon the
village slept, and all my ancestors rose from the waves,
preserved in the tang of my sea-dreams.

Time was at anchor here.

7

Summer Hunt and
South Harvest

Juty was the janitor that clanged shut the school gates for a sweet seven weeks. It seemed like the eternity promised by the evangelists, except that we were a long way from angels. Inevitably we looked for trouble.

Smoking out Harry Watson was a game we learned early and which never lost its appeal. Harry Watson was the harbour master, his office at the head of the middle pier not much bigger than a drifter's wheelhouse. He was a wrinkled kipper of a man, his skin cured by years of dozing his days away in his tiny cabin, his feet up on his sloping desk, the coke stove glowing a hellish red, and the walls blackened by the tobacco that he smoked till he fell asleep, his chair on the tilt, and not a cubic ounce of oxygen left to explain why he was still alive.

In winter the office was a haven of heat, and as many old men as could squeeze inside stood bunched around the recumbent Harry, like strings of herring smouldering over sawdust. They were keeping in touch. The cold weather had put an end to Nancy's prancing about in her knickers up Petticoat Lane, and so they left the bench and added their pipe smoke to Harry's.

But in the hot summer weather only Harry could bear the engine-room torture of the place. He kept the stove at full steam even through the dog days that melted the tar on the piers, and he lay back in his chair in a sulphurous paradise, snoring like a funnel, the pipe hanging slackly from the lolling head. Standing on Golly's shoulders, I hoisted myself up the tarred wall and on to the hot corrugated roof. Then Peem threw up some old torn netting which I stuffed in fistfuls into the saw-toothed tin chimney before dropping back down to watch the fun. The last of the smoke drifted across the harbour and was gone. We waited behind a barricade of fishboxes for Harry to emerge.

It was astonishing how long it took. Sometimes there were anxious moments. Had we asphyxiated him? But always the door was flung open and the white-bearded old devil flew out with the fumes, toothless, pipeless, spitting and snarling, his eyes streaming and his arms waving as he tried to disperse the clouds. We shoved over a few fishboxes and ran out with our water pistols.

'Satan's on fire! Quick, call the fire brigade!'

We ran off along Shore Street, leaving a drenched and steaming Harry shaking his fist and gasping out scripture. 'The wicked fleeth while no man pursueth!'

Reaching the west pier in triumph we looked back to enjoy the spectacle of the old men trying to hoist Harry shakily to his roof to free his choked funnel. Out of the clutches of our teachers, and with most of the able-bodied men away at sea, we ran wild like this for some days with the first taste of liberty.

When Harry had cooled off and was asleep again, we came back to the harbour with a bucketful of sea-scorpions which we'd trapped along the shore. We fixed a good-sized cork to each one, jabbing them on to their spiny backs, tossed them into the water, then stood back and waited for the swimming gala to begin. The cork was a deadly burden for these short-spined fish, popping them skywards when they tried to dive, and producing agonized aquabatics to rounds of applause. Like comic torpedoes they traced crazy lines all about the harbour and we joined in the fun, tearing off our clothes down to our pants, diving into a harbour emptied of its boats, chasing them in dolphin droves with screams and splashes and salt-caked laughter. But we always freed them in the end, returning them to the sanity of their cool cellars among the rocks and weeds of the shore.

One summer a bigger specimen came into harbour. I saw it from the backyard first thing in the morning, swimming between the May and the shore – a black boomerang that ripped open the firth, shot up higher than the lighthouse, crossing the white orbits of the gannets, and crashed back into the sea, sending mountains of snow cascading to the clouds.

I ran up to George's room. He was standing at his open window, not fully dressed as he usually was, but with his spyglass at his eye. The pages of his bible were fluttering in the blue breeze.

'What is it, Gramps? Can I see?'

He passed me the glass and I saw for the first time the savage cut and thrust of that living scimitar slashing and thrashing the waves, the battling bull head, the powerful fin, and the tigerish tail that mauled the water, churning it like a propeller.

'What is it? Is it a whale?'

'Aye, they call it a whale,' muttered George, 'but I wouldn't. It's liker a wolf.'

'Is it like the ones you used to hunt?'

'No,' he said quietly, 'that's a killer out there. And compared to the beasts I went after, that one is a butcher, let me tell you, a bad black devil!'

He told me how he had once seen a pack of killers tear out the tongue of a great blue whale.

'It was nearly ninety feet long, and its tongue in its jaws must have weighed a ton. They just ripped it out and fed on it while it was bleeding to death from the mouth, the fuckers!'

I knew he had said a bad word. He was grown up, so he

was allowed to. All the same it shocked me. I'd never heard
George swear before.

'Didn't you catch killers, Gramps?'

He turned, and I saw his back making for the door.

'Come with me,' he said.

I followed him down to the lumber room. It was like
the interior of a shipwreck. He clambered stiffly over piles
of dog-torn, mouse-eaten nets, throwing aside shredded
baskets and punctured dahns in his struggle to reach what
he was after. I frisked after him, sniffing at this and that.
He was in the corner, tugging heavily at a stiff tarpaulin
wrapped around what looked like a long pole.

'Pull it off,' he breathed, 'you that has so much life in you.'
My great-grandfather was no more the man who had taken
the Jehovah's Witness by the throat.

He tilted the pole and I pulled at the faded green sheeting
till it came away.

My mouth opened. It was his old harpoon – nine feet
of lacquered larch and a further foot of solid iron, tipped
with a brutal barb that made even a great-line hook seem
like a bent pin. The everyday working weapon of my great-
grandfather's youth, unveiled after nearly three-quarters of
a century.

'Bring it outside,' he said. 'Take care.'

I followed him through the transe and into the yard,
amazed at the sheer weight and size of the arrow that had
pierced a whale to the heart. We looked out at the killer, still
ploughing up the firth.

'That fish out there wasn't made by God,' George said.
'It's one of Satan's playthings. Do you know what it'll do?
It'll slash open the bellies of seals for sheer sport and leave
them dying among the rocks. It'll bite the heads off their
bairns just out of its badness.'

He steadied himself against the seaward wall and reached
out for his old weapon.

'And I'll tell you this too. If I had seventy years off my

back, I'd take that harpoon and a boat and go out there right now and bring about the death of that brute in the name of the Lord.'

I looked at him as he trembled whitely beside me, putting up his hand to his blurred old eye.

'But this is the nearest I'll ever come to it now.' He reached out suddenly and held on to the nearest support – the handle of old Leebie's mangle.

'And I'm heartsore at what I once did to the great whales.' His voice cracked. 'The days of my folly – too late now.'

Then came the first surge of sorrow for one of my own family, one whom I would never have dared pity. But just a few short years of my own life had begun in him the slow stiffening that was a rehearsal for death. I looked quickly away from him and out again at the whale, still whipping up the waves.

'I think it's coming in, Gramps.'

He peered hard over the rooftops.

'So it is,' he said slowly. 'It's coming into shore. It's coming in to die.'

The killer came in with the forenoon tide and the ebb left it stranded in the harbour, stuck in the mud between the middle and east pier. Everybody that was alive and walking that day came down to stare at it. Even wheelchairs were trundled down the brae, though my grandmother stayed at home, having no wish, she said, to see any animal in torment. But the whole village strung itself out along piers and street, galleries of spectators come to scrutinize its immobility, its utter possession of agony. The old men said that it couldn't survive on land for long, that it was being slowly crushed by its own terrific weight, the vanquished victor victim now to its own bullying bulk, the pitiless unpitied.

When they saw its helplessness a few boys descended the steps and plodded soggily across the mud to show their bravery. They swaggered right up to the slumped warhead, punching its defused, defenceless sides. The whale ignored

them. Trapped inside its carcass, netted in air, only its tail
flapped idly, like a tangle at low tide. Encouraged, they
clambered up on to the huge back and raised their arms
aloft and cheered, cheap little toreadors mocking the bull.
Nobody laughed.

But word had spread to the farms. A coarse drunken
ploughman called Robert Mackie came down the steps and
took sole possession of the summit. He started to fumble
with his flies.

'We'll see if it survives my harpoon!' he brayed boozily,
standing over the whale's blowhole and making it clear
what he was about to do.

The women shrieked and the men muttered under their
breaths.

Then the minister arrived.

In a sudden kirk silence he materialized out of the mud
and bellowed at the drunk.

'Get down from there, you bastard!'

The village as one drew in its breath. The huge rush of air
was followed by an almighty hush. But lacking the sobriety
to measure the mood of the moment, the ploughman began
to execute a vulgar parody of the hornpipe on the whale's
back.

The Reverend Kinnear heaved himself up. Without
wasting another word he drove his fist straight into the
slack side of the drunkard's leering jaw. Mackie teetered on
one leg for a fraction, then keeled over in slow motion into
the sucking slime, where he lay like a felled tree.

Hoots and jeers and applause all round for the minister.
He was still standing on the whale, breathing fiercely
through flared nostrils, his eyes like live coals, his huge
fingers clenching and unclenching, his knuckles white and
red. But he couldn't speak for rage. He jumped down and
sank up to his ankles. The silence was awesome, as if he
were in the pulpit, holding forth. He trudged with soiled
shoes and red face across the harbour bed.

'Get me a hose!' he roared as he came up the harbour steps.

A long hosepipe was produced in seconds, led from the tap outside Harry's office and fed into his hands. He pointed it over the wall and down below at the whale, quieter now without its tormentors.

'Turn it on!'

A fountain of water flowered and fell – and a great sigh rippled through the whole slow length of the whale. Everybody sighed along with it.

'Now you can all go home!' roared Kinnear.

But he stayed there himself all through the rest of the afternoon and into evening, hosing down the grateful killer until the first blue fingers of tide touched its dying sides. Some of the newer seine-net boats were in harbour, their crews not part of the older work-rhythms that took grandfather up north. One of them tied ropes to the flicking tail and towed it slowly out past the breakwater, releasing it a mile out to sea. And there it died.

But for weeks afterwards it was washed up at various places along the coast, haunting one harbour after another on the flood tide. Finally it came to rest on the west rocks, right beneath the Old Kirk. By this time it was stinking.

Kinnear preached a sermon about it.

'O, thy offence is rank, it smells to heaven!' he thundered at his flock, telling them about the cruelty of man and the innocence of the animal kingdom.

George always made a point of asking me what the Sunday sermon had been about. When he heard what Kinnear had preached he grunted.

'He should go to the whales for a winter or two. He'd not come back with a bleeding heart for killers.'

Then he looked at his quivering hands.

'There was a time it could have taken its chances with me in the sea. I'd have brained it stone dead.'

It wasn't until the drifters came home the following

month that we were finally rid of what Kinnear called the
wages of sin. But the whale keeps on returning, on those
tides that ebb and flow in sleep, deep in the brain.

The sea was always bringing in something or other to
provide us with fun or food for thought: a massive spar of
pitch pine which we tried to sell to the boat-builder, a turtle-
shell in which we boiled potatoes, a tailor's dummy (female)
to which Peem and Golly added anatomical details, propped
it up at Pussy Starr's front door, rang the bell and ran away.
Masses of driftwood for building into rafts or drying out
and setting alight. Somebody's wooden leg which we all
tried on before hanging it from the red-and-white striped
pole of Sam, the one-legged barber. A crate of sodden
oranges which we did our best to eat. Once, a wooden crate,
found half sunken in the sands at lowest ebb, and containing
two bottles still intact. Golly pronounced it to be Spanish
wine. There was no label to authenticate its Spanishness
or otherwise but we needed neither label nor language to
confirm its potency. Peem broke the neck of a bottle over
a boulder, picked up a large scallop shell and filled it till it
brimmed with gold.

'This is Sangster's skull!' he tittered, swigging it off.

We all followed him.

'This is old Gourlay's!'

'We're the One-Gallus Gang!'

Drinking out of the dead heads of the dominies, our
ancestral enemies, gorging ourselves to glory on their sea-
scoured brains.

We filled and refilled the shells, clapped them on our
heads and went staggering about the beach with long
prowling strides, whacking the air around us.

'Open your sum books at the end!'

'Open your mouths wide, you stupid wee buggers!'

'Open another bloody bottle, boys!'

'Damn me if I don't, Miss Shagster!'

'Have one for the road, you lemon-faced old nanny-goat!'

'Go and meet your maker in hell!'

'How do you fancy being ravished first?'

'Three times!'

'By Spanish sailors!'

'I'd rather have Spanish women!'

'And kiss them too!'

We laughed as long and loudly as we could, out of our ignorance, our undefined longings, at the thought of kisses that lay beyond the Spanish seas.

'Get out your Oxford Song Books, you drunken dunderheads!'

'You're tone deaf, boy, you're dumb as the devil made you!'

'You're dumb as they come and daft as they go!'

'Daft as a duster!'

'Get your hands off these dusters!'

'Off these garters!'

'Off these girls!'

'Off these Spanish ladies, I say!'

'Are you ready then?'

'Farewell and adieu to you fair Spanish ladies.'

'One, two, three . . '

> *Now let every man drink off a full bumper,*
> *Now let every man drink off a full bowl,*
> *For we will be jolly and drown melancholy,*
> *With a health to each jovial true-hearted soul.*

The shore was rolling underneath our feet and the skyline tilted. So we stood splay-footed on the bouldery deck, sea-legged, as we ranted and raved like true British Spaniards, tossed and pitched and lurched and heeled, and then we ran into the sea and sang *Blow the man down.*

The waves pounded us. But we knew our Oxford Song Books, year in, year out, cover to cover.

> *The gale she is raging far out on the deep,*
> *Away-hay, blow the man down.*

We blew mightily on one another. Struggling back to shore, I blew on Peem and he dropped like a tree in a storm. Golly blew on me and I fell alongside Peem. From the beach the two of us blew up at Golly and he toppled and rolled, crashing on top of us. We became insensible as spars, and the sea broke over us.

When we woke up we were dead men. Leebie threatened to knock me back into final senselessness with the leg of a chair. George, who had once thundered at me that the drunkard was an affront to God, stared into space and said nothing. My mother and grandmother brought me through the hangover with aspirins, soda from a siphon, hot sweet blackcurrant drinks, eyeshades, smothering blankets, a few whispered words and a great deal of sympathy. After that my father thrashed me, and my aunts laughed till they had to lie down for the soreness of their sides.

'If it's not drink, it's women,' old George used to say. 'Man has only two ways to fall,' adding that if Adam had had the technology, he'd have made cider out of the apple.

July proved him right. When the trains pulled into the station in the first week of the month, they disgorged dozens of Glaswegians, who emerged out of the steam with a clattering of accents and carriage doors. They threw their suitcases before them out on to the platform and jumped from the footplates with whoops of jubilation. They were determined to squeeze every drop of enjoyment out of their two-week respite from Glasgow's daily grind. There were children and couples of all ages, married and single, linking arms or slinking off to their separate pleasures, the twin ingredients of which were, just as George said, either Eve or the apple.

The apple was consumed in the Cabin Bar, the May View Hotel – or out in the street. Eve required some privacy and we spent part of our summer holidays shadowing the courting couples as they made their way hand in hand to the old castle. Once a fortress, the castle was now a stronghold of concealment for the lovers who occupied it. On the south and east sides it was approachable from the village only by toiling up steep green slopes. On the west and north sides was the sheer crag on which it was built, dropping a hundred feet to rocks and sea. But the killing times were over, time itself was now the killer, and folk simply walked in through the gaping holes, unchallenged and untriumphant. Its roof was the blue sky, the sea its window panes, tussock and turf its floors. Dog roses decorated the green tapestries, grew in the cracked hearthstones, leapt up the cold chimneys.

Here the local boys also took their girls when they had at last grown tired of making tinny fires and had started talking to mirrors instead. Here they were out of sight of all the houses in the town – apart from God's house, of course, only half a mile east. And God was always at home. But when we saw them heading west, holding hands, shy, secretive, subtle, we followed their slow feet through the tall grasses of July, allowing them ample time to disappear between the castle walls before closing in on them, giggling guiltily, frantically afraid of what we would miss, of what we would see.

And what did Peem and I see as we crawled through the grass, approaching our twelfth year?

Golly and a big-eyed Glasgow girl, leaning back in the

grass, etched against the sea, their hands cemented, their breath intermingled, their lips feeding off one another. They were like statues. They had a beauty all of their own, unprecedented, impregnable, excluding us absolutely.

We brayed our hatred of Golly. We threw down fistfuls of insults and stones, letting him know that we had sullied his secret, and we ran off across the fields, howling and hooting our jealous derision. For the next five minutes we tore up dog roses, kicked the heads off dandelions, hurled huge boulders into space, watching them smash on the rocks below. Then we ran to the castle's crumbling old dovecot and shook our fists at the pigeons.

Golly had broken the code. Peem and I parted sullenly and went back to nature.

July was a blaze of blood-red poppies, heavy with the smell of elderflower and tall with nettles and willowherb, waving at us from the dry ditches and the kirkyard burn, where the loosestrife ran free. The dog days were sweetened by dog roses and wild roses, and by wild strawberries that lay in the hedgerows like fallen sunburned moons.

Yet it was a sad month too. The leaves were already losing their gloss and rustled now with a drier sound in the early morning breeze. Birdsong was dwindling. Towards the end of the month the swithers and bladderwrack and green sleet came in on the tide in large quantities, the slack heads of the tangles washing ashore in the south-east gales. Heavy rains drenched the harebells, drove the bees from the lime-flowers and clover, and gave the meadowsweet an even madder fragrance. The old men looked up from their benches, glanced over their shoulders and commented on the mass of seaweed floating in the harbour, nodding at it with a grim satisfaction.

'Well, there's another summer almost gone.'

And as I walked along the shore, I could see the summer slipping away and life going back fast. The whelks that had spawned in June now began to creep back underneath the stones. The oystercatchers had returned but the shelducks had gone and wouldn't be seen again this year. At nine in the evening Cassiopeia stood like a gathering of old friends, their cigarette ends glowing faintly in the dark. Autumnal Pegasus reared above the sea. The afterglow was dimming fast by midnight, the firth darkening during the lengthening nights, ghost-moths fluttering here and there, and the air full of the crushed peppery nettledust of life, drifting over the fields, cooled by the first evening mists.

Old Leebie came back to the house after one of her rare summer visits to the braes.

'Summer comes with a white flower and goes with a white flower,' she said.

She was holding a daisy in her right hand and a bindweed in her left – life and death in either hand.

By August the north fishing was played out and the drifters came down past Fife to the Northumberland coast and landed their herring at Shields during the week. On Friday nights they shot their nets in a northwards direction, hoping for a modest catch which they could carry straight home and sell on the pier on Saturday mornings for twenty shillings a cran. But if they made a heavy catch when shooting on the way back to port, they had to turn about and steam all the way back to Shields, for only smaller shots could be handled by the St Monans buyers. Small for Shields but enormous for me – the harbour at the weekend all fish and funnels and shouting and bargaining, with Northumberland herring for tea. They were the biggest and best that I ever saw taken out of the sea.

The days were long gone of the Lammas Drave, the local fishing in the firth during August, when colossal catches had been taken from the stretches of water at Pittenweem,

and especially off Fife Ness – the area known as the Old
Haikes. Grandfather remembered this over and over.

'The shoals were so dense you could have walked on their
backs right across to the Bass.'

I took it literally at five years old, and even at ten.

'Yes, you could have walked across the sea all the way to
Edinburgh – no need to take a train!'

Behind mindshut eyes I saw the busy boats, the plum-
meting white gannets striking the shoals, heard the shouts
and screechings, and sensed in my soul the wonder of the
moment – man and bird and fish brought together in a
miracle of sudden abundance, the whole cosmos killing and
recreating itself in a circle of sacrifice and sustenance. And
grandfather walking across the water, his arms outspread
to enfold me.

For weeks they never stopped, he said, landing at
Anstruther and Pittenweem and St Monans in turn, sharing
out the catches among the saturated buyers, and steaming
across to Newhaven and Dunbar and right back again to
Fife Ness round the long clock of the month.

'I still dream about it,' grandfather said.

Sometimes he dreamed that after half a century the
herring had returned in August, and he woke up with the
cry ringing round the room, though it was only in his head:
There's herring in the Haikes! There's herring in the Haikes!

Some folk had dreams, he said, that one day King Arthur
would return to Britain, that he had never really died but
had gone to a mysterious place called Avalon. 'But King
Arthur's dead and gone – and the fish'll follow him, just you
wait and see.'

Prophet or realist, grandfather said they were killing
the sea. And I didn't have long to wait. But the boom-
before-the-bust stays with me till I die: one single blinding
image of St Monans harbour seen from the braehead, lying
beneath my feet, glittering in the morning sun, with what
looked like a billion fish, silver bullion in boxes, but also

lying loose everywhere, littering the piers and pavements, spilling out into the streets and slipping back into the water, the swooping gulls going mad as they gorged and circled and swung, nobody to stop them sharing the excitement, the wild bonanza.

After that it was the East Anglian fishing. But before he left for Yarmouth grandfather liked to accompany the Dyker to the lobsters. They had cast their shells in June and July, coming inshore when the increasing temperature of the sea told them that the time had come. And as they provided tasty bites for fish with their armour off, they sought the seclusion of holes in the rocks rather than engage in an unequal jousting on the seabed. They were easily caught by fishermen in August when they needed food to build up the calcium in their new shells. By September their flesh was at its sweetest, but the meat grew tougher later in the year, when the wintry tail in particular became hard to eat.

Every year at the extreme end of the summer, grandfather and the Dyker made new lobster creels, and they took me with them up to Balcaskie, where the ash trees were growing wild. If somebody had beaten us to the best ash-boughs, they took dog-rose stems instead, whittling away the thorns with their penknives, the blades of which had dwindled to slivers with decades of honing. They had been using them since they were boys. The Dyker liked the stems of the whins best of all, but grandfather said that only a man whose hands were filled with time would take the trouble that whin-stems required. They were best because they were the strongest, but they refused to bend into the required half moons unless they were given a good steaming over the backyard boiler.

They also disagreed about lobster bait. Fish-heads failed to satisfy the Dyker, who went to enormous lengths to entice the lobsters into his creels. He stretched herring nets across the harbour mouth to the annoyance of the other fishermen, weighting the nets with chains along the

bottom. Or he dropped fresh herring guts into muslin bags
and pinned these to the bottom of the creel. But grandfather
always insisted that stinking mackerel were good enough
bait for a lobster.

'A lobster is different from a crab,' he told the Dyker.
'Crabs go into creels on scent, lobsters on sight. You don't
even have to use flesh for bait – anything will do.'

The Dyker looked away, smiling at the sea. But to prove
his point grandfather set three of the creels aside. He baited
one with a piece of white rubber from a sea-boot, another
with a shiny piece of tin, and a third with a broken white
plate. To the Dyker's dismay some of his own creels came
in empty whereas grandfather's were full, and the one with
the piece of tin had two lobsters in it.

'There's your answer,' said grandfather. 'They go in with
their eyes and not their snouts, just like I told you.'

I showed this trick to Peem and Golly. Peem's brother
had become a plumber and Peem himself was soon to lose
all interest in seawater. Golly's interest in girls was short-
lived. Girls cost money, he argued with a maturity beyond
his years – lobsters made it for you. He stole a creel and tied
it to a tangle in a rock-ringed puddle just behind the west
pier. A lobster was taken with the very first tide. Then he
stole the blacksmith's long poker, and using it as a cleek, he
raked out lobsters from the rocks as if they were magne-
tized. His nickname adapted to his success and he became
known as Lobster Golly.

August threaded our noons with dragonflies and stroked
our faces with thistle seeds. Summer had stood still for a
time but now its settled silences were over. Berries replaced
blossoms, and seed vessels rattled where flowers had waved
at us in passing in July. Campion and cow-parsley and dog
roses still filled the ditches, the convolvulus rang its white
straggling bells in the hedges, and harebells embroidered the
braes with their wild clear blue. But the swifts were leaving
in large numbers and the swallows had taken to sitting in

long rows on the telegraph wires. They were waiting for the autumn call. Up in Balcormo Den the big beech with the initials carved in a heart was already beginning to yellow. The hymn boards in the churches reflected the passage of time. If you listened on a Sunday to the voices drifting across the village roofs, you could hear nature making the choice and calling the tune.

> *Change and decay in all around I see,*
> *O Thou who changest not, abide with me.*

But the biggest change in August was in the fields, as the sun wove into them the bright threads of autumn, green turning heavily to gold across the quilted country. They stood like churches emptied of their people, the white heads and colourful hats gone from the pews as daisies and cornflowers and poppies made their straggling exits.

If you closed your eyes, the sound of the wind in the barley told you the time of year. All those secret whisperings and sighs of satisfaction, the long slow susurrations of fulfilment – summer had its special music. But an August wind, no matter how soft and gentle, was always an anxious one. It roamed and probed the waves of grain, sometimes with quick little questionings, sometimes with gustier surges of aimless undefinable longings.

Then the whiteness came on the cornfields, and they rattled like urgent papers turned by an anxious hand. And when the restless sounds died away at dusk, the setting sun slid like a big drop of blood into meadows where the trees stood half shrouded in the early evening mists and the cattle sometimes disappeared in a sea of milk. The earth hoisted the stars on its shoulder, the afterglow had gone. When I saw Pegasus breaking the waves with the first stars and making his way to the fields by nine o'clock, I knew that autumn had come. The horse was now a reaper, pawing the corn, swinging Andromeda all the way to the west like a great silver scythe.

It was time for grandfather to sail to Yarmouth. Before he left, the nets had to be mended. This was work for old women who had nothing left to do but talk, and old men whose last pleasure was tobacco. But grandfather never minded putting in a needleful himself when he had nothing else to do, always insisting on mending every last broken leg on a mesh, and frequently whittling away at old bone needles, which he preferred to the wooden ones, and which he made as a hobby, decorating them with tiny carvings of the old sailing ships, tea-clippers and Fifies and Zulus.

For the Yarmouth fishing there could be up to a hundred nets at a time in the *Venus*'s fleet. A net cost anything between three and five pounds, not including its four ropes. A two-mile messenger warp for the whole fleet of nets could cost over twenty pounds. Even a box of cutch to bark them was thirty shillings, and a hundredweight was needed to the tub every time they were treated. With the herring dropping to only ten shillings a cran, many hundreds of cran had to be hauled before the crews could even cover their costs. Grandfather used to say that they were fishing for four weeks in every season just to keep the boat afloat and the nets in the water.

Mended, boiled and barked, all the nets were then taken back down to the boat, and by the end of the first week in September the fleet had sailed for Yarmouth.

The East Anglian fishing was the highlight of the drifterman's year but it was always accompanied by loss of life, and some children were allowed out of school to see their fathers away, in recognition of the possibility that they might never see them again. I went down to the pier with my mother and aunts to see the men off, grandfather and Alec and Billy, and even grandmother managed to come down with Leebie, arm in crooked arm. There was a colossal noise going on in the harbour – too much steam on the boats, and they were blowing it off. The wind was a hard south-easter, blowing the smoke from the funnels straight across the town. The crews handed out some of their biscuits and grandfather gave me an apple. Then the ropes were slackened and flung back, the engines gathered like lions, stems bristling for the harbour mouth, pennies were thrown on deck for luck as they passed beneath us, hands waving and grinning faces looking up from the water, last goodbyes shouted out hoarsely in the grateful confusion, masking our emotion, that sick fear that the sea would take one of ours – and then they were gone.

'Aye,' said Leebie, 'and somebody's body will never come home again. That's always the way with Yarmouth.'

Nobody said anything. We came home in silence, my mother holding my hand hard. I wanted to eat the apple that grandfather had given me but my stomach was too tight. I went along to the braehead house, up to the garret, and looked out over the town, emptied yet again of its men. And the days were drawing in.

September started with the saturation of summer in the earth and ended with winter pre-echoing emptily in the rising winds, with their early autumnal liking to the north-west. The jam-making had moved through all the crops, strawberries, raspberries, gooseberries and apples, in that order, and finished up with plums and pears, the wasps pirouetting like dying dancers in the midnight purple ballrooms of half-emptied plums, the fallen golden-drops lying like eggs in the cool grass. The bees winged their way wearily from flower to fading flower, overtaken by the lighter air-traffic of floating seeds, and the failing bluebottles blundered drunkenly into dew-beaded spider-traps that glittered and shivered among rose-hips and brambles.

The harvesting that had started in late August went on daily in the wide fields, all the efforts of men concentrated on the land, now that the fishermen had gone south, taking with them their new chaff mattresses made from the first cuts of corn. The golden tide receded as the combines cut down wave after wave of shining grain and soon summer's murmurings were a forgotten dream. Distance stood heavy with the annual lament from the stubble fields, piping farewell to the earth. The sharp still sound of the dead seasons hung in the air like a scent, forgotten, then remembered.

But these were not the thoughts of the workers. They stood the sheaves of corn in stooks to face the Bass Rock and dry out in the sun. Peter Hughes set down three huge barrels in the centre of his field. One contained treacle, a second baps, and the third beer. Only the men drank from the beer barrel, but men, women, children and horses clustered round the treacle. I dipped in Guthrie's floury baps, holding each one like the infant Achilles for a near-as-damn-it total immersion, and brought them out again dripping with sweet black molasses. When I could eat no more I staggered off to the burn, drank it down in deep gurgling gulletfuls, and let my head and hands hang in the cold clear water until there was nothing left of existence except the pearled pebbles on the paperweight world of the bottom, and a billion silver bubbles singing in my ears.

The month went on, tingeing the leaves, peeling the petals from the last of the roses, dropping them in slow cold circles round the ginger-jar's blue mouth. The southbound swallows assembled in their flocks, the robin's autumn song reddened the wind, and shoals of jellyfish purpled the tide.

'It's getting right back-end now,' Leebie would say.

The goosey mornings arrived, so called by the old folk either because of the coming of the geese or because of the pimples raised on our shivering flesh as we stood in the cold dim light of dawn, hurrying into our clothes. With the swing of winter already in legs and lungs we strode up to Balcaskie to look for conkers. The field-flowers and feathered grasses that had brushed our wrists and knees

as we walked had been cut away. The roadmen had scythed
the verges and cleared the ditches. All that was left was a
flowerless aftermath, strewn with dead daisies and lopped
pink poppies – and the dandelion clocks were the dead heads
of the dominies drifting across the stubble fields, fading
bubbles from the backyard boiler, the morning ghosts of
the harvest moon, dematerializing into day.

In the frosty sunsets a milky stillness settled on the earth,
the dew fell heavier now from tall clear skies, and the old
winter friends were reaching down to us again – Capella
glittering in the north-east and Aldebaran well up by
midnight. The mellow harvest moon rose like Jockie Bett's
big burned face over the beds of stubble, and stone jars of
cider appeared from nowhere.

We had arrived at the equinox. Light and darkness held
one another, two dancers in perfect harmony, poised on a
pin-point of rest. After this moment the music of the dying
year would grow stronger, darker, and the fall-away of life
and light would throb like a lament.

Towards the end of the month the weather was different
in the ears and nostrils and on the tongue. Sharp winds
came in from the east, ruffling the water, and soon the
gales were growling round the gable-ends of the houses,
breaking the stained-glass lattices of the trees. One after
another the leaves began to fall in like windows and the cold
sky came pouring through. A great coldness returned to
the sea, which resumed its autumnal roaring. The shadows
clustered thickly on the walls. The black roses are back,
the old folk said – and they drew their chairs closer to the
fireside and began muttering about hot toddies and long
johns and porridge again in the mornings.

George's porridge pot stood cold now over an unlit fire.
He refused to have one on. He'd stopped eating as well as
speaking. Only the wind turned the pages of the big black
bible by the window. And even Leebie couldn't nag him into
turning back to life.

Leebie used to say that if Jack Frost didn't appear by October he'd be late in the year and his visit would be long and hard. But the goosey mornings often came early – a dark purplish-blue sky glaring white at the horizon, with a shiver in the air, and later in the day you'd look up at the sound of the huge arrowheads of geese winging their way over firth and fields. The frost was on its way. You could even hear it coming in the sea, a sonorous echo as the full tide splashed among the smaller stones of the beach, crackling like tinfoil, a sound not heard since last winter.

'She's got her head on a north-west pillow tonight,' the old men would say of the October wind, as they heard the north-westerlies falling away at sunset, ghostly over the fields.

And in the morning, sure enough, came the frost. Winter's first white fingertips parted the curtains of the year. The frost set fire to the trees and they burned like braziers black and gold in the foggy fields, yellows and oranges and reds, torches of rowan and ash sending up flares through the falling leaves, signalling the death of the year. A single poppy, drained of blood, stood stiffly in a ditch, the stopped heart of summer on the edge of the stubble.

October washed the streets and sky a pale gold. Mornings arrived like the postman, throwing open the gate and marching up the path to hammer on the door. I awoke to the farmers breaking up their fields again, the ploughs pulling behind them long black-and-white streamers of seagulls and rooks. Engines throbbed far and near as the tractors lorded it over the land. The four-legged kings of the fields were out to grass and fewer horses now stood in the streets. The sun's white fist was punching holes in the clouds that charged along the tops of the low dykes, the swift wild rains blowing by, the last shows of light sweeping the fields in broken golden arcs. Splinters of sunlight lay in the cart-tracks like broken bottles and winked at me from wisps of straw stuck in the scattered lumps of dung.

Out in the bay the gulls rode at anchor, ruffled by strong cold winds. The town stood as if I'd never seen it before – etched sharply against the black and silver sea, the chimney-smoke from all the houses scrollworked across the clouds. Raindrops glittered on the kirk spires and all the grave-stones were on fire.

Suddenly afraid of the vast unstoppable nature of change, I ran madly up into the country where the hands and arms of the trees were now showing through as the winds stripped them down, producing a paper pantomime of coloured snowflakes. Rose-hips blazed out from the hedgerows, and on the shining black coffins of the last brambleberries the flies laid themselves down and died, like the lovers in Georgina's songs.

> *Not a flower, not a flower sweet,*
> *On my black coffin let there be strewn,*
> *Not a friend, not a friend greet*
> *My poor corpse, where my bones shall be thrown.*

Love lay like the bird's egg I came across in a ditch, cold and unnoticed as a stone since the spring. I came back heavily at sunset and sat in the garret, thinking of Georgina in Yarmouth now with the men, remembering her songs, her gentleness. The moon rose out of the sea like an old drowned skull and the clouds quickly shrouded it. I tiptoed up to George's door and listened. At one time he'd have caught the footfall of a spider. Now he'd stopped listening altogether. *Vanity of vanities, all is vanity.* Was he talking in his sleep? *All go unto one place, all are of the dust, and all turn to dust again.* I looked through the keyhole. The window was open and the hooded moon looked in at the fluttering pages. The voice seemed to be coming out of the bible itself. *There is no new thing under the sun.*

I tried to sleep. But the winds were blasting the walls and windows, while the sea shattered itself uselessly on the cold sands night after night, the tides coming in and going out endlessly and to no purpose. The foghorns started up, baying like brutes in the darkness, voices out of hell. I lay awake asking myself for the first time who I really was, while the night turned over and over without sleep.

But nobody wanted to sleep on Hallowe'en, the last night of the month.

I dressed myself up one more time in my father's old navy uniform – next year I'd be too old for guising, I was told – and bell-bottomed, striped and navy-blue, went out into the darkness to meet my friends, pretending for the last time to be my father, before returning him to the bottom drawer.

Golly was a caped lady in crinoline and yellowed pearls. Lipsticked, powdered and rouged, he was bestoled with fox furs stolen from his grandmother's best wardrobe. Peem was a Red Indian, Big Chief Sitting Bull, with seagull feathers dyed scarlet and green, and the hatchet from the woodshed in his hand for a tomahawk, whooping all to himself by his back door.

We went into the turnip fields to make our witches' heads, and as we crouched down in the damp earth with clasp-knives and candles, we saw the scattered lights of other guisers come bobbing through the dark, the jagged teeth and orange eyes floating through the field at various levels, depending on the ages and heights of the decapitated ghosts who approached us with strangely thrilling invisibility. Who were they? We grinned uncertainly, trying to see beyond, into the false faces of our friends. Once up close we could relax again. Boys and girls, that was all, in long trailing skirts, feathered hats and strings of beads, soot and satisfaction all over their unrecognizable faces, grinning behind the warpaint.

'Who is it? Who is it?'

'You first!'

'No, don't you come near! Not till you tell me who you are!'

'Don't you know my voice, you idiot?'

And when the recognition scenes were over, we pointed and screeched at one another and joined up in a band with our communal tin, to knock on all the doors and beg a few coppers to help the guisers. Some doors never opened, year after year, but most folk let us in, and we stood in a weird wet huddle in halls and vestibules and warm yellow kitchens, or in front of roaring fires that made our make-up run.

'Right then, do your turns. You first, Lady Muck. And what about you, Buffalo Bill?'

Sweating and self-conscious, even under our disguises, we all sang or recited something, one by one or all together – 'Old Meg she was a gypsy', 'Oh I do like to be beside the seaside', 'O wha will shoe my bonny foot?'

'You with the sailor's clothes, whose are you?' an old crone cawed at me from the inglenook.

I gave my name.

'But you're Christina Marr's laddie, aren't you?'

I shook my head. I'd never heard of Christina Marr. But my grandmother's mother's maiden name was indeed Marr, and old wives who wanted an answer to the usual question would blithely omit the males of four generations and ignore your father. Especially if he was an incoming English sailor. Insular and matriarchal, that was St Monans.

'Well, give us a sea song anyway. Your dad was a sailor. But Captain Marr was a much greater one.'

I knew all about Captain Marr from Leebie, my four times great-uncle who'd captained a man-o'-war against Napoleon. The exact replica of his ship still swung suspended above the pulpit of the Old Kirk by the age-old umbilical that connected religion and the sea. So I astonished them by singing about Francis Drake, lying in his hammock, slung between the round shot in Nombre Dios Bay

'What kind of a song is that now?'

'Is that one of Georgina's weird numbers?'

'Can't you sing the Skye boat song?'

'Ssh! We all sail the same sea.'

After that we walked the mile to Balcaskie and made our way through the moaning woods, huddling as close as we could along the Bishop's Walk where the trees reached out and touched and our feet waded through cold rustling waves of leaves. At last we arrived at the mansion, hidden behind its ivy, except for the chimneys crenellating the sky. Hardly any lights were on. Enormous cockerels were pretending to be hedges. Lions stood on guard. We rang the bell and waited. Nothing happened.

'Let's ring again,' insisted Golly.

The rest of us were ready to turn tail, secretly relieved that the nobs hadn't come to look round-eyed at us for our audacity. But Golly explained that they'd all be busy dancing and drinking champagne and that the butler wouldn't come to see who it was until all the ladies had smoked their cigarettes right down to the silver holders and gone to the bathroom to check their make-up.

'And have a pee,' somebody said.

'Shut up! Ring again.'

And after the third ring the sound of shuffling footsteps could be heard, approaching so slowly that at times they almost seemed to be receding. But eventually the door was opened and we all stood staring at a wizened little old man almost lost in a pale-green tweed suit. A drooping moustache, a pale dome shining through the last of his hair, eyebrows out of control, and the eyes themselves moist blind blue sapphires that had long since ceased to register astonishment – or any other emotion.

'Ah, the guisers,' he nodded to himself. 'Of course.' And

he waved us inside as ceremoniously as if we were long expected honoured guests.

It was decided that 'Auntie Mary had a canary' would not be in order and that I was best qualified to come up with something congenial to the occasion. Stared at by stags' heads and standing among pieces of furniture made for titans, I sang the whole of the song about love and death which I had unearthed from Georgina's piano stool.

> *Come away, come away, death,*
> *And in sad cypress let me be laid;*
> *Fly away, fly away, breath;*
> *I am slain by a fair cruel maid.*
> *My shroud of white, stuck all with yew,*
> *O prepare it!*
> *My part of death, no one so true*
> *Did share it.*

The old man listened gravely, standing with both hands on the knobbly head of his black stick as I went on to the verse about the flowerless coffin and the solitary grave and the corpse without a sigh or a tear to mourn it. He stared intently into the worn carpet while his little wisp of a wife sat by the fire with her faded head to the side, nodding and smiling faintly. Then he tottered towards me.

'Good man, good man.'

We waited while he fumbled in his pocket.

'A most unusual piece for a young man, yes. And it's by a very great writer. Well done, well done.'

He pressed into my palm the clinking coins, cold from his stone cold fingers. Then we were offered some fruit to take away from a gleaming bowl on the sideboard – some shrivelled apples and oranges whose skins had turned to bark.

We went outside into the wind.

'What did he give you? Let's see.'

Two half-crowns.

'Five bob! It's a bloody fortune!'

After that the group made me sing Georgina's songs back at the village. But they never made an impression on anyone else.

Then it was home to the braeheads to dook for apples and eat treacle scones and count our winnings. We sat by the fireside in our creased and muddied costumes, our faces streaked with treacle and the remains of our make-up. The dowsed turnip lanterns, too close to the grate, started to stink and shrivel in the hearth. And Leebie told us stories of ghosts and ghouls, and of witches and vampires flying about the cobwebbed sky.

'Those born tonight', she croaked, 'will have the *taish*.'

'What's that?' we gaped.

'The *taish* is the second sight – you see something happening before it happens, sometimes years and years before.' And she told us the story of Captain Meldrum.

His grandmother had the second sight, and on the day he was born, the old woman pointed at him in the bed where he lay on his mother's breast, and this is what she said: 'Many's the green wave will he go over – and many's the green wave will go over him.'

And that's how it turned out. Agnes married him much against her mother's wishes, the old woman being herself a seer, and he died in the China seas, drowned there for ever.

I shivered at the thought of knowing the future, like Saul who knew in the middle of the night before the battle that he was going to die the next day. I was tired and cold and it was after midnight now. We were into November – the gloomiest month of the year.

The wind month. Not the clear winds from the north-west and north that brought quiet frosty weather, but the heavy easterlies that ferried the Flanders frosts to the coast. The wild winds, together with the fierce groundswells in the sea, ran for such a long time that mountains of weed were thrown up all along the sands — not the slack heads now but whole masses of oarweed and tangle, torn up by ground-swell and gale from the seabed and dragged inshore. They stretched for miles and the farmers came and collected them for manure.

These heavy swells, and the gales ceaselessly blowing in the North Sea, kept the big white waves pounding the shore. The divided labours of sun and moon conspired with them to stop the waters from ebbing effectively, and so the sea never went to sleep but went on with its worrying all through the month, when wind and water, the oldest sounds in the world, seemed to be all that ever were. When the tides did recede, the coast was strewn with bare rock pools in which nothing winked or waved, only the bitter ruffling of water all day long under a stiff wind. Standing disconsolately in one of these pools, I lost sight of my rubber-booted feet in just three or four inches of muddy water. The clarity would not return to it now until spring.

The harpist wind played everywhere, accompanied by rain. There was uproar in Balcaskie, where the Bishop's Walk was a long whirling mile of leaves and the wind screamed through the trees. Rotting sodden flowers and their dead seed-vessels were beaten into the earth, the black smells answering them, oozing out of the ground. This was November, the dismal trough of the year, choked with filth and fallen black branches streaming wetly. It was rawness and rotting and rain, the bleak blasting month when the earth's empty stage was swept by curtains of fog and the old men of the woods went storming to their graves. It was voices in the wind and clouds trailing thin rags of light, armies always on the march. When it seemed things couldn't get worse, they did. The rains fell harder, the skyline disap-peared, the gales gathered again, the trees tightening their toes in the earth, screeching and bending in the sea of wind, clutching at stones and bones.

And yet it was at this time, when you thought nothing could live, that the winter migrants came back to the coast – flocks of fieldfares clinging to the softer ground of the shore, where they scratched for their existence. Tough as they were, I often found one of them after a few days of hard frost, huddled in behind a dyke, dead where it had lain for shelter. Snow swaddled it in the Christmas month, and when spring came there would be a few feathers left in a tiny cage of bones – and in last year's nests some deserted eggs, staring out like cracked blue moons.

The curlews too were active on the land along with the lapwings and crows, the sky echoed with arrows of geese, whistling wintrily down from the north, and just offshore great flocks of mallards came in on the smooth water made by the north wind. All day they bobbed silently in the bay, as if they had come for no special purpose. Then at sunset they rose and flew in over the bare fields to pick up any stray potatoes that the onslaughts of frost and rain hadn't yet turned to purple stones and black mush. Often as I stood on the landward side of the house I could hear their quack-quacking coming from the moonlit fields where they continued to feed well into the night.

But by the end of the month I was listening for a different sound – the throb of returning engines on the water. They would all be coming home with the changing weather, back from Yarmouth with the hardening moons and the first dustings of snow. If there had been heavy rains early in the month, with the swollen streams running high, then a period of dry quiet weather followed by a hard and rapid frost, the waterdrops clinging to the over-hanging grasses quickly froze, and the weeds hung like wintry chandeliers across the solid ballroom floors of the streams, whorled and patterned as if by ghostly dancers during the night. That first whiteness was the sign of the last month of the year, when winter would blow through our bones.

Every day grew colder. There was no wind with it, just this huge hand, hard and cold as iron, gripping the earth, its fingers creeping out of the north, tighter during the soundless nights when only the stars tingled in space, and the black sea snapped at the shore. I took to creeping out of the house when everyone else was asleep and walking along to the kirkyard. Staring at the gravestones, glittering against the crackling sea, I knew that George's April lesson would prove true, that the time would come when I'd be nothing more than white bones frozen beneath an impenetrable armour of ice.

But April was a long way away and George's lessons had stopped. Something told me that my own fate was as nothing compared to the sheer splendour of the suffering world and its extremes, and the unutterable iciness of the stars. I knew this and yet exulted in it – knowing it was a kind of triumph over a universe that didn't know it, because it couldn't think at all, unlike the unprecedented unrepeatable me. I'd never heard of Descartes or Pascal, but my nocturnal senses told me then what reason taught later.

Tighter and whiter gripped the fingers in the clenched fist. In the sparkling mornings Geordie Haines's milk horse still stood in the meal-white streets like a horse of bronze, newly forged, the steam coming out of it and its head fuming in its nosebag as it snorted and stamped. Geordie himself stood slamming his arms across his chest and round his back, beating the ends of his frozen fingers and laughing and cursing loudly.

'Right brass monkeys' weather, this, bugger me!' he roared. 'Hang in there, you young fry, watch your tits don't drop off out here! The milk's frozen solid near enough!'

I ran out behind Jenny with the pitcher, holding it beneath Geordie's urn to catch the rich white waterfall that he sloshed carelessly off the back end of his cart, together with the frozen chunks that clashed in a welter of bubbles into the jug. In the wake of his cart the pools of spilt milk were already starting to freeze the whole length of the glazed street.

'All the way from the North Pole this morning, my lad!'

Once he handed me a long frozen poker of milk.

'There you are now, cockie, stick that in the hottest place you can find!' And he bent down from the cart and whispered something into Jenny's tingling ear.

She screamed and let fly at him with her jug. He bellowed loud laughter, his hands on his hips, while I hugged the pillar of milk and ran gasping with it into the house, crashing it into the sink among the startled women, then stood back slapping my burning finger-ends round my back and howling and hopping up and down as if the ghost of Shuggie had risen from the ice-bound graveyard and given me six of the best.

'Right brass monkeys' weather, this, bugger me!' I roared at them. 'Watch your tits don't drop off into the milk!'

Then I ran out whooping into the white tight world.

The day came when the great hand relaxed its grip a fraction, releasing the first few flakes of snow. They drifted down like the early gannets sometimes seen round the Bass in mid-December. But the sky darkened and the flakes thickened, fell in soft fast flurries into the fields and streets, wove a quick white shroud about the bare bodies of the trees. Sky and sea disappeared as the ghostly shoal enveloped us and we swam all night without bearings, bound for nowhere, prisoners of this soundless drifting.

But in the morning the shoal had vanished and the world was a white bride, clutching a bouquet of winter jasmine, the only flame in our garden. Somebody had stood the sun like a pitcher of cider on a high blue shelf. The whole countryside

glittered like an army, distant ponds flashing their shields
at us. Even the rock pools had frozen, and the seawater on
the sands, where the marram-grasses glinted like swords in
the sun. The seagulls standing sentinel on the kirk steeples
had turned to stone, their hearts cracked in the cold like the
sculptured doves on the kirkyard tombs. A robin turned his
breast up to the sun, a rusted brazier. Now and again a tiny
red footprint in the snow appeared – the blood of a rabbit
or hare, wounding the immaculate fields. Even indoors we
gulped down freezing draughts of air, drunk in dark dawns
before the first hot cups of tea, when our numb fingers
fiddled blindly with buttons and strings and we stood and
shivered uncontrollably. And on Sundays sprays of kirkyard
coughs were passed round like wreaths in the pews.

There were mixtures of syrup and honey and rum for the
coughs. Or there were kill-or-cure sledgings and slither-
ings and daredevillings on studded feet down braes become
glaciers and wynds that were lumpy rivers of glass. We were
soldiers and explorers. The Bass was a giant white polar
bear, asleep on the skyline, liable to be wakened by the first
gannets that had perched on his back since October. Glued
leaves crackled like rifle-shots underfoot, alerting us to the
retreat from Moscow, and with Cossacks picking us off all
the way from Balcaskie to the Blocks, we had no option but
to run the slippery zigzag all the way to the furthermost
point, while giant waves crashed across our path and rose
into the air like white churches before collapsing thunder-
ously on the other side, tons of water thundering down in
smithereens and salt. And not a man was lost on the final
run.

Our blood was up. Back we came, running red-faced and
sea-splashed all the way to the white frozen wave of the
kirkyard where we yelled fit to waken the dead. Then we
made for the homes of the aristocrats, Mr Brock the banker
and Mr Pagan-Grace the lawyer, their houses side by side,
their gardens always immaculate, just as they were now,

not a crumb of bread for the birds disturbing the spotless
tablecloths of pure white snow spread out from window to
wall. Conquest by division was our strategy. One platoon
prepared the snowballs while the other crept up to the
doors and laid hold of the knockers – doorknockers that
burned our fingers yearly with their flickering white fire –
and hammered loudly and long with the iron heads of lions
and Greeks before running back to the gate and waiting
for the fun. Two doors opened simultaneously, a brace of
astonished red faces – and the combined force hurled its
missiles, peppering the slippered, becardiganed enemy with
double-barrelled white fire.

'Come back, you blackguards! I'm phoning the bobby!'

'I know all your names! I know every one of you!'

But we were all behind our balaclavas and running like
snow leopards in all directions.

'You'll pay for it! You'll pay for it!'

'I'll be up at the school tomorrow! I'll pick you all out!'

We ran on and on into the eternal world of snow, our
chests bursting like Jamieson's bellows, our hearts like his
forge, each one a red pulsation in the whiteness of the dead
bewintered world.

Word came through then that the fleet had left.

Thirty hours later, in the smallness of the morning, we
were gathered at the harbour, a huddle of families waiting
to see the lights flecking the firth. Yarmouth brought back
rock for the youngsters, perfume for the young women,
glasses and presentation china for the old. The wedding-
flags were run up with cheers on the bridegrooms' boats,
and the brides brought out their house-fillings from below
the bed, the vases and pictures, the linen and crystal and

crockery that they'd been saving bit by bit since they left the school, and which their fathers and grandfathers had been bringing back from Yarmouth and Lowestoft and Shields year after year, piece by precious piece. For now was the marrying time and at last old Leebie found a verse to throw in the brazen face of time.

> *When December snows fall fast*
> *Marry and true love will last.*

Each man also brought back with him a barrel of salt herring for himself and his family. Grandfather's was a half-barrel and Alec and Billy brought a quarter-barrel each. The first salt herring from Yarmouth were rinsed, then roasted on the brander and served with heaps of potatoes, rifled from the clamps in the fields. There were cauldrons of kale and boiled beef. And as Christmas drew closer Guthrie's windows filled up with rounds of shortbread, each one bearing the design of a different drifter and its name and number.

Work was over now for the drifterman till the second day of January. Only the fireman spent a laborious week inside the boat's boiler, chipping away at three months of encrusted salt. But grandfather was hardly home a day before his restless legs were off again, gathering sea-coal from the shore, which sparked and spat in the grate all night long. For coal was often scarce and the braehead fire was never allowed to die.

Sitting in front of the fire at last, grandfather celebrated the fish which multiplied so miraculously and fed so many thousands of families and yet which he killed in its millions. Along with all the old men of his time, he believed that the herring swam down from the Arctic and made a circuit round the British Islands once in the course of a year, and that for every ring that it completed, time put a ring on each of its scales. By counting the number of rings you could tell the age of the fish, just as you could with a tree – just as he counted the ring of candles on my twelfth birthday, for the last time.

Mystical cycle or complete myth, what mattered was that he believed it, just as he believed in the fish itself, almost worshipping it. He sat me down on the pier once and showed me the features that made it so unique, the rings on the scales, the streamlined shape and forked tail which made it swim so far and fast, the silvery-white belly and blue-green back, the one merging with the sea, the other with the sky, giving it its double protection from predators of fur and fin, though not from a man with a net. He held a female in his hand and stroked its belly.

'Thirty thousand eggs a year come out of that one little belly. If I didn't catch them the seas would be solid with herring from coast to coast. Can you imagine that?'

I imagined it – and once again saw grandfather walking on the water.

He laughed at my expression.

'As long as they keep on coming I'll have to keep on catching them, I suppose.'

'Won't they ever stop coming?' I asked.

'Not till I stop catching them,' he said. 'When I stop, they'll stop. We're inseparable, just you wait and see.'

Then he was off to sea again, leaving me with his words for the rest of my life.

'Northerlies bring you nothing,' he used to say. 'Give me a good steady south-west breeze and I'll bring you back a hundred cran with every shot.'

He knew from observation what marine science confirms. Always the fish swam into the wind in the unseen currents between the surface and the seabed, and a compensating flow in this stream took them in the opposite direction to the wind and at a faster rate of drift, and so the herring made their way. A north wind held up the southward movement of the shoals and an east wind lured them further from the coast. But a south-west breeze brought them down and close to shore, where the nets were waiting and the old men stood with their nostrils flared, grandfather on deck with a smile on his face.

'I don't have to sniff for herring,' he once said. 'If they're there I can taste them in the air.'

So the crews cast their curtains over the starboard side, fifty feet deep and two miles long, steaming on their way till the long meshed wall was unfurled in the water. And it hung there while the boat drifted quietly with the tide, coming back on board like a sheet of shining silver shivering madly in the moon. They steamed furiously for harbour then with their perishable cargo, and the sweat would barely grow cold on their faces before they returned to the herring grounds, fishing in the same old way all through the months of September and October and November, and back again in winter and summer and autumn the following year, year in year out. And they did all this on little sleep and wet sea legs, on beef puddings and suet duffs. Their medicines were Friar's Balsam and Sloane's Liniment, Gregory's Powder and Carlton's Dutch Drops, and their bandages were of red flannel, cut from their women's petticoats and soaked in paraffin to take out the sting of the saltwater boils.

And finally they came in to rest.

It was Christmas Eve. After dark I went out with grandfather and we took the deserted road to Balcaskie, white in the moon. We were off for our Christmas tree. Grandfather walked slightly ahead of me, the end of his cigarette glowing redly in his cupped palm as he shaded it from the wind. We sang together as we walked.

> *Brightly shone the moon that night,*
> *Though the frost was cruel,*
> *When a poor man came in sight,*
> *Gathering winter fuel.*

When we neared the wood we stopped our singing and went in whispers, walking in silence through the trees, the snow starting to fall again in the world outside. The Bishop's Walk, roofed and carpeted by nature, kept us dry. Grandfather still led the way, his cigarette end bobbing like a red boat-lamp through the dark. I followed it as it veered off into the spruces and firs and pines, then stopped. I knelt down beside him as he opened his jacket and took out the saw. Quietly, gently, his cigarette in his mouth the whole time, he took down a small fir, the property of the rich man in his mansion. I remembered Hallowe'en and suggested to grandfather that if I sang the old man a carol he might let us take an even bigger one.

'Better not bother him,' grandfather said, 'he might tell you to take the whole wood!'

On the way out grandfather picked us some greenery and a sizeable log for the fire, a Yule, and we lifted up our voices again when we were well clear of the estate, the thickly falling flakes burning our open mouths.

> *Page and monarch, forth they went,*
> *Forth they went together,*
> *Through the rude wind's wild lament*
> *And the bitter weather.*

The tree spread the secrets of the wood around the room, a totem glittering in its tinsel. Some gifts were laid in front of it. The holly and the ivy made a grove of the walls. Birdsong whistled from the wet firewood and the screwtops were opened and cigarettes lit, grandfather rolling his with one hand and without even looking. His stockinged feet were on the fender and his head was back, eyes closed. He'd be asleep soon.

But Georgina sang us a carol about a spotless rose blowing at midnight in a cold cold winter, and he opened his eyes again for a bit. Then she sang 'In the Bleak Midwinter' and he closed them again. When he woke up he took the half-burned Yule log out of the fire, saving it to light up the new log next Christmas. He ran out with it on the shovel into the yard, where he threw it, spitting and snarling into the snow, dying among clouds of smoke and steam and popping sparks. Our chimney smoke was drifting up into the stars. George's window was an open blackness and his chimney was cold.

'He's not long for this earth,' grandfather said, putting his hand on my shoulder, 'and he'll go out in his own way.'

The gravestones glittered like sentinels on the kirkyard hill. Down beneath us, over the rooftops of the town, the breakers foamed, pounding the shore. An alien eternity was grinding its teeth.

I went to bed to wait for Santa Claus to swing into our tiny port, tie up on the pier, and perform his secret ministry. But I knew that grandfather was really Father Christmas, and the unseen presents from Yarmouth were waiting downstairs. Midnight was striking in the black belfry of the year, flinging out the wild white chimes of Christmas. And I knew that in just a week's time Regulus would be rising on the first day of January at nine o'clock, a starseed of spring sown in the dark, and that grandfather too would be rising for his last day at home. The following morning he'd be off again to the winter herring.

As always.

8

The Village Spade

If the worlds of work and nature wove a double rhythmic spell, sealing off childhood terrors, the seal was broken every time I headed for Alec Fergusson's house by the church, or looked in on him at his work. It would have made perfect sense to stay away. But there was another sense, a moth-and-candle-flame sense, in which Alec was always waiting for you. So I went slowly by the back gardens, past the old ladies washing their long white hair in the rain barrels. Or I detoured the streets, where the same old ladies, their hair now up in netted buns, were out shopping, their string bags dangling as low as their hems, even with the pitiful contents – a half loaf, a couple of carrots, an onion, a scraggy pork chop from Grant's, just enough to keep them from their Saviour for one more day, before Alec dug a hole for them. As he did for all of us.

There in the kirkyard, his black bent outline etched against the glimmering sea, Alec toiled among his grave-stones. He considered his gravedigger's duties a calling, no mere crust-of-bread occupation, he left you in no doubt about that. But let him speak for himself now, just as he spoke to me fifty years ago.

Sexton here sixty years (he always started by telling you

that, as if a thousand tellings hadn't registered it with you) and just a day off eighty now.

(Curiously, he was always just a day off eighty. He never moved in that respect. Maybe he was eighty. Maybe he was a hundred and eighty. I don't know. I do know I'm interrupting him, though.)

Yes, sixty years, man and boy. I worked with my father when I was ten, and took over the job from him when he died. Literally. I was twenty and the first grave I had to dig was my father's. He was digging a grave the day he died, and had almost done when he collapsed on the spot and died in the grave. And do you know what his immortal last words were? 'Finish it for me, son!' That's all he had to say. I suppose it was all he had time to say, but you'd think a man would use that last precious breath for something a bit more memorable, wouldn't you? 'Finish it for me!' It's quite practical but hardly encourages philosophical contemplation, now does it? Me, on the other hand, I'm something of a philosopher as well as a practical man.

Puff puff. (Sometimes Alec remembered to put a match to his pipe, but in or out, it was always clenched in his teeth, and he either talked through it or through the blue narcotic haze, Death drawing nicely and making the silence fragrant. Then after a few puffs he'd get into his stride.)

I've never actually taken an exact count, though I could work it out from the records, but I reckon I've put upwards of six thousand folk into the ground. That's near six times the town's population today. Just think, I've buried the whole village six times over, single-handed. That's a lot of digging. What do you think has kept me so fit? That – and going to the lobsters.

Most folk imagine there's a thousand jobs they'd rather do than dig a grave for a living, and sure enough, it wouldn't suit everybody. But look at it this way. The kirkyard here is right hard against the sea, and it's a cold enough business in winter – but I'm breathing the best fresh air to be had on God's earth, I'm out here in the open, and I'm doing a lot of bending and stretching that keeps my joints supple, in spite of my age. I've never had a sore back in my life.

Look at it another way. I'm more or less my own master. Nobody breathes down your neck when you're digging a grave, least of all the one you're digging it for. It's a trouble-free occupation. You make a hole in the ground, deposit a box in a safe place, pile on the earth and put back the turf. What could be simpler?

Mind you, it's surprising the lengths some folk will go just to avoid an hour or two of labour. A mile up the coast you'll find a man in my trade who's made up a hexagonal frame, shaped like a coffin and not much bigger. He lays it on the earth and digs inside it. He drew me a diagram once to show me how he was saving himself nearly half the digging. He worked it out exactly by geometry. To me that's no way to dig a grave – by geometry, and with your eye on the clock. No way at all.

In some places they use mechanical diggers. The grave-digger just touches a button and pulls a lever and watches a load of metal do the rest. Gravedigger? He doesn't even deserve the title. To me that's soulless. It's possible, believe me, to dig a grave with feeling, especially if it's for somebody you've known. You can take pride in it, just as if you were building a house for the man – which in a sense you are, a house that lasts till doomsday, which makes you a better builder than the mason, the shipwright or the carpenter. You see? I'm not an uneducated man for an old spade. I've read some Shakespeare and I've read the *Prince of Denmark*. Hamlet says to his friend Horatio, about one of the gravediggers, 'Hath this fellow no feeling of his business that he sings at gravemaking?' And Horatio says, 'Custom hath made it in him a property of easiness.' He's used to it, in other words. Well, I think that misses the point. No professional ever dug a grave with a long face. It's a job. There's no question of having to get accustomed to it. But that doesn't mean you can't dig with dignity.

That's something a machine can't do. The least one man can do for another is to personalize his resting-place for him. Mechanical diggers! Can you imagine? Next they'll be having mechanical ministers to conduct the service, just you wait and see.

In a manner of speaking we've got some of them around here as it is. Dull of soul, that's what they are. Not Kinnear, mind you, he's got fire in his belly all right, but when you listen to some of them reading the Order for the Burial of the Dead, they might as well be reciting from the back of a cornflakes packet. For as many times as I've heard it, the funeral service is one of my favourite pieces of reading. I used to enjoy hearing the bits from the Book of Job.

Man that is born of woman hath but a short time to live and his days are full of sorrow . . . My days are swifter than a weaver's shuttle and are spent without hope . . . We brought nothing into this world and it is certain we can carry nothing out.

Passages like that fairly put life in perspective for you, so that you can see death as not so bad after all, if life's so terrible.

Few things used to be so grand as one of the old-style ministers pointing his finger at the coffin in the open grave and proclaiming that worms would destroy that body. That was impressive, dramatic. One old stager was fond of quoting from one of the Paraphrases.

The wood shall hear the voice of spring
And flourish green again,
But man forsakes this earthly scene,
Ah! never to return!

That sort of thing made you come away from a funeral with something to think about. But some of them these days are happy enough with the earth-to-earth, ashes-to-ashes bit, and even that they get over with as quick as they can, as if it were indecent to remind the mourners that their loved one is just a pile of dust, and that that's all they are too, kirkyard mould. Some of them even tell me not to bother stepping up to the grave with my spadeful of dirt during that part of the service – that's when I scatter some soil on to the coffin – and I'm always disappointed when that happens. I feel I haven't done my job.

In the old days the ministers weren't frightened of dirtying their own hands from my shovel, even on a wet and muddy day. One man used to grab a fistful of clay as tightly as he could, and hold it up to the mourners, shaking it in their faces before he threw it on to the coffin. That was one way of showing a man what he really is. But not any more. Folk just can't look death squarely in the face these days and that's a fact.

I think it all stems from the modern attitude to death. What with all these clever operations and medical machines and pills being pumped into folk to keep them pegging on long after they ought to have died – they start seeing death as something unnatural instead of the most obvious thing in the world. I'll tell you, nothing strikes me as simpler than the fact that one day I'll just be a few shards of bone lying in the earth somewhere, and after that just kirkyard clay and nothing more.

It's not that I'm not frightened of death. Everybody's frightened of death in one way or another, whether they're religious or not. I don't fancy the actual process of dying, for one thing. There might be nothing in it, of course, like falling asleep after dinner. But you can never tell. There could be pain and prostration, and nobody actually looks forward to that, the indignity and hopelessness of it all. I don't want to die in my sleep, though. I can't understand folk who say a man was lucky to have died in his sleep. Lucky? To have missed the big scene? The curtain call? I'd feel cheated.

I'll tell you something else. Old as I am, I still don't feel I've had enough of the world. I enjoy my job, whether it's a fine rimy morning in November or an afternoon of butter-flies and bees. I like reading and listening to the wireless, smoking my pipe and drinking a jug of beer. Most of all I enjoy just watching the world go by, the boats going up and down the firth, the gulls sailing about me, coming down for the worms, the seasons turning over. When I think that all that can still go on without me, I suppose I do feel a sort of fear, stronger than fear even – a kind of black panic, a rebel-lious frenzy, an unwillingness to accept extinction. You have to control that sometimes.

And then there's the fear of what comes next. You just don't know – and there's nothing more frightening than not knowing. Even a bairn knows that kind of fear, fear of the dark. And the older you get, let me tell you, the more of a bairn you become, maybe because you're getting closer to the dark again.

Not that I'm an atheist – don't think that. I don't think I could do the job if I was an atheist. If I thought death was just a mass grave, a bottomless pit into which the genera-tions have been tumbling blindly since the beginning of time, I'm sure I'd go off my head. I don't know what happens to the mystery that is me once they sling the rubbish that's left into the kirkyard here, but I do know that a man is more than muscle and bone and brains and blood.

Once when I was opening up a really old grave, a man came and looked in at what I was doing. He said he was a lecturer from the university at St Andrews – a geologist, that's what he said he was, so he must have been one of the clever folk. I came on some bones that were so old they were badly discoloured and just flaked away like rotten wood when I touched them with the spade.

He said to me, 'The bible says that these bones will live again. Looking at them now, can you really believe that?'

I said to him, 'Looking at them now, can you really believe that they ever lived in the first place?'

That quietened him. But that's the thing, you see. When you're in my job you're coming across human remains all the time – teeth, bones, skulls, they're all over the place. It's hard to picture flesh on them again, and to remember that muscles once moved them, that they danced and sang and steered ships, that they had eyes that looked at the sea, a brain that understood it, a soul that loved it and lips that spoke about it. All that's hard to believe and yet everybody knows it's true. Frankly I don't find the reverse any harder to credit – that they'll live again, I mean.

From that point of view I reckon my job puts me in a privileged position. There are some folk that have never seen a corpse in their lives. The undertaker comes between them and the dead, saves them from even having to look. But even the undertaker sees a body much as it looked in life. I see further than that, further than any man, after corruption has done its work and the spirit has gone to God. Between the undertaker and God there's only me. That's quite a field, believe me.

I see them all on their way – schoolteacher, doctor, provost. They may have had better brains than some, and they may have better headstones than the town drunkard, but the same grass covers them, and beneath that it's a classless society, let me tell you. Coffins? Don't talk to me about coffins. Solid oak or pitch pine, they all rot away and earth's what you're left with. An orange box would have done the business. Or nothing at all. After that, break up the honeycomb and you find one man smells as sweet as another. Pride, arrogance, selfishness, good looks – all have an ending here.

I'll tell you another thing. There's folk buried side by side here that would never have given each other as much as the time of day. They would have passed each other in the street with their faces turned and their noses in the air. And now they're sleeping partners till the last trumpet. There's families too that bitched among themselves till there weren't two left to row with one another. Now they're lying together as peaceful as you like, them that would never have shared the same room, let alone a bed. I've crammed them all in. Sometimes it's been a squeeze and I've had to go down deep and pack them like kippers, cheek by jowl. But there's never a murmur, you can be sure of that.

Which suits me just fine, the peace and quiet. Fine decent folk, the dead – that was the punch line of a sexton up north, in a story I once read, and he hit the nail on the head.

Mind you, this place has its horrors. There was a typhoid epidemic here just before the first war and it had me working myself down to a shadow. It got so busy that some of the bereaved had to come and do their own digging. I just didn't have enough hours in the day. The kirkyard looked like a field of giant mole-hills. Sometimes the doctor told me not to bother filling in the grave after a burial – it would be needed again within the week, or even within the hour, with members of the same family falling victim to the disease. It went like wildfire.

Anyway, it had only just blown itself out, the weeping and wailing were over, and the whole town was walking about wearing black, when somebody reported that an old tinker who camped in the field opposite where the school is now – Tinker Johnny, they called him – had caught the tail-end of the storm and died.

Six men were paid a high price to take a coffin up to his tent, and they nailed him down on the spot. They were all wrapped up in gloves and masks. Then they hoisted him shoulder-high and started off with him to the kirkyard. That's the other end of the town, as you know, so it was a long haul. There was no minister and no procession. He got a hymn, though.

They were only halfway to the kirkyard when one of the pallbearers thought he heard something. But they were passing the boat-building shed and with all that commotion going on they weren't sure. Then after a while they all heard it and they stopped and listened. Sure enough, there was a groaning coming from inside the box. They laid it down and looked at one another. Then without a word they hoisted it back up on their shoulders and walked on. They didn't want the whole thing starting off again, did they? No, the sick man was safer inside his box.

Then the old tinker actually started knocking on the lid of the coffin. By this time they were in Shore Street, where folk were going about their business, and the man was fairly hammering away and shouting. So to drown out his cries for help, they struck up one of the Paraphrases.

> O may the grave become to me
> The bed of peaceful rest,
> Whence I shall gladly rise at length
> And mingle with the blest!

That's what one of them started to sing, so I'm told, and they all joined in. Raising their voices like a congregation, they carried him all the way to the grave I'd already dug for him. I couldn't believe my eyes and ears.

'But the man's alive!' I said. 'Good God Almighty, he's as alive as you or me!'

And all these eyes looked at me, staring at me between the hats and the black crêpe masks.

'Yes, he's alive, Alec,' one of them said. 'But he's going to die anyway. Are you going to die along with him? Take off that lid and you might as well lie down in the grave with him!'

What would you have done? Would you have opened the box? And taken a blast of all that diseased air, right in your face? I'm sorry to say I turned my back and said it was up to them. I was off to the lobsters. They lowered him into his grave then, and all six of them went mad, spading in the earth, and him screaming and hammering all the while.

Can you imagine what it must have been like for him, hearing the first clods come thudding on to the coffin lid, and the sound of the spades gradually dying away? Then a darkness and a silence that you just can't conceive.

Worse than that, though, is picturing what it was like for them. How long before the earth muffled his cries, if at all? Would cries like that ever leave you, even in your sleep? For the old tinker the struggle would have been short compared to theirs. Every time they looked up from their work, in the direction of the kirkyard hill, wouldn't they hear that endless scream coming out of it?

Well, that's not the end of it either. Seeing as it was a tinker's grave and never paid for, the plot was reserved for victims of fortune – vagrants, suicides, corpses washed up on shore, that sort of thing. You'd think there would have been a taker or two, wouldn't you? But it was quite some years till I had occasion to open up that plot again. And I'll never forget the sight that met my eyes. It made my blood run cold. The man had gnawed off the fingers of one hand in his despair. You could see it at a glance. The rest of the bones were like a Chinese puzzle, all twisted into the most awful shapes you could imagine. It was the sound-picture of a scream, white as you like against the black earth, a scream that had never stopped. They had a voice, those bones. And I'll tell you what, I was damned if I was going to be the only one left with the nightmares. So I rounded them up, the men that had done it, and made them come up and look. They cursed me for it, I can tell you. After that I smashed the pattern to bits with my spade and the noise in my ears went away. But it was hellish, the worst thing I've ever seen in my life. And I dream about it to this day.

That's one of the few disadvantages of the job – you see some sad sights. It's not folks' remains that bother me, it's the things they get buried with that sometimes get me. Wedding rings, still round the bone, though mostly they're taken off. But on occasion a partner refuses to have the ring removed. Photographs are usually blotted out by the time you get to them, but now and again you can make them out. What I hate most are bairns' toys, dolls and stuff like that. In fact it's these tiny wee skeletons that bother me the most. I can never get used to them. There are precious few infant burials these days, but they happen all the same, and the older graves are full of them. What's the point of being born at all, I ask myself, if you're buried within a year? I've never yet heard a decent answer to that one. Another cherub in heaven. One more sunbeam for God. Hasn't he got enough of them? What kind of answer is that to a heart-broken mother?

Digging up somebody you've known, to make room for a relative, that's something that puts me neither up nor down as a rule. I do it all the time. But every now and then it gets under my skin. It depends on who it is.

I felt like that when I came across Rob Lumsden, for example, eleven years after I'd put him in. Lord Lumsden, they called him – he was the chimneysweep for years and years, and a kinder man you couldn't hope to meet. He'd a heart of gold and a fund of funny stories, and he told more lies than there are hairs on a cat, though they made good listening, that's for sure. But the bottle was what made and unmade him. It was great to see him up there, roaring drunk and lurching along the rooftops in all weathers, singing like a lark among the lums. Maybe that's why they called him Lord Lumsden – that and his fondness for the drink. He was always as drunk as a lord. It was drink that put him to his grave, with a broken neck.

I remember the morning I looked in on him. I'd never seen him with anything but a black face. Even his wife begged Jimmy Miller not to clean him up for his coffin. 'Let him go with a bit of soot on him,' she said, 'just the way he always was.' And for some reason the sight of that white skull – not a spot of soot to be seen – gave me a bad turn. I just sat down on the edge of his grave and blubbed.

I felt weird too when I came across Peggy Wilson, the day I was putting her old father to bed. She was a local beauty here fifty years ago, a real stunner she was. The young men would give anything just to walk her along the braes and hold her hand for half an hour by the kirkyard wall. I often used to see her hereabouts and she always gave me the time of day, not like most of the women round here. Who wants to go out with the gravedigger, after all? Even a young gravedigger, as I was then.

She stopped speaking to me, though, after what happened one Sunday. I was taking a walk up at Balcaskie when I heard these screams coming from an open field. It was Peggy Wilson. There were hives in the field and she'd got over-curious. I dare say she fancied some honey. She didn't know much about bees, though, that's for sure. They were fizzing round her in a great big swarm, hundreds of them, and she was going frantic. There was nobody else about. I ran across the field like mad, but by the time I got to her they were all over her like she was jam, and right inside her clothes, underwear and all. There was only one thing to be done. She was wearing a light summer dress and I just gripped her and ripped every stitch off her back in one go. Then I ran with her bare buff to the cattle trough at the edge of the field and plunged her in. I had to shoulder my way through the beasts, they were that thirsty with the heat, but it got rid of the bees, all right. After that I carried her dripping wet into the farmhouse. You should have seen their faces. She was nearly unconscious by that time, she'd been so badly stung, and I'd collected a few stings myself. Lucky for her there happened to be a doctor there at the time, otherwise she'd have died for sure.

Well, she avoided me after that, she was so embarrassed that I'd seen her all. Little did she know that I'd see her

down to the bare bone. Less than a year later she was gored
to death by the Balcaskie bull, running mad in the meadows
– a right bad beast that was – and the young man that was
with her was maimed for life trying to save her. Lord, you'd
think she'd have stayed away from Balcaskie, but the young
folk liked to do their courting up there, it being nice and
private like, and Balcaskie had marked her card for her. She
was put to an early grave and a bloody shame that was.

I had to dig into that ground twenty years back. What
a turn it gave me! Her hair used to light up her face like
sunlight. God, she was lovely! And to look at her then! 'To
this favour she must come.' That's what Hamlet says, you
see. Talking about Lord Lumsden too, it puts me in mind of
another verse.

> *Golden lads and girls all must*
> *As chimney-sweepers come to dust.*

That's Shakespeare too, isn't it? Anyway, these are some
of the shocks you get.

You wouldn't think gravedigging had its lighter moments,
but it does. One time I had to fill up a grave I'd just dug
because it turned out the old man it was for wasn't dead
after all. They call him Cheat-the-Grave round here. He got
the length of the mortuary then sat up and asked for a cup
of tea. Since then he's been on his death-bed times without
number, till his family are fed up to the back teeth with him.
To make matters worse he's a Catholic, and the priest in
Pittenweem who just has his push bike for transport, he's
pedalled that journey God knows how often to administer
the last rites. Once he had a puncture and just turned back.
He said it was a sign, and that by the time he got back to
the chapel the old bugger would be well again. And that's
the way it turned out. I heard somebody say that if there's
one more false alarm he's threatened to send the last rites
by telegram.

As for me, I'm like doubting Thomas. I'll want to poke him in the ribs a few times, and maybe stick a pin in, before I lift up my spade to turn a foot of soil on his behalf again. He's unkillable. Sometimes you just have to laugh.

A real killer, though, and anything but a laugh, is one of the Flanders frosts in January or February, which is my busy time. I know some men that will use a drill to break up the first foot or two of earth. But not me. I don't hold with machinery under any circumstances. Mattock and spade, these are my tools, even in a Flanders frost. And a pickaxe if I'm stuck. One winter I couldn't get the leeks out of my garden even with the pickaxe. That season the frost went on for three months solid without a break, and folk were dying at the rate of knots. Digging graves that year was no joke, let me tell you.

Trees can be a pest as well. The roots spread everywhere and I've sometimes had to put down the spade and get out the saw. I've seen skeletons looking as if an underground octopus had got hold of them, roots twisting right through eye-sockets and everything, it's incredible.

I must tell you, though, there's one compensation and that's my elderberry trees – these are the trees that line the west wall. I make my own wine from the berries and I can tell you I've had some great vintages from them. What else would you expect? They're fed with the best compost you can get, these trees, their toes are right in among the boxes, tapping all the goodness. I offered the last minister a glass of the stuff and he just couldn't get enough of it. It made him fair tipsy. He wanted the recipe. Then, when I told him what it was and where it had come from, he was mortified. Literally. Now that's something I can't understand. All flesh is grass, I told him – he ought to have known that, it's his business to know it, after all. The whole universe is eating and drinking itself, isn't it? But he thought it was gruesome, my store of elderberry wine, made from mortality and drawn from the cellars of the dead. Château La Mort, I call it. Kinnear's not squeamish about it, though. He'll drink any amount.

I've an elderberry tree in my own garden and I make wine from that as well. Not with human compost, though. I'll tell you what I do. I dig in dead cats wherever I can find them. They're the best. The farmer once gave me a whole sheep, but a sheep can't compete with a cat. Cats improve the flavour of your fruit no end. I won't take cats from McCreevie, though. I don't approve of drownings. I've got nothing against cats. I've got a cat at home myself and we're the best of friends. But after he's dead he'll do me one last service. Why not? Waste not, want not, that's what I say.

If anybody sees anything wrong in that, it just goes to show that what I was saying earlier is true. There's too much squeamishness about death these days, and not enough poetry. Every year, before the fruit forms on these elders, you get the white flowers. On summer nights the fragrance can be really piercing and they're like scented stars hanging just above your head. As if the dead had come out for the night in another form. That's when I'm always put in mind of that other bit from Omar Khayyám.

> Now the New Year reviving old Desires,
> The thoughtful Soul to Solitude retires,
> Where the White Hand of Moses on the Bough
> Puts out, and Jesus from the Ground suspires.

But folk just don't think like that any more. They don't write like that either.

You can see that from most of the modern-day headstones and their epitaphs. They used to take some trouble over a stone in the old days, with the emblems of mortality carved along the top and sides – skull and bones, the sexton's tools, the hour-glass and the Angel of Death. And usually a grand-sounding verse on the back. I know all the headstone poems by heart. This one, for example:

Naked as from the earth we came,
And entered life at first;
Naked we to the earth return,
And mix with kindred dust.
How still and peaceful is the grave!
Where, life's vain tumults past,
Th'appointed house, by Heav'n's decree
Receives us all at last.

They didn't have to be as long as that either, to be impressive, these old inscriptions. One of them here just reads, 'Here lies all that *could* die of John Brown.' Think of the faith that lies behind that one little word, 'could'. You've got to admire it. You don't get faith like that nowadays.

The stones got smaller in this century – and so the verses got smaller too. Still, up to a wee while ago they always left room at the bottom for a nice bit of scripture, a consoling sort of text, like *Until the day break and the shadows flee away,* or just *The morn cometh,* something like that. But these days you usually get palmed off with something really uninspiring. *Sadly missed.* What do you think of that? No religious feeling behind it at all, not even any poetry. That's what I miss most of all, the poetry.

Some of the really recent ones have nothing at all on them, apart from the names and dates of the deceased. Can you imagine anything more dull of soul? There's one here that was put up just the other day – that young chap that was killed on his motorbike. Do you know what his epitaph is? I'll tell you. *A great Elvis fan.* I ask you! What will that mean to somebody clearing away rubble and dust from here in a couple of centuries from now? A great Elvis fan! What kind of immortality is that? I suppose it's appropriate enough to our age, with its cheap tin gods that don't even last out the age itself. It's as I say, there's no poetry left in death now. It's not just a matter of economics, though there's that to consider. It's the spirit that's missing as well as the flesh.

From the point of view of feeling as well as finance, folk are just no longer giving death his due. That's a fact.

The gravestones in Alec's kirkyard were my first books, I suppose, stories written in stone, some of which he showed me and all of which I devoured for myself as soon as I was able to read. The kirkyard was an open library, sprayed by the sea. Crystals of salt illuminated the letters so that they sparkled in the sun, lichens blotched the lines like mildew. Soon the fragrance of fried herring came dancing among the gravestones from the direction of Alec's open window, mingling with the butterflies. It was easy to sit here and submit to time and heat, while summer was gold-plating the firth and the sun's unstrung necklace lay broken over the bay, a scattering of beads, bouncing in front of my half-closed eyes. Just over the wall the sea's pale-blue dress whispered like silk, drew back its curving hem, petti-coats of surf, and I knew then that all my ancestors were doomed lovers. The sea was their femme fatale. She wove webs of sunlight that netted them like lobsters, bewitching even the strongest, the bible-boatmen who had steered a straight course through life, till she took them from wives to waves, and the cold caress of conger and crab. Out there somewhere they were salt and coral, vague as the shifting of the sands on the shore, lines of hair parted by the wind, time's whispers along the skull, wrinkles imperceptible as ageing. The tides ebbed and flowed over them without desti-nation, irrational and inarticulate as the years. There was something safer about the graveyard's green memory bank, where the generations slept, too deep for tears. And so for a time I haunted the place like a revenant, resurrecting the sleepers in my mind, saying their names to the sea air, whis-pering their years to a wind of weathers. I fed deeper and deeper on their vanished lives, still available by the volume, on permanent loan. In spite of Alec's horror stories, there was something satisfyingly fixed and final about this place, free from the frightening flux of life. Here I was at peace.

It wasn't to last. It was the family funerals that put an end to my safe house and personal library.

The funerals were my first acquaintance with drama. Refining the rawness of human grief, they elevated it to the status of tragedy, played out on the coast's rocky colosseum to the listening amphitheatre of the sea. Penman's bell rang in the streets, summoning the audience, beating open a black hole in the kirkyard turf, which Alec covered with boards until the day of the funeral. And the gods took their seats.

Always the funeral service was held in the house of the departed, where the corpse was laid out, given the last longing, lingering looks – a black procession of eyes – and finally screwed down. Eternity lay just behind those closed eyelids and it was always a relief when they were hidden from sight. A house of death was recognizable by its drawn blinds. I used to hurry past in the street, wondering what it would be like to be on the inside of such an establishment.

My time came soon enough. Uncle Jimmy, the sailmaker, died in his sleep one night, and three days later we all sat in silence in the Elm Grove kitchen, a solid black circle of suits and shoes and dresses, so seldom worn that they creaked and squeaked and whispered whenever anyone made the slightest movement. So nobody moved. You could hear everybody breathing, though, packed together round the fire, sitting on borrowed chairs, not speaking, waiting for the minister. The coffin was apart from us in the best room, old uncle Jimmy lying in state behind polished oak and brass, alone among the faded family photographs in their cold frames, alone in the cold and darkness of wherever he was – nobody knew where for sure, but we could all hear the continuous hushed roar of the silence he now inhabited. It deafened us as we listened to it between the hideously slow and heavy tickings of the grandfather clock. Eternity, eternity, eternity. Hell, hell, hell. Tick, tick, tick.

Rat-a-tat-tat, bang, bang. The knocking on the door – no timid fist, that one. It shattered the closed circle with the relief of the outside world breaking in.

'That'll be the minister now, let him in, somebody.'

Mr Kinnear filled up what was left of the room when he came in. A big, black-coated bear, blowing heavily, unnecessarily, smelling of the pews, he rubbed his huge hands together briskly, a hale and hearty antidote to death, and nodded to the fire.

'Nice blaze there, yes, grand to see a fire today, the year's drawing in now. How are you, Mrs Main?'

Silence.

The fire burned. The clock ticked. The silence roared. We adjusted ties, hats, handkerchiefs. What was it we were waiting for exactly?

Then Mr Kinnear put his back to the fire, looked up at the low ceiling, and cleared his throat. 'In the midst of life we are in death . . .'

I had never heard the words till that day, not even in church. They were reserved for the funeral service. Now they hit me like a gong, confirming the triumph of death over my decade. In the midst of life we are in death. It was true. It had always been true. One of the sea-facing stones Alec had shown me had long since lost its names and dates. But the epitaph survived on the reverse side. It read simply, *O! thou Adam, what hast thou done?* This said it all. The whole promiscuous boneyard was Adam's work, the whole thrust of life itself stifled and negated by the first great sinner. The wages of sin is death. And now uncle Jimmy had reaped Adam's reward. As would we all.

Mr Kinnear's bellowing was filling up the room.

We are like grass which groweth up. In the morning it flour-isheth and in the evening it is cut down and withereth . . .

And then a few words on uncle Jimmy, who had sat on his low, dark brown bench all the days of his life, now defined as futile, with his sailmaker's tools and his heavy drooping moustaches; uncle Jimmy, who had always looked so sad because he was born of woman and his days were few and full of sorrow; uncle Jimmy, who was being moved out of the best room now, feet first, and into the waiting hearse, to take his last journey. The rooms were small and the hallway narrow. The undertakers were having a hard time manoeuvring the coffin. There were six feet of uncle Jimmy, one of Miller's biggest boxes.

Yet it was only yesterday he'd been a boy, so he'd told me, running down the brae for the butcher's fat, the day he spoke about barking the sails. I remembered the sea's blue immensity at our backs and how he'd sat in the sun, shading his eyes as he talked. Soon he would be with his friends, he said, and he took off his cap, revealing just a few fronds of sea-bleached hair. I couldn't fathom the net of veins on that wrinkled head. So I'd sat there and watched him die, sentence by slow sentence in the sun. There was a picture of him on the mantelpiece, the sail spread stiffly over his knees and tumbling on to the floor like solid water. Only when the four winds blew into his canvases did the stillness of his life's work take on form and movement, when the dark fins of the Fifies cut the sky and a forest waved in the firth. Now they'd wrapped a shroud round the tall mast of his years and taken him down.

'That's him left the house now,' said auntie Elspeth, dabbing her eyes, 'for the last time.'

But uncle Jimmy was going to God, said Mr Kinnear. For the souls of the righteous are in the hands of God, and there shall no torment touch them.

All the men went away then, and I was left with the women.

'He had a long haul, old Jimmy.'

'Do you mind how he laughed that day?'

'Aye, they're not long in getting you into the ground.'

'And to think we've all to come to it!'

I wasn't allowed to accompany the hearse to the kirkyard. Auntie Elspeth had said I should wait till I was twelve till I got involved in all that. If she'd known about the grisly conversations with Alec, she'd have been horrified. The graveyard was visited mostly by women, and shawled old wives were frequent figures up there, sitting knitting among the graves. 'Oh well, we're among our own folk,' they would say with a shrug. But the women were not expected to attend the actual funerals. They stayed at home among the unbroken shortbread, the unstoppered sherry, waiting for the men to return from that most harrowing of journeys. It was a man's business. Fumbling with coffin cords, handling the heavy box, watching it swing slowly down into that awful hole in the ground. The grim practicalities of death.

But on the day of uncle Jimmy's funeral I asked to go out for a walk, and I stole after the cortège, darting across the fields to watch the business from the shelter of a dyke. The hearse wound its way up the steep green mound of the kirkyard hill like a giant beetle gleaming in the sun, and the figures followed it like ants. I moved closer, scaling a rock and scuffing my new shoes, to look down on them. They gathered round the graveside, black statues, all holding their hats, and the words came floating up to me, resonant with life and death.

Since by man came death, by man came also the resurrection of the dead. For as in Adam all die, even so in Christ shall all be made alive.

I am the Resurrection and the Life saith the Lord; he that believeth in me, though he were dead, yet shall he live; and whosoever liveth and believeth in me shall never die.

Forasmuch as it hath pleased Almighty God of his great

mercy to take unto himself the soul of our dear brother here departed, we therefore commit his body to the ground, earth to earth, ashes to ashes, dust to dust, in sure and certain hope of the resurrection to eternal life through our Lord Jesus Christ.

At that point Kinnear turned slightly and nodded, and Alec came up to the graveside with his spadeful of earth. I could see the slight smile on his face. He looked in my direction, right over the heads of the mourners, and seemed to wink up at me as the minister grabbed a fistful of dirt and scattered it over the coffin. I ducked down further behind the rock.

And so into that cold hole in the ground, where the worm feedeth sweetly, as old George used to say, uncle Jimmy went to join Epp and Chae Marr, Hodgie Dickson, Miss McNeil, Sangster, Shuggie and the whole host of the earth's anonymous. The Reverend Kinnear's voice boomed through the boneyard like a trumpet.

I know that my Redeemer liveth, and that he shall stand at the latter day upon the earth. And though worms destroy this body, yet in my flesh shall I see God.

The men put on their hats and filed away, and the first clods came thudding on to the coffin lid. Alec would have been pleased with the performance.

I ran back to the house, my heart beating for fear and yet with a wild vibrant thrilling to the triumphant sound of the words, the message of hope boomed out from the mound of bones, where all hope seemed to have died.

The next day I went back to the kirkyard and looked at uncle Jimmy's grave. The grass had been desecrated by his death, the squares of turf stitched crudely together by the hand of the old sexton and battered flat by his spade. But in a year from now I knew the grass would be blowing sweetly over his bones like a seamless green sea.

Close to the grave a dandelion clock faded like a white moon into morning – the clock and the tomb, the two things by which our lives are bound, standing side by side in the graveyard, the one so quickly blown, the other not to be worn down by a world of winds. The image was not my own. Alec had preached on the subject often enough.

I left the new grave and wandered among the older stones that I'd come to know so well. What was death? Thousands of bones and skulls separated from me by only a few feet of earth. But Jesus, who had raised Lazarus and Jairus's daughter, had said that these people were not really dead, they were simply asleep. I lay down on one of the graves and shut my eyes, my feet to the east, ready to rise and face my Saviour, my head to the stone, pointing in the same direction as all the other heads in that green hill, one flicker of life in the whole sleeping shoal, adrift on the dreamless tide.

But was it really dreamless? Nobody knew for sure. I opened my eyes again and stared up into the blue sky, trying to see where it began and where it ended, whether it existed at all or was some vast empty illusion. Would being dead be much different from this? I shouldn't see the sky, of course. Nor would I hear the sea, or the spray splashing on my stone or the raindrop ploughing down the carved letters of my name, turning to fire in the sudden sun. But I might just be dimly aware, in my six feet of slumber, that I was lying waiting, and that the great and terrible day was lying in wait for me too, when Judgement would rip off the green covers and rumple the sheets of clay, and the bright golden trumpets and sunrise would erupt irrevocably.

In the fields behind the kirkyard the farmer's men were busy bringing in the harvest, and their shouts mingled strangely with the soundless roaring of the dead all around me, and the words of yesterday's service, still filling my ears, telling me that uncle Jimmy would wake up one day with a new body.

Behold I shew you a mystery: we shall not all sleep, but we
shall all be changed, in a moment, in the twinkling of an eye,
at the last trump: for the trumpet shall sound, and the dead
shall be raised incorruptible, and we shall be changed.

The shouting grew louder and I tried to sink back into
sleep so as to avoid the terrible day, but the time of the
harvesting of the world had come at last. The graveyard
was raggled and crumpled, its stones cracked and capsized,
and all Alec's work was undone. In a thousand broken beds
the sleepers stood, dazed with day, rubbing the long sleep
from their eyes. They were all new made. Kate the Kist
threw away her coffin to be fitted for the New Jerusalem.
Jean Jeff's ears were opened and she turned and pointed her
finger. Peter Cleek held up his hook in a bright new fist and
flung it with a whoop into the sea.

They all came at me then, out of earliest childhood –
Hodgie Dickson pointing at me with solemn warning as
he advanced, Chae Marr thumping his chest to show off
his bright new heart, beating it like a drum, Tom Tarvit
growing teeth and toes and standing up straight again, and
the Blind Man opening his red eyes for the first time and
running at me in his rage. He hurled his stick away over the
kirkyard wall. It fell whirling like Excalibur into the waves
and he charged with eyes of fire, his fists and feet flailing.

Now I've got you, fishbait! Break open your head . . . feed
your brains to the fish!

I screamed and fell to my knees, covering my head with
my arms.

And the sea gave up its dead, all the drowned bones of my
ancestors, coral skulls answering the call. Mad Maria stood
up to her knees in the water and roared and laughed. Bella
Bonnysocks ran into the tide that had taken her Tam for
forty years and he came reeling off the end of the great line

that had wound him into eternity. It was the day of reckoning and all the shopkeepers lined the shore, clamouring to be paid. Then Honeybunch rose out of the waves, new washed and shining and singing to herself, naked as the day she was born, straddling the grave of Alec Fergusson, demanding to be dressed.

Was Alec dead then?

We were all dead, and we all stood before God, and the books were opened. And another book was opened, which was the Book of Life.

There are a great many souls in the world, and you have to make very sure that yours will not be a lost one. Supposing, just supposing, that you were such a borderline case that the recording angel missed out your name by mistake? Imagine all the saved souls of the world to be written down, and just one little error to exist, a scribal error in heaven, so small that not even God would notice – and that error to be the omission of your own name! Left out not because you were exceptionally wicked but because your life had simply not made it clear enough whether you were sheep or goat. Why not put that beyond doubt right now, while there is time?

But there was no question of error, for there was no doubt where I was bound for now.

Epp appeared, dressed in white, her jaw still knotted and leering, and the poker still in her hand.

There's nothing more for you now!
You will go to hell now – you will go to the burning fire!

I tried to run out of the kirkyard but Sangster stood at the gates, whirling a flaming sword, forcing me back in my terror, backwards and downwards, downwards and into my grave.

When I woke up the last of the field had been cut. The workers had gone home and all was silence and stubble. Only Alec was standing there, looking down at me curiously and grinning, lighting up his pipe.

'If you stay there much longer I'll have to charge you for the plot.'

He reached down and pulled me up with one hand. I rose stiffly.

'Nightmares?'

I nodded.

Nightmares.

They worsened with the weather, when the nights were wild and eerie. The heartbeat of the hearth, to compensate, grew stronger, redder, and I felt the simple things more keenly – steaming mugs of tea at ten, a stone hot-water bottle like a volcanic island in the arctic drift of the bed, a Georgina song to break up the monotonous monochrome dribbling at the windows, the wolves in the roof and the bears in the chimneys, wind and rain sweeping the earth and making the sea smoulder and hiss.

But sometimes when everyone but granny was away from the braehead house and my mother and father were both on night shift, I crept along to Alec's house to see if there was a red glow in his window. He kept long hours.

'When you get to my age,' he said, 'you sleep less and less. The closer you get to the long sleep, the less you need the naps. It's logical.'

So he'd stick a mug in my hand, climb aboard his rocking chair with the big foot-rest, light up his pipe and swing and smoke for hours, like a steam drifter gliding through the dark. A crowd of shadows joined us round the fire.

'Some folk ask me how I can sleep at all – sleeping next to a crowd of dead folk.'

Looking through Alec's window, I could just make out the dark humps of the headstones, crowding the mound that rose to meet the moon, just a step away from his cottage.

'I tell them that's the most peaceful place on earth out there. It's the poor lost souls that worry me – the ones I can't bury because they're rolling about in the dark, known only unto God, with the sea rolling over them.'

There was Fergus Hughes, for example, who appeared to his old mother Alice at the moment of his death. He left for the sea one wicked night on the *Harvest Reaper* with the rest of the boat's crew. It was their last chance to save their anchored nets off Kingsbarns. Fergus was on duty at the halyards when the tackle snapped and he was pitched into the sea.

Less than half an hour after he'd left the house, as his mother sat with her knitting by the kitchen fire, she saw him suddenly appear in front of her. One arm was leaning on the mantelpiece and he seemed to be warming himself in front of the coals. But he was still wearing his oilskins and she knew from the old stories that this meant only one thing. He was a dead man. Sure enough he turned his head then and looked at her. His white lips moved without the sound of words and she saw the water streaming down his face before he disappeared into the fire, like steam sucked up the chimney by the wind.

'I've never seen a ghost.'

Ah, but it wasn't a ghost old Alice saw, it was his spirit double, what the old folks used to call a fetch.

I tried to picture people older than Alec, who'd buried the village six times over. Or old Leebie, with her white walnut head, who also talked about fetches.

'But how, how . . . ?'

How does a fetch appear?

'Yes, how?'

Easily.

Picture yourself drowning. It's a dark night and you're tossed into the water with your oilskins and boots and all your heavy gear. You kick your arms and legs and try to gather the sea to yourself like a sheaf of corn. But the harvest is too big. Soon your arms are full of the sea and your legs are tired. You think you might go to sleep. So you stop your threshing and let the sea do the harvesting. The firth is filling your boots. You go down like a stone. You think you can hear your shipmates crying to you far above the waves and you vaguely wonder how they're going to get you out on a night like this when every man is fighting for his own life. But it's only the roaring in your ears that you're hearing – the roaring of the darkness telling you that you're a drowning man.

At such a moment where would you most wish to be, do you think?

'At home.'

That's right. At home, with your mother, and drying off at your own fireside. Grown men cry out for their mothers, you know, at the point of death. We're all our mothers' sons. That's where the drowning Fergus Hughes most wanted to be in his dying seconds, and that's where the force of his longing projected that last image of himself, making it materialize before his mother's eyes. It was her son's last wish that she saw, and not his ghost.

'Did they ever find his body?'

But Alec wasn't listening now. He was a remembering mouth, nothing more, rocking in the dark.

The same thing happened to Euphemia Christie.

She was just a young thing, poor lass, her man at Yarmouth for three whole months, and a month-old bairn that he'd never seen, lying sleeping in the crib on the floor. She was making infant clothes and her foot was rocking the cradle as she worked. Andrew Christie was caught in the chest by a swinging boom and went straight into a heavy sea. He was never seen again – except by Euphemia. She looked up from her work. Her foot and fingers froze. He was coming across the kitchen floor in his oilskins, dripping wet, and so real that she spoke out loud to him.

'Mercy me, Andrew, what's this that you're home from Yarmouth with never a breath of warning?'

He answered her never a word, but he bent down and looked hard and long into the cradle, his sea-swept eyes taking their fill of the bairn he'd never seen. Then he faded into the fire, like Fergus Hughes. And when she looked across the kitchen floor there wasn't a drop of water to be seen.

The telegram came the next morning, but she hardly needed that. She was already wearing black when she answered the door to the boy from the post office, and he read it through to her without her so much as turning a hair. She had shawled the bairn in black as well. The crib was like a coffin. A message like that – typed out on post office paper – that was nothing to the one she'd had the night before, when her husband came to her for the first and last look at the son he'd never seen and would never see in the flesh. It was exactly the same situation, you see – the man appearing in his mortal struggle just where he yearned to be. That's what the power of thought can do.

And that's just single drownings. Imagine what happens when a whole crew goes down or when a whole fleet is lost. The day I was born, 19 November 1875, was the blackest day ever for the east coast of Fife. Five sailing boats went down with all hands on the way back from Yarmouth, the *Vigilant,* the *Janet Anderson,* the *Excelsior,* the *Agnes* and the *Rising Moon.* Thirty-five men lost their lives and a hundred and thirty children on just a few miles of coastline lost their fathers. Some of the fathers saw their children – just like Andrew Christie. Can you imagine the sheer force of human emotion that ran through the sea that night, with all those men drowning? That was a power bigger than anything you could invent. Who needs a wireless or a telephone when you've got a wave like that, running up the North Sea, through the air, through bricks and mortar, and into the human mind?

As Alec catalogued the disasters and the apparitions, I saw them over and over, my ancestors, rising and falling like the sea, rolling in drowned generations through my head. Pale upturned faces sank slowly through the water, dreaming their last bitter dreams of kirk and kin, a quiet cradle and a pair of milky breasts. Then the waves closed like curtains over the sea-dreams, saltwater filled up every corner of the skull, the last particle of longing fell out like a silver coin from a turned-out pocket, and the dreamless head bumped gently on the seabed and lay there for ever for the tiny fish to take the place of darting thought.

But the strangest drowning of all was Mary Prett's – one that still sends shivers up my spine, though I'm not one for the terrors, as you know.

She had seventy years on her back. She'd had a good life, and she still had a good man to help her while away the hours left between them and the kirkyard. Every Saturday night they went to the whist drive in Anstruther, and that's where they'd come from on the night she took her life, home on the last bus, happy with a few wee drams inside them, and her talking nineteen to the dozen as usual all the road home.

Well, it was three in the morning maybe, by John Prett's reckoning, when she rose, and pitch black it was too, and the worst night of the year for gales and rain that folk could remember for years. He thought she'd gone down to the water closet when he heard the back door bang, and so, with him a bit befuddled, he dug down deeper into the blankets and went back to sleep. When he woke up it was as light as it could be on such a terrible morning, but there was no Mary to be found inside the house or at the neighbours or anywhere round about. They searched the town from east to west without finding a hair of her. Fearing the worst

by then, they combed the shore and looked over the end of
every pier, probing the tangles round the point of the Blocks
as it was a low tide.

'Wasn't she drowned?'

Oh, she was drowned and dead all right, no doubt about
that, but it was the manner of it that was the weirdest
thing. It was late afternoon when the bobby came up to
John's door and informed him that she'd been found – at
Kilconquhar, of all places, which as you know is more
than a two-mile walk from here. They're later risers up
there – too many retired and retarded folk, if you ask me.
Anyway they finally got up out of their beds to find the
body of an unknown woman floating face down in the loch,
a white nightgowned thing among the reeds and rushes
and nothing on her feet.

'Why did she do it?'

That's the first mystery. But there are other questions,
don't you think? A woman perfectly right in the head gets
up from her sleep in the dead of night and decides to drown
herself. She has less than ten steps to walk to the harbour.
It would have taken her the same number of seconds. But
instead of that she battles two miles in her bare feet, and
nothing on but her nightgown, along a road she's never
travelled, and to a place she's never been. Why? She makes
her way through solid sheets of rain, ripped and shredded
by the winds. Her nightgown was in tatters. My God, I can
remember that night. It was so bad that if she'd just turned
at the loch and walked all the way back again, she'd have
been dead by the time she reached her doorstep, through
sheer exposure. But she threw herself into that dark and
freezing water, far from her own fireside, and left other folk
to work out the whys and the wherefores.

'Maybe she was . . . made to, somehow.'

Cold covers to look for in the middle of the night, that's
for sure. They closed over her all the same, and she went
back to sleep, this time for ever. Nobody knows what kind

of mind she had that night or what went through her head
on that journey.

'I've never been to Kilconquhar loch.'

Don't go there. Do you have any need to go? Stay away
then. It's an unholy place, that loch. Maybe she was called
there by something. Some spirit of the water. You know
what the power of thought can do. It can draw a woman
out of her sleep, out of her bed, two miles away, take her on
a pointless journey, and make her take her life. Kilconquhar
loch – in the old days, you know, that's where they drowned
the witches.

'Were there witches in Fife?'

There were witches everywhere. They cursed the corn,
blighted women's bellies and made all the fish forsake
the firth. Lighthouse lamps went black and barns became
beacons, luring ships to the reefs. A fall from a horse, a lost
footing on a slippery deck, a bloated cow, a dead infant, a
man's member shrivelled up to nothing between his legs
– oh yes, the witches were busy enough round here, and
they sowed skulls in kirkyard and sea.

It's a long time now, but they used to burn them here
between the kirk and the castle. My predecessors had the
job of scattering the ashes to the four winds – they wouldn't
bury them in consecrated ground, you see – and the charred
bones that were left were lodged in the kirk loft just under
the steeple, and there they stay to this day. I can take you
up and show you if you've the stomach for it. A funny thing
when you think of the folk sitting in the pews on a Sunday
– a vault of black bones right over their godly heads, just
behind the whitewash. A rotten roof for kirk folk, but fine
enough for whited sepulchres, what do you think? It was
either that or they tied them to a stake at low water and
condemned them to suffer the washing of two tides.

'I'd rather be drowned than burned.'

Would you? Drowned at the stake? How would you feel,
watching the tide coming in that day, I wonder? Would you

think of apple-blossom, seeing the lines of surf advance?
First it tickles your toes and washes your feet – that's all
right. Then it's slapping at your legs and thighs, and chilly
fingers are grabbing at your groin – not so nice. Think of it
up to your chest, with the sound of the waves like thunder
in your ears. You take your first mouthful of cold salt water
– it tastes bitter. You don't want too much of that. But it's
filling your nostrils now, sucked up in hard hurting lumps
into your lungs. You struggle with the combined powers
of wind and tide for two paltry minutes. Then all your
struggles cease. Your eyes are sightless as water, the waves
are combing your hair – tossing like tangles, without a wish
in the world. Your head is filled with foam – it lolls and
lollops with the turning tide. Now all's still. A drowned
statue stands at the stake, underneath the sea. The crabs
and conger eels advance.

Wouldn't you rather suffer the red tide of the other stake?
Spreading from your toes to the top of your head again, a
million times more agonizing, but faster than watching a
six-hour flood lapping your way. Would you live to hear
your own skull burst like a bomb in the blaze? And your
heart crack like a roasted black chestnut, a shrivelled-
up stink? I wouldn't think it likely. They say the heart is
a bugger to burn. But what terrible ways to have to die,
burning or drowning, cinders or salt on your tongue, ashes
or silt behind your eyes, your skull a white-hot shard or a
cold coral stone. What a decision, eh? Hopefully you won't
have to make it, though. With any luck you'll die in your
bed. Many years from now.

With any luck.

But many years later, with Alec long dead, the nightmares he gave me are still alive.

One final irony gave him the last laugh. In his closing
winter he suffered a very short illness and pneumonia set
in, which proved fatal. Some people joked that that was one
grave he'd at least be spared from preparing.

When they got to the kirkyard it was snowing. The marble maidens stood in their stone petticoats, over their ankles in snow. And the grave was already dug.

9

The King My Father

Alec once said he'd very likely given me enough nightmares to fill a book. He spoke truer than he or I knew at the time. But of all the fears that darkened my days, none was worse than the fear of my own father. Why I call him king I have no idea, but it's clearly something to do with Hamlet. The king my father. He was more of the wicked uncle than the father, more of the cutpurse than the king, a usurper whose reign of terror I resented, an alien figure, never absorbed by the culture that surrounded him, never woven into the fabric of my mother's fishing upbringing.

Every Eden has its snake. And so let me bring mine out of the undergrowth, to supplant the beautiful Adam I longed for and never got, the intruding serpent who made my mother's life a misery, and still haunts mine.

My father was born on 9 May 1919 in Middlesbrough, the son of Elizabeth Hicks, housewife, and Jack Rush, bricklayer, journeyman.

A small black-and-white snapshot falls out of the folder of documents along with the certificates of birth and marriage and death, and I can see now with a shock something of what produced me. My father has conveniently dated and inscribed it for me, 'Dad and myself, 1937', so I know I am looking at my eighteen-year-old father and my paternal grandfather standing at the open door of No. 24 Bank Street two years before the outbreak of war.

My grandfather Jack is a Lawrentian figure: out for the occasion in his stocking soles and braces and collarless shirt, metal sleeve-garters clamped around his upper arms. He's a small man (I can see where my lack of height comes from) but his shoulders are like a bull's. And there's the belt which he'd unbuckle to thrash his son. One hand is thrust in his pocket, the other is round my father's much less impressive shoulders. My father is not yet fully formed, though in two years he will be classed as able-bodied. He's much more smartly dressed however, quite a dandy in fact. Wide striped trousers and waistcoat to match, and what looks like a nice silk tie, also striped. I can see the gleam on his shoes. He has taken trouble with himself for the photograph. His thick glossy hair is full of waves, falling away from the period-style middle parting. Good pronounced eyebrows – I wish I had them. I have his nose, though, long enough and straight enough, and I'm thankful for that.

One thing is missing – the wedding ring that will be slipped on to his finger in 1944. And the smile of the proud father – he doesn't yet know that I am waiting for him in the womb of time, to be delivered by Caesarean section from the belly of his Christina, whom he has not yet met. He's probably never even heard of Fife, though he'll have heard of Hitler. So the finger is ringless as yet. But I'm struck by the artistic quality of the hands. Perhaps that's because he's holding his favourite prop to help conceal his teenage embarrassment that his father is gesturing apparent affection. The prop is a banjo – an instrument that will feature in this interlude, now that I have been visually reminded of it.

But it's the faces that fascinate me in the end: my father's handsome, no doubt of that, and acutely uneasy. Why had he lost all that uncertainty by the time I knew him? Was it five years of war? Was that what brutalized him? Or had that been achieved already, by his father Jack? Jack too has good thick hair, but beneath it the battered face stands out like a relief map of the Himalayas (he once beat up two policemen, my father proudly told me, who'd come to tick him off for being drunk and disorderly), and though he's probably fifty, he looks seventy. Except for the black hair. The eyes too are black, black caves lost under bushy brows. The great gash of a mouth seems slack – but when I look closely, I can see that it's pursed and firm and unforgiving.

Photographs are old emotional territories, maps of the past, charts of the heart. I lay the 1937 one of my father beside one of my teenage mother, leaning against that now vanished iron gate. It was taken in the same year, though she's two years younger, at sixteen. She too is innocent of what's in store for her: a brief wartime romance, followed by marriage to a violent and vengeful drunkard. That's why she smiles so sweetly, with unclouded eyes and wide grinning mouth. Outside No. 32 Gourlay Crescent, St Monans. Where ignorance is bliss.

My next photograph is of a wedding. It is February 1944, and my parents have met, courted and married. And somewhere along the way, to use that quaint old phrase, fallen in love.

So there's the photograph, the visual accompaniment to the marriage certificate. It would have been a black-and-white photograph – except that the artistry I noticed in those banjo-toting hands was no illusion. The hands have tinted the wedding photograph delicately, allowing us to get close to the colours of the occasion. My father was skilled at this, and villagers would bring their family photos to him to be tinted, for a few shillings or perhaps a few bottles of beer. No amount of skill, however, can tint away the poverty, or colour in the absence of ceremony. It seems to have taken place in a guesthouse, not in the Congregational Church, though its minister, the Reverend Lodge, did the honours.

Six decades later I have a better understanding of my father, one of the millions of young men who hadn't gone to graveyards and to flowers, every one, but had gone to girls instead, surviving a five-year relationship with 32,000 tons of cold wet metal to enter a postwar period of much dreamed-of peace and plenty and to dig their hands deep into chronically empty pockets. But they were ripe for romance when they came up to the Scottish naval airbase of Crail, HMS *Jackdaw*, a few miles from my mother's village and a few yards from where I live now, and met girls like my mother at the sixpenny hops – girls who were equally entranced by the sudden disembarkation into their lives of shiploads of clean-shaven southern sailors. Can you wonder that they fell in love, in the way that people did in the forties? I used to thumb through those tinted photographs of my father, looking ridiculously lean and impossibly handsome, and saw at once why my mother had fallen for him, though I spent my childhood wishing she hadn't. But I've been busy unspending my childhood since it ended, and it has taken the death of my father and years of sweated prose to achieve this moment of – what can I call it – reconciliation? Not quite, but let's say recognition.

My father is in a sailor's uniform – which simply means he didn't have to spend the money, which wasn't there anyway, on a bridegroom's outfit. The demob suit will come later. But his telephonist bride has no uniform to disguise the fact that she can't afford a white wedding. Instead she does the best she can: a feathered forties hat, rather stylish actually, dark brown coat open to show the painfully thin pink dress, handbag and gloves found somehow to almost match the coat, borrowed probably. If she's wearing anything blue, it's not on show. And those shoes – too clumpy for her slender but shapely legs. God, she's lovely! All slenderness and smile, a strawberry blonde, a beauty.

That night they take off all those wartime togs, my mother carefully removing the green leaf brooch pinned over her left breast, and suddenly he's all over her. And a cold coming he must have had of it in the unheated accommodation in which I was conceived: rented rooms on a steep windy hill overlooking the harbour, a fishmonger across the street and a blacksmith next door. Once she told me she was a virgin till her wedding night, and urged on me the same restraint. I was off to be a student in the swinging sixties and I followed neither her precept nor her example, but her theory was that a man quickly loses respect for a woman who has submitted to him before marriage. An unfounded belief, but it reflected the starchier forties. What she didn't know, on 25 February 1944, was how quickly her own matelot would lose respect for her, no matter how pure she'd kept herself.

Exactly nine months later (less two days) I was born, the punctual product of honeymoon passion. But well before then the Emperor Hirohito had sent his greetings once again, and passion was put on hold till the end of the war.

That's when the trouble started. The outbreak of peace spelt bad news at No. 16 Shore Road, where hostilities were waiting to happen.

I struck the first blow, as you know, and the blow was followed by banishment from my mother's bed. The sailor was home from the sea.

As soon as I could walk I used to join the cats in the gutting sheds before graduating to the fierier delights of the smiddy, watching the brief lives of sparks. Born in the forge, they flew out on the wind, where they died like bees in the street. Briefer still the stars struck by the hooves of the Clydesdales, clashing on the cobbled floors, the sound of iron on stone, mingling with the hooting boats, the screaming gulls.

My father soon realized that life in an east coast Scottish fishing village was not the paradise he'd dreamed of, and he urged my mother to turn her back on her people and return with him to Middlesbrough. It was asking the impossible. So the able-bodied seaman, who'd learned the art of signalling in the employment of His Majesty, settled for signalling of a different sort at the local railway station on the princely wage of two pounds ten shillings a week. Bricklaying in

Bank Street or signalling in St Monans – there was little financial difference and not much else to do. He saw the trains in and out, and I saw myself as a two-year-old engine driver – till one day I was lifted up on to the footplate, saw the red furnace roaring within, and looked straight into the mouth of Epp's hell. Death by water seemed preferable and I returned to my first fancy, to be a fisherman.

But the earliest Christmas present that I can remember was not a boat, it was a Hornby railway set. I can picture it nearly six decades later: the curved lines of track that fitted together to form a circuit, the smart moss-green engine with pistons that actually operated the wheels, the tender, heaped with shining black plastic coal, and all the carriages with their doors and windows. It was beautifully made and doubtless expensive. A world of signalling and telephone operating had gone into its purchase. So it was a pity that I broke it on its first day. How was he to know that the son he had produced was destined to be useless with tools and a menace with his hands? Before the Hornby I had played with gas masks, which looked, felt and smelt mysterious. I took some stupefied and fleeting interest in the Hornby and then damaged it, not hugely or deliberately but through innate practical clumsiness. I was sitting on the floor at the time, holding in my hands two pieces that should have been one, when I looked up and saw a strange sight. My parents were dancing. No, they weren't dancing exactly, they were gently wrestling. Recollection has made sense of it. He'd made to strike me, and my mother, fiercely protective always, had intervened, grasping both his hands. I can see the sweet winning smile on her face as she looked up into his eyes, quietly pleading, and the reluctant smile on his as he submitted to her soft words and strokes, her face in his chest, so petite. She wooed him away from me and I was saved, unaware at the time that I had been in danger of the first return blow. He glared at me. 'Next time you're for it,' he seemed to say.

I didn't have long to wait. As soon as I discovered language he discovered that his son, apart from being clumsy, was also a linguistic dunce who couldn't pronounce the letter *r* – a malady common to two-year-olds. But in my case it was obviously a sign of stupidity or stubbornness, or it was sheer laziness, the Scots, so he maintained, being slovenly in their speech through their innate indolence. They just couldn't be bothered to get the pronunciation right. Later it was decreed by him that only English should be spoken at home, or anywhere else for that matter, and although I slipped into Scots in playground and street, and in the braehead house, it was always with my head turned over my shoulder, to ensure he wasn't within earshot. Otherwise there would have been trouble. As a matter of fact he rarely visited grandfather's, but when he did I was struck dumb, unable to identify myself comfortably with either camp. Then I was accused of being a rude mumbler and told to speak up, for God's sake – 'Or I'll make you sing out, sonny boy, if I 'ave to clip you across the bleedin' 'ead!'

Such was the noble English that rolled from his tongue. One day I unwisely pointed out that his omission of certain letters was not dissimilar to my own. I don't suppose I argued a particularly cogent case, but I put my toddler's point of view and was thrashed for bloody cheek.

By an unfortunate coincidence I didn't like rice pudding either, which also began with the offending letter. This led to a scene of sadistic bullying in the gloomy Shore Road house, in front of a dark green curtain which screened off the marital bedroom. I was something short of three, I think, and he'd be twenty-eight. My mother was not at home and so the master of language and cuisine was in charge.

He made me a massive bowl of rice pudding and put me on a stool. I was ordered not to move a muscle except to eat. There was no way I was going to get off that stool until I'd eaten it up – every bleedin' spoonful, every bleedin' drop!

The spooning began. I gagged and was slapped, gagged

again and again and was slapped each time. Concentration to prevent this was difficult. Tears filled my eyes and fell into the bowl. I was slapped again. This went on until the bowl was empty.

And after each hateful swallow I was ordered, 'Now say "rice".'

' 'ice.'

Slap.

Rice!

'Wice.'

Slap.

Rice!

' 'ice.'

Slap.

Rice! Rice! Rice! And at the end of this you'll be saying 'rice' or I'll be making you another bleedin' bowl, sonny boy!

Personal tidiness was another of his obsessions. A boy on the loose with other boys in the salt-and-tar environment of a working fishing village is not going to stay spotless. I was as physically adventurous as my friends and came home stained and torn. Each missing button, each scuff and snag were punished by clouts across the head, punctuating the tongue-lashings and the black looks. Complete bedragglement meant a belting.

'You come 'ome like that again if you bleedin' dare!'

Even my injuries – bruised forehead, grazed elbows, skinned knees – were thrashing matters, whereas in granny's house they meant hot water and ointment applied with smiles and shakes of the head. Tender loving care had been left out of his vocabulary, perhaps as a result of his own experience of the father-and-son relationship. Not that I could have understood that at the time. I simply saw how other boys ran into their homes bleeding and begrimed, with never a hesitation or a tremble at the front door. I usually crept in at the back.

I envied my friends their fathers, and often daydreamed

that mine was this one or that. Why couldn't I have had uncle Alec as a dad? Or Billy? Or grandfather? He was old but he was kindly. And he put his arm round me. And called me 'son'.

Money – or the lack of it – lay at the gnawed heart of my father's bitterness, and I suppose I symbolized the frustration of his hopes. He'd had five years of youth ripped out of his life by war, and he'd come up to Scotland to settle for life as a railway worker. Not that there would have been money in Middlesbrough. The family he left behind could tell him that, and did. But it was natural and easy to blame the place he was stuck in, and to lash out at those who were nearest and most vulnerable. For some reason he had chosen not to be a fisherman, though his naval experience would have given him a good start. Possibly, like many wartime sailors, he was simply sick of the sea and had vowed never to leave the shore again. I don't know what was in his head, because he never told me. We never talked.

So here he was, a two-pound-ten-a-week signalman with no prospects and a useless sort of son. Was this what victory amounted to? And those years of dodging torpedoes and dive-bombers – for this?

For some men the love of a good woman is enough to banish discontent. But my father was a malcontent, and the good woman failed to satisfy him. My mother worked long shifts at the telephone exchange, also for a meagre wage, but somehow even their combined pittances couldn't pay the rent and the bills and leave enough over to eat. Holidays were out of the question.

The other consoler of bitterness is the bottle – and this is what my father took to. But he who drains the bottle drains his pocket and his pride. And so the vicious circle ran round us, closing tighter and tighter till it erupted in violence, violence that went beyond the level of the seemingly statutory thrashings, and embraced my mother too.

She was a thrifty and selfless soul who spent little on

herself all the days of her life. All her care and concern was
for those around her, her mother, father, siblings, me – and
even the man who abused her. Only once do I remember my
gentle grandmother breaking out in black anger, when I
was maybe seven.

'Look at you!' she addressed my father. 'Waltzing in here
all done up like a tailor's dummy in your three-piece suit
and your fancy tie! And your wife bare-legged and it bitter
winter out there! Haven't you more need to go and buy her
a pair of stockings and a decent pair of shoes?'

He walked out. And bought not a pair of shoes or nylons
but a skinful of beer. When he came home that night, raging
drunk, I could hear the slaps and shouts going on for so
long, I got up and ran to the bedroom. She was cowering
in a corner of the bed and he was over her with his arm
raised.

'I'll bleedin' kill you! I will an' all! I'll bleedin' swing for
you!'

I believed him. In my terror I ran to the woodshed and
came back with the axe. By the time I reached the bedroom
he'd slipped in his stupor and was sprawled on all fours in
front of the bed, his head lowered, as if for execution.

I lifted the axe and looked straight into the horrified eyes
of my mother. She screamed and I dropped the axe. This
roused him and he turned, reached up and seized me by the
hair.

'You get back to your bleedin' bed! And you get up again
if you bleedin' dare!'

Everything was bleeding – including my mother. That
was the night that fear turned to hatred.

There were many such nights. Arguments about money
– why wasn't she a better housekeeper? Arguments about
drinking – he never took her out. Drinking was a man's
affair. But I watched other married couples, my friends'
parents, walking arm in arm to take the bus to the Regal
and Empire picture-houses in Anstruther. They seemed so

normal, so serene, and trod the streets like saints in some heaven they inhabited, the impossibly distanced dimension of the ordinary, the everyday, the country from which we were somehow excluded, to which we didn't belong.

My mother stayed at home, except when she was working nights. And he came home legless, starting up the minute he swayed in through the door. Even when she never said a word, he erupted, seeing the reproach in her eyes.

'Money, money, money! All I ever bloody hear from you! Well there's your bleedin' money!'

And he dug into his coarse black railway uniform trouser pockets and took out fistfuls of coins, coppers mostly, flecked with glinting silver, hurling them at her head, turning his back on her and scattering them behind him up the long dark corridor as he stormed his way to bed, leaving her weeping in the corner.

That is how my crimes began.

We had a good-hearted neighbour called Lizzie, also poor, but whose husband, a quiet man, stayed at home. 'He's happy with a glass in the house,' she said.

Occasionally my mother would send me across the garden to Lizzie's back door, to borrow a shilling to feed the gas meter, so that she could make a meal. After a time I took it upon myself to go to Lizzie's unbidden and borrow a shilling for this or that – a loaf of bread, a pound of margarine, 'some tea for the pot'. These shillings I squirrelled away in an old tobacco tin at the back of a cupboard. As the weeks went by I grew bolder and begged for two shillings – to buy some messages, to pay the insurance man, 'to tide us over'. I stepped it up to half a crown. And still Lizzie never came and asked for the money to be repaid, never as much as mentioned it to my mother, too decent for that. It seemed to me that it could go on like this for ever. I went up to five shillings, two half-crowns. Things were getting serious and the tin was heavy. I recall no feelings of guilt. I knew it was wrong – that's why I kept concealing the money – but at the same time I was accumulating a hoard of treasure that would save the day.

Inevitably the day came when Lizzie knocked at our door, grown suspicious by my latest request for ten shillings, and by the fact that she'd lent out more than a month's wages. It didn't matter that I hadn't spent a penny of it. Nothing would convince my father that I hadn't intended it for myself, that I was simply trying to help. And I lacked the vocabulary to explain. Words froze in my mouth whenever he turned on me. His anger and my fear made me inarticulate. The evidence was against me. If I'd intended the money for the family, why hadn't I produced it? For the obvious reason – my mother defended me – that if I'd produced it I'd have had to explain where it had come from. I'd simply followed my instincts without thinking it through.

'Instincts nothing! The boy's a bleedin' thief!'

Even by his standards it was a brutal thrashing. My mother stroked the weals on my backside and applied calamine lotion. Then she went off to her night shift, telling me to stay off school the next day if sitting down proved too painful. But as I lay face down in bed in the morning, he appeared holding my coat and ordered me to get ready. We were going out. I thought I was going to be marched to school but he propelled me in a different direction, his hand on my collar. I asked him where we were going.

'To the station.'

But we'd passed the turning to the railway, I pointed out uneasily.

'Not that station, you fool! This is a police matter.'

I panicked. What would be done with me?

I'd be locked away, was his answer.

Would my mother be able to see me?

No, I'd be sent far away, to Glasgow or Dundee. And there I'd be put in the company of boys who knew a thing or two. They'd be worse than the jailers. But most probably it would be neither place. Because of my age, too young for borstal, the likeliest sentence would be the *Marship*.

'And there they'll 'ave you for bleedin' breakfast!'

Fear, sick fear took hold of me as I pictured this bleeding breakfast, quite literally, and I tried to run away. He dragged me along by the scruff of the neck, people staring in the street.

I pleaded. I had other money saved up that he didn't know about – in another tin. It was mine. He could have it all.

'I don't need your bleedin' money, boy! You ain't 'alf goin' to cop it, and that's all there bleedin' is about it!'

As we turned the corner to the policeman's house at the end of the village, my mother came off the bus from her shift. She ran up and asked what had happened now.

'I'm taking this bleedin' thief to the police,' he said. 'He's got to be charged and punished, 'asn't he? He's broken the bleedin' law!'

I saw the withering look on my mother's face, a look from which all love had drained. The years have defined it for me (emotion recollected in tranquillity, maturity) as contempt.

'My God! What kind of man are you? And how many laws have *you* broken? Ask yourself that.'

With that she loosened his grip on me, put my hand in hers and took me home, turning before she did so to say one more thing to him.

'And can you speak a single sentence without that horrible word *bleedin'* in it?'

It surprised me that he said nothing and showed no resistance. Maybe he was startled by the look on the face of this woman whose ancestors had faced the wrath of the sea and whose emotions had turned to sudden anger. She left him standing in the street, to wander off in the direction of the Cabin Bar, where he achieved such a state of blind

drunkenness that he was unable to carry out the thrashing
that he threatened as he blundered through the back door.
He passed out instead and I helped my mother to get him
into bed. As I did so many times.

Only occasionally did the drinking lead to such total
penury that there was literally nothing in the house
to eat, though it was a hand-to-mouth life at times. One
morning there was a cup of water for breakfast, and my
mother's wretchedness led me to risk the *Marship* again. I
started slipping down to Agnes Meldrum's and asking for
minuscule amounts of groceries, to be put on the slate. The
massive slabs of butter and cheese on the counter meant
that if you were really stretched – and many were – you
could ask for just a couple of ounces, which Agnes would
cut off with hairline precision, never erring on your side,
not like Mrs Guthrie and her baker's dozens. Even a penny-
worth would go on the slate. In this way I stowed crumbs of
food behind jars and pans in the pantry and left my mother
to discover them with little cries of surprise that made me
feel like Santa Claus.

'Oh, look what we have – and we never even knew!'

'Oh, Chris, see what's been forgotten!'

She called him Chris but me Christopher. How strange
that he gave me his name but saw nothing in me to identify
with.

This scheme of mine also had a limited life. Agnes sent
up a bill after a decent interval and I was bent over the chair
again. This time there was no threat of the *Marship*, as my
altruism was evident, even though it still resulted in a good
thrashing. After all, I had to be taught a lesson. I was always
being taught a lesson. And it was always a *good* thrashing, a
phrase whose irony struck me as often as he did.

But even this did not deter me in my determination to
save us from starvation. I stole off to the harbour at nights,
dropping silently out of my bedroom window in the small
hours and darting like a shadow down to the boats. I knew

which ones had been stocked up ready for departure, and so I clambered quietly down the iron rungs of the piers, thrilling to the mysterious movements of the moonlit water, the bobbing boats, the green and red harbour lamps turning the tide to emeralds and rubies, winking at me in connivance. Down below decks and into the galley, stepping from vessel to vessel, taking just a little from each, I built up my own set of stores in our garden shed, taking from it as occasion demanded, planting things in the larder like a night-tripping Lapland elf – a couple of slices of bread and bacon, a knob of margarine, a pickled egg.

Word went round that there was a thief in the town, a robber of poor fishermen. Grandfather took a dim view of it and I cringed in secret shame, ceased my pilferings and lay low. But I forgot about the store in the shed and it mouldered and was mouse-eaten. Eventually it was discovered. It was long enough after the boat-thief period to pass as a purely domestic crime. I'd been stealing from the larder, that was all. A simple thrashing matter. But my father questioned me closely and was convinced there was more to it than met his narrow eye.

'Well,' he said, 'when I thrash you, which I'm going to do in a minute from now, I'll just make extra bleedin' sure, that's all. Bend over that chair!'

The thrashing that followed made bleeding certain.

Later the doctor called to see my mother on another matter and examined me with owlish concern. There was a long low conversation between them. He made repeated suggestions, quietly, seriously, and my mother kept helplessly shaking her head and crying. Nothing happened.

And all of this when I was still in the early years of primary school.

The move to the new council house came in my second year of primary school, and for some reason things deteriorated. The drinking deepened and took a more regular hold, the thrashings reflecting the change. The violence was always worst when my mother's menfolk were at sea. When they were ashore my father was quieter. But sometimes they were at hand when he was being abusive, and there were physical fights, blood on the wallpaper, broken furniture, doors off their hinges. Uncle Billy stood up to him once when he made to strike my mother after a drinking bout, and a fearful fist fight followed. Neighbours ran to the end of the village – few owned telephones in those days – and now there really was a police matter, only it was the father, not the son, who stood in the dock. Not literally. The bobby simply came along on his bike and took charge of the chaos that was our house that night.

Far from being terrified by the arm of the law, I remember feeling impressed and empowered by the policeman's sudden palpable presence. The black uniform and heavy glossy gloves, the polished shoes, silver buttons, cap and badge, the truncheon, the notepad – they all combined to produce this overwhelmingly tactile sensation of power – power to bring peace and restore order and sanity again. The notepad especially had quite an effect on me. The pen was busy on the paper: when, where, why, what exactly? Who threw the first punch? Was it a blow, or was it a form of restraint? Some of the language eluded me, but its drift and effect were enthralling. Chaos was being quelled and emotions controlled by a few words, quietly committed to paper. I noticed how my father had gone meek as a lamb under the policeman's questioning. He was pointing his pen at him, a slender stiletto, like a little silver dagger, and the bully lowered his eyes. Where was the spirit of Jack Rush? Wasn't he going to let him have it? No, the officer was a huge man. Jack Rush's offspring beat up those who were smaller, younger.

So things went quiet for a time.

One night he came to me with a smile on his face. My mother was working a night shift. He called me by my name. Did I remember that time he pretended he was taking me to the policeman, just as a joke?

I remembered it. I didn't remember the joke.

And I'd offered him all the money I'd saved?

So I had.

How much money had I saved, exactly?

Every weekend I did some sort of work for my grand-mother – shopping, grass-cutting, weeding. She couldn't pay me much, but as the months went by the pile grew heavier with threepenny bits, sixpences, shillings, half-crowns. I'd followed my mother's philosophy of thrift. Proudly now I went for the tin and presented my fortune. Fifty shillings. A week's wages.

How would I like to make twice that much? Even ten times that much? In one night?

But how could it be done? I asked, intrigued.

It was easy. In fact I didn't have to do a thing. He would see to everything. All I had to do was give him the money, to take with him to the pub. I felt uneasy at the mention of the pub, but he said he was going to have only one drink. After that he was going to take part in a game. It was called gambling.

'If I win,' he said, 'I'll bring you home a fortune.'

'What happens if you don't win?'

'I'll win,' he grinned. And he pocketed the money.

He was brought home in the small hours, swearing and staggering. His gambling friends left him on the floor, where he produced not the promised fortune but pools of puke and piss. I tried to move him to the bed but he was a dead weight – blindly, snoringly, senselessly drunk. I gave up and went back to bed.

Unable to sleep, I left the house with the drunkard in it and walked the three and a half miles of darkened coast to Anstruther. The men were at sea. The firth was a black glimmering, emptied of life. Not a light to be seen, except for the lonely lighthouse flashing off the May. The stars glittered like coffin nails in a black sky. It was winter. I was frozen by the time I reached Anstruther. When I arrived at the little telephone exchange I could see the dim glow from the first-floor window, telling me that my mother was on duty. I opened the back door and went up the winding stone steps.

'Mercy me,' she gasped, 'is somebody dead?'

'No,' I said, 'it's, it's – him.' I could never say the word 'father'. Or 'dad'.

'He's not drunk is he?'

I nodded. 'Blind.' I had learned the gradations.

'But he hasn't got a nail to claw himself with. Where did he get the money?'

I explained, and she buried her face in her hands. Then she made up the fold-down bed for me and covered me with a blanket.

Many's the night I walked that stretch of coast to the exchange, getting to know every twist in the road, and slept beside her, often wakening to watch her white pensive face in the semi-gloom, listening to her calm tones as she took the calls. Her voice was measured. In spite of her troubles she remained a tranquil instrument of information. But there was a heart in the assured, official voice which all the local folk adored. When they stopped to chat on the line her voice changed immediately to the soft, cosy one that I knew so well. And there was a background calm to the mysterious tickings and clickings of the switchboard, a soothing testimony to order and efficiency, which sent me to sleep. It was like the policeman's pen, processing the mysterious passions of life. Who, after all, made calls at three in the morning? And why? But they did. People who were frightened, people who were ill. And my mother's voice was like an angel's in the dark. She was always there.

When we got home after that particular night he was still there on the floor, cold and soaked in what he had expelled, and gradually coming to. With a lot of effort we got him to his feet and he staggered to the bathroom, leaving the door wide open as he pissed my savings into the toilet.

'Ask him if he won,' my mother said in a tight voice, her switchboard serenity left behind.

I stood right behind the bent, degraded figure.

'Did you win?' I asked.

'Nope!'

That was all the answer I ever got out of him, and I have detested the sound of that slang word ever since. Whenever I hear it I see him bent over there in the bathroom, his uncaring back to me. I see the look of shame and misery on my mother's face. And I hear her murmuring the words in disbelief.

'How could you stoop so low as to rob your own child of his money?'

My grandfather gave her the answer.

'A man who will stoop so low as to raise his hand to a woman, will stoop to anything.'

I used that line in the only piece of writing for which I ever won a prize. When I was ten, the churchy village ladies who belonged to the local Temperance Association decided to put up the money for the best essay to be written on the evils of alcohol, the competition to be administered by the school. This was my first conscious piece of creative writing, and if it still exists, which I doubt, it will be lodged in some mouldering folder labelled 'St Monans Temperance Association Essay Prize 1955'. The prize was presented the following year.

Apparently the essay created a profound impression. I'd

written from the heart and had left out no details. The joke
went round the school that I could hardly fail to win – I was
the boy with the worst drunkard in town for a dad.

But it was no joke at home. The Temperance Ladies spoke
to the headmaster, who made phone calls. The policeman
arrived for the second time at our house, accompanied by
a man in plain clothes. The notepad came out again. I was
not made privy to the talk that took place between them
and my mother, but I was questioned by the man in plain
clothes about what I'd said in the essay. Was it all true? Had
it all happened exactly as I'd described it, or had I used my
imagination?

'Did you deliberately exaggerate?'

I wasn't entirely sure what he meant, but sensing retribution I clammed up and said very little. It was just an essay. I
just wrote it, that was all. When my father came in from his
shift he was astonished to find officialdom waiting for him.
He'd threatened to throw the policeman out if he appeared
again, but again the spirit of Jack Rush deserted him. After
the two men left he turned on me fiercely.

'You write another word about anything   if you bleedin'
dare!'

That was all he said. No thrashing ensued. I felt a warm
glow. The power of the written word had made itself felt.
And I ignored my father's warning.

When the prize was presented at the end of the school
session, it was a book, *Stories of King Arthur and His Knights*,
retold by Barbara Leonie Picard for the Oxford Illustrated
Classics, and it cost twelve shillings and sixpence.

'More than a day's wages,' said my father, glaring at the
dust-jacket. 'Why couldn't they have given him the money
instead?'

Congratulations were not in order.

I read it from cover to cover, cried when Gawain died, and
wept again with Bedivere when Arthur was taken away in
the barge by the black–clad damsels. Naturally I read it not as

fiction but as a chronicle of the truth, overwhelmed by sheer sadness that an entire culture and fellowship could simply die and disappear, leaving nothing but a story behind.

But the story was there, and the book is still on my shelves. Even if I were to win the Nobel Prize for Literature, it would not mean as much to me as this little book did at the time, and still does.

My father was one of those black knights who stood in the way. Often I wished him dead – I even prayed that he would die and leave us in peace. No Galahad was going to ride up to our front door and smite him through the body with a fifteen-foot lance. No black dwarf would bar his way on the railway bridge. I imagined alternative scenarios, an accident on the line, a drunken fall into the harbour on the way back from the Cabin Bar.

There was a partial answer to my prayer. He suffered headaches and began to act oddly, leaving the house and saying he was going away. My heart lifted – but he always returned, strangely sober. The sobriety was even more frightening than the drunkenness. He sat blackly in his chair, like a bomb waiting to go off. For a time he entered a mental hospital for assessment. They returned him to us, saying they could find nothing wrong with him – his personality was his problem (and ours) and he was not in any way unbalanced. He scoffed at their stupidity.

'They know nothing, them bleeders!'

For another period he did leave home, went back to Middlesbrough and worked in the foundries, staying with his sister, my auntie Bessie, and her family. Within a year or two he was back again, strangely chastened, never to break out again into such terrible rages, such blind fits of drunkenness, but still a smouldering presence, causing a gloom to descend whenever he came through the door. He got back his old job on the railway.

While he was away from home I rummaged through bags and boxes that he'd left behind in cupboards, and discovered his old love-letters to my mother, written in his navy days, when all he ever wanted was to have her beside him, to kiss and cuddle at the fireside, as he put it, and as he imagined it, lying in his bunk, writing on cobweb-thin paper and going over home in his head.

Sea-dreams. He'd wanted a lot more than that and hadn't got it. Bitter frustration lay at the heart of his wasted life. Plucked at nineteen from a grimy red-brick box, in which he'd been thrashed by his own father, he was set down by the iron claw of European politics in an even less inviting habitat: the wet and slippery deck of one of His Majesty's battle-cruisers, where the combined attacks of U-boats and the Luftwaffe had a way of making your legs quiver on an already less than stable surface. I didn't understand that at ten years old. But I did ask myself a question as I sat on the floor surrounded by a sea of skeletal letters. What happens to all that love, that youthful adoration? How can it simply disappear? Where does it go? Where is it stored? You can still make out the words on the tracing paper. But where is the love itself? A question not so much rhetorical as unanswerable.

I also discovered a series of erotic drawings he'd done. He had a draughtsman's ability rather than an artist's. The hand that tinted the photographs had taken care and pleasure in depicting women's breasts. The nipples stood out erect and dripping.

He was musically talented too. He played the piano by ear with astonishing confidence and precision, and if tutored would certainly have flourished. He was best of all on the banjo, and in his quieter periods strummed away on this for hours at a time. It was always a relief to come along the street with slow and wary steps and hear the sound of the banjo coming from the house. Then my pace would quicken again. He was in a safe mood.

But even that safety valve was soon closed off. A man at the other end of the village died, and his widow, who'd heard my father play at some of the town hall concerts, came along to the house with her late husband's mandolin. It was a beautifully made instrument and my father took to it easily.

The first night he played it we heard a terrible crying sound out in the street. I went to the front door and looked out. The dead man's dog, a black-and-white collie, was sitting in the middle of the road, staring at the house, and howling.

'Oh, my God,' my mother said, coming up behind me, 'that poor poor beast.'

'Throw a bleedin' stone at the thing!' my father shouted through his playing.

I ran out into the road and sat down beside the animal, putting my arms round his neck and stroking him, trying to comfort him. But nothing could cure his heartbreak. He had heard his master's voice. So we sat there and cried together. Then my father appeared in the doorway, mandolin in one hand, stone in the other.

'Get out of the bleedin' way!' he shouted.

I got out of the way just in time and he flung the stone. The dog ran howling down the street but then stopped at a safe distance. He reappeared any time the mandolin came out of its case, even if the instrument was never actually played. All my father had to do was take out the instrument and lay it on the table. It was uncanny. My mother cried too and my father stopped playing – 'because of the bleedin' noise'. But perhaps a dog had found a way to his heart.

Perhaps.

My mother cried again on 28 January 1953 at eight o'clock in the morning, when the mentally deficient Derek Bentley was hanged for a murder that was committed by his accomplice, Chris Craig. On a Croydon rooftop during a bungled robbery, the eighteen-year-old had told the sixteen-year-old with the gun to let the policeman have it, just as Jack Rush had done in Bank Street, letting the coppers have it, using his fists and his feet and those very words. My mother watched the clock, dabbing her eyes and wondering what that poor woman, his mother, was going through as the seconds ticked by. She told me it was wrong, that it was not beyond reasonable doubt that the words were unambiguous. 'Let him have it, Chris!' could easily have meant 'Give him the gun', which is what the policeman had asked him to do. My father disagreed and shed no tears. How often had he said to me that he was going to let me have it. And it had been all right for Jack Rush to let the coppers have it – 'nearly killed the bleeders, he did' – but Derek Bentley was not excused. He was not excused from hanging either, sentenced by a sexual deviant, a bully got up in robes. I knew all about bullying, and I cried with my mother for Derek Bentley.

I cried again after my father died.

It was 1989 and he was seventy. Decades had passed, and many changes had taken place. We'd left St Monans and gone to Edinburgh. I'd gone from there to Aberdeen University, had graduated, married, become a teacher, a writer. And he'd actually taken a pride in me at last.

'This is my son – he's an author, you know.'

Another time, another place. Different house, different people, a wife and family for me, grandchildren for him, and a long slow mellowing. We drank together in the pub. From time to time.

Too late, alas, much too late. It's the first five years that count. The damage was done. When he lay dying of cancer of the throat in a hospital bed, looking like a skinned rabbit, we said goodbye. It was painfully constrained. He reached out and shook me by the hand. That was it. Father and son knowing they would never meet again – and we were dumb

to one another. There were no words. I should have been
the one. But I couldn't find them. They have had to wait
till now.

On the day of his death I didn't cry. But some years later I
cried at the end of Kenneth Branagh's film of Mary Shelley's
Frankenstein. Robert de Niro, playing the monster, stands by
the funeral pyre of his creator in that famous scene on the
Arctic ice. He is weeping uncontrollably, now that he has
had his revenge.

'But why', asks the captain of the ship, 'do you weep for a
man who has caused you so much pain?'

The answer from the ice-raft, forced out of him by bitterness and grief, was not Mary Shelley's but de Niro's. And
it is mine too.

'He was my father.'

End of the Idyll

Paradise Lost?

Yes, there really was a garden, a golden age of childhood, in spite of my father, the serpent in Eden. Except that in this case it wasn't the intruding serpent who ended it. There were other intrusions, unforetold actions, and everything came to an end with astonishing swiftness.

They killed the pig, my grinning companion in ignorance, he who shared my solitary moments on the way to school and responded to my scratchings with that idiotic smile. They gave him another grin one morning, a wider one, split him from ear to ear, and I ran howling into the woods.

The pig was killed to be eaten, so they told me, calming me down and sending me back to school – that's why it was bred in the first place. It's what it was born for. You feed it, tickle its snout, stick daisies in its ears, scratch it till it grins, give it a name so that it comes running to you when you call – and then you kill it. That's how it goes.

There were other signs that marked the exit from Eden. The pig was only an individual casualty. Soon the braes were bedecked by hundreds of little cases of living death. Myxomatosis had been introduced – a free gift from man to the rabbit population of Europe, to help them control themselves.

One day I was out with grandfather, up near Balcaskie, when we saw a man lashing out with a stick at one of the crouched grey bundles.

'He's putting it out of its misery,' I said.

Grandfather grimaced.

'Maybe,' he said. 'But do you know what that man does? He works for the nobs in the woods. If there are rabbits about, he goes along to their burrows with a little bit of equipment, and if they're nice and healthy and the disease hasn't got to them, he gasses them. He gassed a lot of rabbits before this disease was ever heard of.'

We passed by, and I saw the stick coming down on another of the inert little ornaments that were decorating the fields, like garden bric-à-brac. The man shouted something and grandfather ignored him.

'Would you do that for a living?' he asked. 'Gas rabbits?'

'Would you?' I asked.

'Me? I wouldn't lower myself.'

Not long after that there were no rabbit warrens around Balcaskie. There wasn't even a Balcaskie, except in name. The entire wood was ripped up – so that the nobs could enjoy an uninterrupted view of the sea, so it was said in the village. The Bishop's Walk became a memory, a scented echo. It was a headrush of snowdrops, a girl in green, a woman wheeling a pram. A way through the woods. It was the beat of a horse's hooves and the swish of a skirt in the dew.

Landscapes, like language, get turned around. Cultures vanish overnight, like knights of old. The herring, that had been the life-force of the tribe, disappeared like its dialect, harried out of existence by the laissez-faire system of the day that gave it no protection, and by modern methods of fishing. The herring had the misfortune to be the only marketable fish that laid its eggs on the seabed, and so the birth-beds were destroyed by the new seine nets that dragged the bottom of the world, looking for cod, the few young herring that survived being easily swept up.

The day of the drifter was over, grandfather said, and with it the life of the herring. Why couldn't politicians have seen what he saw? Even if they could they would never have thought fifty years ahead. Five was their mental span.

Grandfather watched one of the new boats leaving the harbour. 'Look at that stupid little tub,' he said. 'The sea needs something to hit, something good and solid, not that piece of nonsense.'

With their high heads and long keels and the draught of water they commanded, the drifters were the fisher kings of their day and withstood the stress of storm. The last one left harbour for Yarmouth when I was twelve – another signpost on the move, marking the end of economic innocence.

'And the men on her,' grandfather said, looking at the seine-netter, 'they may be fishermen today, but tomorrow they'll be labourers at sea, that's all. Fishing will just be a wage-packet for these young lads, not a way of life.'

He looked at his nets piled up on the pier.

'And they won't be interested in mending these either, you'll see. It'll be left to old-timers like me, sitting in the sheds, earning their cigarette money.'

So the firth was fished out, just as he said, the boat-building sheds fell silent, and the old men were left to puff their pipes and work their needles. The village churches dwindled and emptied, one by one the shops disappeared – no butcher, no baker, no grocer, no chemist, not even a fishmonger – and a mini-supermarket took over. St Monans settled down to await its swift extinction as a place of second homes for people with more money in their pockets than grandfather could have earned in a year. Blair's Britain was still a long way off, but Dr Beeching's axe was poised to hack away all the local railway stations, and Thatcher's government to remove local control from the councils, so that problem families and drug addicts could be moved in to vandalize the village churchyard and desecrate the memorials to the dead, my own dead included.

The eccentrics decayed too. The village grew saner – and less safe. People started to lock their doors.

Every gain implies a loss, they say. Is the reverse also true? The hellfire went out with the herring, and that was no bad thing. But what did we acquire in place of our lost innocence?

In 1954, when I was ten, the first twelve-inch black-and-white television set was carried into the upstairs living-room of our neighbours across the street – and life in that house died instantly. Living-room? It became a morgue. The shapes of the dead could be seen silhouetted against the ghostly grey-blue flickering of those upstairs windows. Soon there was a set in every house in the street except ours, and the whole street died. But our turn arrived eventually – and we joined the ranks of death. My aunts and uncles stopped dressing up to take the bus to the picture-houses. They folded a few years later.

We also got Buddy Holly and the Crickets, Bill Haley and the Comets, and in March 1956, Elvis Presley. The King was born. A café opened in Shore Street where my friends sat round drinking Coca-Cola, jerking their tight new drainpipe trousers, and singing along to the juke box that thundered out its lyrics across the harbour. Some of the fishermen looked up from their decks and stared, but there were fewer of them now, and they soon grew used to it. Hops and hard men took over the town hall, loudspeakers were set up on the piers and the people flocked to rock to the sound of 'Heartbreak Hotel'. The Holy Rollers and their glad hosannahs were drowned out and swept into the gutter, outcasts in their own country. People were not coming to be saved any more. All the young folk were putting on the agony, putting on the style.

And that splendid family I ran to when troubled? Grandmother died at fifty-nine, her heart weakened by the asthmatic assaults that had plagued her since her twenties. Leebie lived on a little longer but at last she lay like a fallen white candle, its top end guttered and gone out. Alec emigrated to Australia, driven out by lack of work. Billy stayed at the fishing but drove his crew in a minibus to Glasgow airport. From there he flew them to Holland, where he berthed his boat. What was the point of setting sail from Scotland?

'I'm up among the polar bears these days before I even smell a fish,' he said

Jenny married a boat-builder – who lost his job when the sheds shut down. Georgina came back pregnant from one of her trips, crushed with shame. She had a baby girl who died when she was two. The father became an alcoholic and fell between the boat and the pier one night, dead drunk, dead drowned. She married again but was unable to have any more children. After that she worked for years in a shoeshop in Anstruther, a dreary divorcee, looking at people's feet. In her house there was an unplayed piano with stained brown keys, long out of tune.

The Dyker died of cancer.

It took five strokes over two years to kill old George. He fell into a coma that lasted for weeks. Nobody knew when exactly he went at last to meet his maker – or indeed if his maker met him.

The little telephone exchange in Anstruther became automated, like all the lighthouses. Unmanned lights, unwomanned switchboards. My mother left Fife and moved in search of work to Edinburgh, where she was joined again by my father.

By that time grandfather was gone. It happened, like so much else, when I was twelve. Death was the wave that washed him over the side of our lives – as it does everybody in the end.

When I was very young, grandfather once told me a story, which went something like this:

A long time ago there was a road that went up to heaven, like a road goes up a hill. You see, there was a hunted whale that had given birth to a ship that was the earth, and had blown all the stars from the seas into the sky.

And the stars formed that road. And the stars were the herring, glinting and flashing.

The whale swam up the road to heaven, to wait there till it was safe to dive again, leaving us alone on the ship that was the earth, alone with our greed. And in our greed we tried to swallow up the silver . . .

The road is gone, I think he meant to say. But sometimes if you look through the glinting and the flashing of the herring, you'll see the whale . . . there, before it dives.

An old man's story, that's all, made up for his grandchild, before he went off to the winter herring, one night by the fire, and on other nights from time to time. He never finished the story – he was obviously making it up as he went along, and was always too tired. And one night he went out like Ulysses, and though fifty years went by, he never came back to his hearth. So the story never had an ending. But now I've remembered it, and given it one, and finished it, and told it over again – this time for him. And for all those that I have loved.

Acknowledgements

I would like to express my continuing gratitude to Dr Anne and Eugene d'Esprémènil of Cellardyke for their unfailing accuracy of observation. Many a slip might have occurred but for their open weather eye. John Beaton, my agent, has once again proved more patient and indeed wiser than I deserve. Nor could I have written this book without the assistance of a list of folk, all dead now, all alive again, I hope, in its pages. Very much alive is the Profile team, all of whom have been helpful and encouraging, especially my publicist Ruth Killick, God love her, and my editor, Gail Pirkis, who has kept on an even keel an author who showed an alarming fondness for the rocks. Many a page might have foundered but for her watchfulness and knowledge of the craft. In watching over this book she has been the sweetest and friendliest of sirens, singing eloquently yet sensibly, and one whom any sailor would be glad to have on board. For my part I cannot thank her enough.